C000194156

PRAISE FOR BANG
AND CHECKIN

"A fascinating collection of interviews, literature reviews, poems and stories from Thailand, and the region. Kevin focuses on one of his favorite expat nightlife venues – Bangkok's Checkinn99 – with accounts of musicians, artists, authors and other night owls."

—Melissa Ray,
four-time Female Muay Thai Champion in Thailand

"Chris Catto-Smith has a pig-headed determination to give a voice to the often unheard talents of writers, poets, actors, singers and artists. Checkinn99 is a highly refreshing venue, in a stagnating entertainment scene that only seems concerned with cheap copy bands that have churned out the same old tunes, forever. Chris could well drag Bangkok kicking and screaming into a brave new world, aided by those who support his vision, such as Thailand Footprint blogger Kevin Cummings, whose new book, *Bangkok Beat*, is a collection of real events including stories involving the colorful history and entertainment of Checkinn99."

—Kevin Wood,
singer, musician, actor and author of *Opium Sparrows*

"Checkinn99 has been awarded one of Trip Advisor's Top Twenty Hidden Gems in the World for two years running."

—TripAdvisor.com

Bangkok

Beat

Kevin Cummings

BANGKOK BEAT
Copyright © 2015 by Kevin Cummings

Contributing authors:
THOMAS H. LOCKE
JOHN GARTLAND
With introduction by:
JAMES A. NEWMAN

City Pulse poem by Alasdair McLeod

First published in USA
by Frog in the Mirror Press

www.peoplethingsliterature.com
ThailandFootprint@gmail.com

Copy Editing by Mark Fenn
Front Cover Design by Colin Cotterill
Book design by Maureen Cutajar

ISBN-10: 0692396454
ISBN-13: 978-0692396452
(Frog in the Mirror Press)

To the two best teachers I ever had during Act I of life:
Tom Barry and Chic Wallgren.

Among many other lessons, Tom taught me poise under pressure,
and Chic taught me how to shake like a dog.

And for Ratree.

"Develop an interest in life as you see it; the people, things, literature, music – the world is so rich, simply throbbing with rich treasures, beautiful souls and interesting people. Forget yourself."

—Henry Miller

"I have never been convinced there's anything inherently wrong in having fun."

—George Plimpton

CONTENTS

Bangkok

Beat

[I]

Introduction by James A. Newman

THE BANGKOK BEAT. Hot night. Bright city. Neon lights. You've been a tourist all your life, hauled suitcases all over the rock, abandoned paperbacks in hotel rooms. You've traveled, dragging those tired legs, memories, just like the rest of them, been elevated up into the clouds in metal birds and down like guava seeds through the smog, through the Bangkok city, drawn to the light, the hum of electricity that rattles and buzzes near the center, the plaza, the epicenter, epidermis, the core of the rock you've called home for as long as you can remember. Yes. Planet Earth. Strange, ain't it? Past motorcycle-taxis and tuk-tuk drivers, past women who may or may not be waiting for buses, may not be women, past it all – offices, bosses, schools, assholes, clowns, colleges, lunch hours, deadlines, a timeless hum. Clocks tick and tock like insect wings on a warm tropical evening. Rubbing, vibrating, anticipating humidity to explode into a stardust hamburger or a messy relationship, or a messier tattoo commiserating the event. A legless beggar rolls past on a skateboard, great set-up, independent trucks, slime-ball wheels, Santa Cruz deck – this beggar is making some serious coin, make no mistake sonny. Serious money. That beggar is making more coinage than Tony Hawk with his beggar-boy coffin board technique for some Italian suit with a luncheon schedule and a penchant for passing the soap in massage emporiums and short-time hotels. We are in a different world now. Yep. We ain't in Kansas anymore, Dorothy, not by a long chalk, and the flying monkeys might just be monkeys – flying monkeys, baby. Apes in the sky. Witches on the street.

So here we are. So much has changed since Bob Hope's days, but so little has, at the same time. Mobile telephones, meter taxis, sky-trains and subway systems, military coups, fast food restaurants, burgers, bugs, sandwiches, kebabs, massage parlors, tourist police, cigarette smoke, perfume, DVDs, death stars, mace spray, pellet guns, T-shirts. The sad-eyed lady, Russian, about 40-something, plies her trade outside Subway sandwiches, a cup of coffee lasting a decade, never cold nor neglected.

The walk to the Checkinn99 along the Sukhumvit sidewalk is never a forgettable experience, night or day. Or for those brave enough for the challenge, why not take 'the tunnel', the alleyway behind the bar flanked either-side by massage parlors and the kind of bars that take some serious mental muscle to feel at home at? Stray dogs and cats, rats, all forms of human life make a living. Nigerian Internet scamsters, drug dealers, and more.

Night after night.

Inside are the poet, the writer, the photographer, the actor, the comedian, the blogger, the critic, the musician, the filmmaker. This is like the Beat Hotel in Paris, Dean's bar in Tangiers, CGBGs or The White Horse in New York – a place where artists of all media talk about art and politics and listen to jazz. It's a Sunday. Outside it's daylight, inside it could be two in the morning. Time stands still at the Checkinn99. Time slips away, before you know it you've been there a decade.

You walk past a gaggle of transsexuals who try to beckon you, with little conviction, into some sort of beauty salon. You walk past. A stall sells plastic toys and tablets that make the little head go up and the big head down.

Then you see it.

The Checkinn99.

[II]

"Take Me There"

"T AKE ME THERE the next time I am in Bangkok," the author wrote. The author was Timothy Hallinan, who has penned six Poke Rafferty novels – which are written about at length in Bangkok Beat – and then there was Checkinn99. That's what Tim had written on my Facebook wall after seeing numerous pictures I had posted showing the Sunday afternoon jazz sessions with William Wait, Keith Nolan, Clifton Hardy, Peter Montalbano and company. Kevin Wood and Ted Lewand doing their acoustic sets in the early evenings. The Music of the Heart Band composed of Kiko, Cherry, Donna, Grace, April, and Jesse. Uncle Wat in his black tie and white shirt, and the legendary Mama Noi. This is not to mention pictures of the green couches and bamboo chairs, and the Soul Food Café. Tim wouldn't have to ask me twice. It's a there that's been a happening place since 1957. It's a there you are happy to share.

Fast forward a few months to late October, and Tim's Facebook GPS showed he was in Bangkok. Nothing ventured, nothing gained. I figured I'd send him a text message and see if he was available for lunch. I did. Tim had previously been nice enough to tell me his Bangkok cell phone number in an email sent from Santa Monica. Cool California guy, I thought at the time. He called back. Timothy Hallinan, the Edgar and Macavity Award nominated author. Writer of 16 novels and a work of non-fiction about Charles Dickens. The guy who inked a three-media deal for his Junior Bender novels that are now being developed for a cable television series, with comedian Eddie Izzard tipped to play Junior, was calling me back. I wasn't sure what to do, exactly, but answering the phone seemed like a good idea. "Tim, what's up?" Evidently Tim hates texting and prefers telephone conversation. That was okay with me, I have a few eccentric friends. We talked. He was human. He was friendly. I got up the nerve to say, "What about getting together for lunch?" Pause. "That's no good for me," he said. Bummer, I thought. "I like to write a lot during the days, how about dinner?" Super. Hemingway's Bangkok Bar and Restaurant it was. Sukhumvit Soi 14. Inside. Away from that absinthe-filled fountain.

It was a Tuesday. It was quiet. I got there first, 15 minutes early just to play it safe. Tim arrived, right on time. "I hope I am not late, it was a long walk for me." He looked friendly enough. We ordered. We ate. We talked about music, mostly. That was by design. I figured if I talked writing to Timothy Hallinan, he would soon be glancing at his watch and telling me he had to leave so he could "take a meeting". I've been around the block a few times. I've watched Big Shorty. I know how these "Hollywood types" are. But music seemed to light Tim on fire. Tim knows his music. He writes to different kinds of music. He has acknowledged the music he has listened to during the writing, at times, in those novels. There is a rumor that without music and coffee there would be no Hallinan novels in existence.

Tim's writing career started early as a lyricist for the popular soft-rock band Bread, which had 13 songs on The Billboard 100 between 1970 and 1977. Nowadays he divides his time between his home in Santa Monica, California and Southeast Asia, which have provided some rich material for his novels and the characters of Junior Bender, Poke Rafferty, Rose and Miaow.

We did, eventually, in the course of our three-hour dinner and conversation, get around to the subject of writing. So I did what doesn't come naturally: I listened, attentively. Tim had spent the day writing about a new character and he said he couldn't get him out of his head. As he talked, it's not an exaggeration to say, his energy increased. Tim's eyes flickered back and forth, left-to-right as he looked off to the side. The joy of his creative writing experience was on full display without him saying a single word. The chicken wings were also good.

The subject of Checkinn99 came up, and when would be a good time to meet there? Tim mentioned that a couple of weeks earlier he had come across the iconic Checkinn99 sign (since removed) for the very first time.

Tim took a walk down the infamous tunnel to check out the Check Inn for himself, only to be told: "Sorry, sir. We are sold out." As timing would have it, Tim's first venture down the tunnel was the night of *The Rocky Horror Show*, written about elsewhere in this book and starring Chris Wegoda, Kevin Wood, John Gartland, Chris Catto-Smith and the Music of the Heart Band among many others. A tough ticket during its four-night run. Not a problem. On that particular night, Tim went back out the tunnel and took a walk down Sukhumvit Road.

The dozen chicken wings were now gone at our Hemingway's table and the main courses were on the way. "I'll be going to *Blues Brothers* night at Checkinn99. Would you like to meet me there for that?" I said. "It's sold out, but I know the owner so I'm sure I can get you a ticket." Trying to impress the Hollywood guy with my Bangkok connections. It turns out Tim would have much rather seen *The Rocky Horror Show* than the *Blues Brothers* concert. "I won't stay for the show but how about if I meet you there before it starts, for dinner?" he suggested. That'll work, I thought.

I got there early on a nice November night. As nice as Thailand weather gets in Bangkok city. The proprietor, Chris Catto-Smith, was informing a crowded house that those without a *Blues Brothers* concert pass would have to leave by 7.30pm. With me was James A. Newman, a British crime fiction writer who authored the Joe Dylan series. Checkinn99 has always been a legendary nightlife venue, but ever since Newman and artist Chris Coles organized the first Bangkok Fiction Night of Noir – with Christopher G. Moore and Dean Barrett headlining

– it has become quite the haven for "creativists". Catto-Smith is fond of using this word, which seems appropriate and encompasses the writers, authors, artists, photographers, poets, journalists, musicians and the occasional trapeze artist, who make it a destination of choice in Bangkok city. From the blue-haired Trip Advisor crowd attending because Checkinn99 is currently one of its Top Twenty Hidden Gems in the World for two years running, to retired bass guitar playing punk rockers formerly known as Blake Cheetah, Checkinn99 has something for everybody.

Hallinan arrived, wide-eyed, and took in the campy ambience for the first time. We sat down next to an artificial tree illuminated by specks of green and blue light, and after I introduced the two writers to each other, Hallinan began to talk.

"They weren't going to let me in," he said. For the second time, in his attempt to gain access to Checkinn99, he had been told by the diligent doorman: "I'm sorry, sir – we are sold out tonight." Denied. Again. What would Poke Rafferty do if he were caught in this situation, one might ask? I have no idea, but I know what Tim told me: "But I know Kevin Cummings," the quick thinker said to the doorman.

"Ah, well then, allow me. Walk this way," the doorman said, in my imagination. Life is full of irony. This was one of those moments – Timothy Hallinan, the novelist, screenplay fixer, expert on Charles Dickens and Shakespeare and an all-round good Hollywood guy, was using the name of a blogger with a modest following to gain access to the historic Checkinn99. It hasn't happened before in my lifetime, and I doubt it ever will again.

Once we were settled in we got menus and quickly ordered New York steak and baked potato times three. The talk once again turned to music. Newman, for all his modest 36 years of age, can talk classic rock and roll, indie and punk-rock music with the best of them. I went back into listening mode, fly-on-the-wall type. I heard talk of Lou Reed, Velvet Underground, Nico, Bob Dylan, Blonde on Blonde, Pet Sounds, Krom and Jackson Browne – all of those I all knew, while some other groups discussed I didn't. It was fun. The place was noisier than usual, with Sunday jazz still going on – trumpets literally blaring. The place was getting packed. The steaks had still not arrived, but the conversation was cooking.

Catto-Smith was in full need-for-speed mode preparing for the *Blues Brothers* show that evening, with the talented Irish keyboardist Keith Nolan getting ready for a great performance in the part of John Belushi's character, Jake Blues. A couple of times I tried to get the proprietor's attention, with no luck. Chris is a first-class publican and arts promoter. He genuinely enjoys getting to know his customers and meeting new ones, all the time. I wanted him to know that Tim Hallinan was in the Checkinn99 house. As he walked toward the Soul Food Café sign, where the food is served, I held up my hand and shouted "Chris!" I got a look back from Chris that I had never seen before – one of stress. How Chris Catto-Smith does what he does, night after night, seven days a week, I have no idea. I'm just glad he does what he does and I am thrilled to write a small piece of what goes on in Bangkok and Checkinn99 for this book, with the help of my friends James Newman, Thom Locke, John Gartland and Alasdair McLeod.

Chris is a former Australian Royal Air Force Pilot. In a city with more fictitious private investigators than perhaps any other in the world, Chris actually was also a real life P.I. with the badge to prove it. From Pinkerton. The folks who stopped an assassination attempt on Abraham Lincoln and acted as his security during the American Civil War. The same folks who caught Jesse James. That Pinkerton. Chris Catto-Smith is the real deal, never boasts even though he has every reason to do so. I tried a second time, "Chris!" And he shook me off. He shook me off like a baseball pitcher would do to his catcher in the bottom of the eighth, when he's been asked for a low fastball and all he has left in the tank is a hanging curve. Shaken off by Chris Catto-Smith. I was with an expert on Shakespearean literature that night, but there was something rotten in the state of Denmark at Checkinn99 that very moment. I just wasn't sure what it was.

Our steaks finally arrived, after a longer wait than I was used to, and they were good, as usual. Collin Piprell, author of *Kicking Dogs*, a review of which is included in the literature section of this book, made a memorable entrance. How he got in to the sold-out event I had no idea, but I am reasonably sure he didn't have to invoke my name to gain entry. Since all the chairs were taken, a small stool for the fit and large

Ernest Hemingway lookalike was brought over and put between James and me. Collin informed me that Chedly Saheb-Ettaba (the magician, Dr. Penguin) was in the now packed audience as well.

Catto-Smith came over on a hit-and-run mission, informing me that the set menu that had been planned for the night had been disregarded and the regular menu was circulating among the sold-out crowd, creating a two-hour backlog for New York steaks alone. It was lucky we were among the first to order – we got ours in 45 minutes. Welcome to the glamorous life of owning and managing a hidden gem of a nightclub. On the one hand, I'd like Checkinn99 to remain a bit hidden. On the other, word of mouth, social media and Trip Advisor are all pretty good forms of advertising these days. In 2015, Checkinn99 made the Trip Advisor Top Thirty Things To Do in Bangkok and was the #1 rated entertainment venue on that list. Think about that. This is Bangkok we are talking about. The club was rated just below Jim Thompson House and above Lumpini Park – where the monitor lizards play. Checkinn99 is not a secret any more. But it used to be, as a private club dating back to 1957 – the oldest continuously operated nightclub in Bangkok. It used to be a safe haven, a bolt hole for stars and non-stars alike. Then trouble occurred. Chris Catto-Smith rescued Checkinn99 and took over the venue after a monk ceremony – a story which will be told later in this book.

Tim Hallinan left before the 8pm start of the *Blues Brothers*. But I got to "take him there" and I know he enjoyed it, as did James, Collin and I. Tim will meet Chris another time on a different day. And smiles and conversation will be exchanged. Bangkok has been described as organized chaos by much better writers than me, and we all shared a piece of chaotic Bangkok that night – Tim, James, Collin, Chris and I. It had already been a memorable night and yet it hadn't even really started. The *Blues Brothers* nine-piece band was coming up next. That's the way it goes at Checkinn99 on any given evening, if you are willing to walk the Bangkok beat.

[III]

I Am Not a Writer –
and Why the World Needs Them

I AM NOT A writer. And yet I like to write. I find no incongruity to this. I am not a breatharian yet I enjoy breathing; I like eating an assortment of vegetables but I am not a vegetarian. I could go on. A writer might. How do I define 'writer'? It's a good question. Certainly I have made a fair amount of money through the written word. But so have English teachers, accident investigators and email spammers. Writer, to me, conjures up images of a manly man like Ernest Hemingway or a Dapper Dan like F. Scott Fitzgerald. In the fictional world, James Caen comes to mind in the movie *Misery*, adapted from a book written by another genuine writer, Stephen King. On the female fictional side, Angela Lansbury from the television series *Murder She Wrote* is my stereotypical writer, no matter how inappropriate that may be.

I have learned again, as so often before, that I am wrong. There is no such thing as a stereotypical writer or novelist. No generalizations can be made, at least not with any accuracy. Except for one. Writers write, creatively. And they do it with such regularity that books appear, electronic ones or old-fashioned ones. And I applaud them for doing this. The world is a much better place because of creative writers. A world without creative writers is a world I would not want to live in. Given the choice between creative physical art or the creative thought-provoking words of a writer, well, I've always been a words guy. That would be an easy call to make.

I like writers. Certainly not all writers. As Jerry Lewis is purported to have said many years ago, before the Internet, before Snopes: "Percentage-wise there are just as many assholes in wheelchairs as any other segment of the population." And if Jerry never said that, well, he should have. My point is that being a writer doesn't make you a nice person any more than being in a wheelchair for life makes you a nice person. But I have drawn some inferences from the writers I have known and spent some time with, both in California and in Thailand. Writers like to live. Writers enjoy living – more than your average Joe or Jane. And I have a theory as to why that is. Writers are just a wee bit more aware of one inevitability, one certainty – we die. We all die. Writers, accountants, lawyers, dentists and trust-fund ageing hippies alike. The writer has just figured out, earlier than most, that we should make the moments count. Be mindful. Be aware. To paraphrase that old country western song: writers were mindful before mindfulness was cool.

I like to think I have gleaned many good qualities from writers. And the great part about that is that you don't have to do any writing to do that. Here is what I have learned. Your results may vary. First, observation. Writers have helped me observe the world better. And what a fascinating world we have to watch. Second, empathy. Writers need this. Writers have this. Third, encouragement. One writer in California once told me: "The world needs more encouragement." He had tracked me down in the parking lot of a gym, just to tell me he thought I had worked out hard that day. He didn't have to do that. But now I try to be more encouraging. Fourth, generosity. Writers are people after all. But these people who call themselves writers have been very generous to me, with their time, their advice, their books and their humor. And I wanted to take this opportunity to thank each and every one of them. Well, except for the assholes. You know who you are.

[IV]

What is a Writer?

SINCE I FIRST wrote *I am not a Writer – and Why the World Needs Them*, a fair number of people have told me, in not so enthusiastic tones, that there was a possibility I was wrong. Chris Coles was the first, before my blog Thailand Footprint ever appeared. "Maybe you're a writer?" the artist said.

Months later I was at the Checkinn99 for a rehearsal of *The Rocky Horror Show*. At that rehearsal, the singer, songwriter, musician and author Kevin Wood sat down next to me and we were able to have a rare face-to-face conversation, as opposed to the long-distance ones we've had many times while Ted Lewand and he played their tunes following the Sunday jazz sessions. Some people call it heckling. I think conversation sounds more polite.

"Are you a writer?" Wood asked me as we sat on one of the green couches near an artificial tree illuminated with tiny lights. "No." I replied. Then I qualified it. "I could tell you I am a writer. But what you do, people cannot fake." What I meant by this is that telling someone you are a writer is the easiest thing in the world. You could also tell people you are a musician. But eventually, people are going to expect you to play a song from time to time. And if you're not very good at playing the guitar or covering Bob Marley's *No Woman, No Cry*, people will figure that out, real quick. Kevin and Ted are very good at what they do. They are professionals. They are paid, regularly, to sing and play instruments and have been for a long time. The audience can quickly tell that they are professionals.

I recently read a wonderful interview about the books and life of a superb writer who lives in Bangkok, who I have never had the benefit of meeting. Just as I like to read a good book review done by a professional, I also enjoy reading interviews with professional writers done by professional interviewers. I'm always hoping I might learn something. I learned a number of things in an interview with Bangkok-based British author Lawrence Osborne in *The Observer*.

There are many things I enjoyed about the interview. It is entertaining, insightful, witty, revealing and with just the right amounts of brutal honesty and self-deprecation. Toward the end of the interview, Lawrence makes the following declaration: "Very few writers live here, of course. But that's quite all right with me." There are, I think, multiple ways those two sentences can be interpreted. I chose to think that Mr Osborne is quite accurate. When you compare Bangkok to New York City, I would wager far more writers live there, and certainly write on a more varied array of themes than the writers do in Bangkok. One criticism I have seen of the expat writers in Bangkok is that you wouldn't have two dozen writers in New York City living within walking distance of Times Square and having them all write about life in Times Square. That criticism seems valid to me.

The interview made my mind ponder who Lawrence Osborne would consider to be among those "very few writers" who live here? There are clues, if you know where to look. John Burdett would certainly be one. He's published by Knopf and has had multiple printings of hardcover books numbering 75,000 and up. John lives here a lot of the time. Stephen Leather would be another writer who would qualify. I have heard the number two million bandied about when it comes to the number of books he has sold, and I have no reason to doubt it. If anything, it's probably a much higher number now. I have read a few Stephen Leather books. He's a fine writer. I particularly liked *The Chinaman* and *The Bombmaker*.

Christopher G. Moore, the author of *A Killing Smile* and the Vincent Calvino series, would also make the list, Osborne describing him in another interview with *The Bangkok Post* as "a good writer". Jerry Hopkins might be another who would make Osborne's list. His books, including biographies of Elvis Presley and Jim Morrison, have sold in the millions – I've seen one estimate of six million in total. There are potentially many other writers who would make Osborne's list, who I am unaware of because of the limited scope of my literary education.

As good a writer as I think Lawrence Osborne is – and I think he is very good – I have some biases about him. He's a Harvard guy. I am a product of the California State University system, as is Timothy Hallinan. Tim is another writer who, unquestionably, would make Osborne's list if he lived primarily in Bangkok, but he doesn't. Osborne is also a Brit, and I've made it my lifelong quest to figure them out before I die.

So it is Lawrence Osborne I credit for the theme of this chapter: What is a writer? It's a good question that deserves contemplation and an attempt at explanation.

Here is the excellent reply from Osborne in that *Observer* interview, when he was asked why it took so long to find a publisher for his novel *The Forgiven*:

"Mostly, just that I was an outsider to the fiction world. Indeed, my American agent at the time urged me not to bother at all. In the end, I sent it myself to an editor I didn't know late on a Friday night after a bottle of good but despair-ridden and lonely Chablis. A push of a button. The manuscript had been rejected by dozens of houses, even by editors I'd published books with. This was a last-chance gamble. He took it with him on the train home to New Jersey that night and somewhere in the darkened satanic mills of Newark or wherever he sent me a message saying that he was 30 pages in and that was enough. He offered for the book on Monday morning."

This process of rejection and acceptance, which Osborne describes so well, is missing among many of the writers of today. And that's a shame – for them. In the age of self-publishing, Facebook author pages, fake book reviews and Twitter follower purchases, one can become a writer in a day. That seems too quick to me. It was the lifestyle of writers that I always found interesting and appealing to my sense of adventure and personal exploration. Start with Henry Miller. Add Jerry Hopkins. Stir in Christopher G. Moore, whether you like any of these guys' books or not. For musical accompaniment I'll take Timothy Hallinan, who started his writing career as a songwriter for the band *Bread* before he wrote his now well-known Simeon Grist, Poke Rafferty and Junior Bender series. I include Lawrence Osborne on my list. All these men have led lives that would still be very interesting had they never published a single word. Read about any of these men and you will read about rejection and acceptance, numerous times, in their careers as writers.

Just as Chance the gardener in the movie *Being There* likes to watch, I like to write. My business involves writing that pays well but isn't very creative. My blogging is, at times, creative but doesn't pay a dime. There is something to be said for the creative process. There is something to be said for creative people. There is much to be said in favor of the arts. That is one reason the very first blog posts at my Thailand Footprint blog were videos of Alfred Hitchcock on happiness and John Cleese on creativity.

Not too many Sundays ago, I was sitting with a group at Checkinn99. We were doing what groups do there: drinking, talking, laughing and listening to live music. It was the 6pm to 8pm time slot occupied by Ted Lewand and Kevin Wood on stage. Ted turned to Kevin as only Ted can and said, somewhat sarcastically, "It doesn't get any better than this." I thought it was perfect. Because I genuinely felt Ted was absolutely right. It made me enjoy a good evening even more. So much so, in fact, that Kevin Wood addressed us at the microphone. "How is the book club doing this evening?" He said. And then it occurred to me that everyone at my table had written more than one book, except me – I hadn't even written a single one. That is, until now.

Ted Lewand and Kevin Wood — Photo by A. McLeod

My companions that night were the British published novelist and poet John Gartland, Canadian author Collin Piprell, who has published a number of fiction and non-fiction books on Thailand, Alasdair McLeod, author of books of poetry, and James A. Newman, author of the Joe Dylan series and short stories too numerous to mention. John, Collin, Alasdair and James appear on my blog often. I am an honorary member of The Book Club. John, Collin, Alasdair and James are all writers, to me. More importantly, they are my friends. I consider myself lucky to know them as people and writers.

Now that this book is out, it should solidify my standing in The Book Club, which meets irregularly at Checkinn99 and Hemingway's Bar and Restaurant in Bangkok. There are no illusions about *Bangkok Beat* becoming a money-spinner, but I hope readers enjoy it. Will *Bangkok Beat* make me a writer in the eyes of Lawrence Osborne? I doubt that it will, and I believe that it shouldn't. Will it make me a writer in the eyes of Kevin Wood? It might. If that happens, it doesn't get any better than that.

[V]

Why Live In Thailand?
A Childhood Story about the Author

FROM 1959 UNTIL June of 1964, I lived with my two sisters and my
mother, Marion, on Balboa Island, California.

That's not entirely true, as even back then the rents on Balboa Island
would double in the summertime. So every summer we headed over to live
in Corona del Mar. And every school year it was back to Balboa Island.
Our family lived in five different houses on Balboa Island – all rented. Four
of them were still standing the last time I was there in the late 1990s. Now,
why would a single mom raising three kids on her own choose to do this
every year? You'd have to ask her, if she were still alive. I can only guess why.
But I can appreciate that she did it, 50 years later. In fairness, my dad, a
career deputy juvenile probation officer for Los Angeles County, gave $65
per month for each child as part of the divorce agreement. So mom got an
extra $195 on top of her salary of maybe $300 a month as an executive
secretary to various Newport Beach bigwigs.

*As the twig is bent, so grows the tree. Often the values of the
influences imposed on us by our mothers and fathers, our teachers*

and certain friends, are not realized until years later, when we, as a sailor does, look back at our wakes to determine the course we have steered that got us to where we are. – Actor Buddy Ebsen (1908-2003).

Although it has been 50 years since I lived on Balboa Island, the memories are still vivid. It seemed like a magical place for a young boy at the time, and it basically was. Friends were plentiful. I still remember their names – Bill Powers, Johnny Miles and Paul Connerty. We used to run around the island, literally at times, and we were also blood brothers, having gone through the cut-and-rub ritual with our thumbs that we saw from watching the Tom Sawyer movie. I've lost track of them, but not the memories.

There are two memories in particular that stand out for me from that time – and I'm not talking about watching Jack Ruby shoot Lee Harvey Oswald on live TV. One was a birthday party for one of my six-year-old friends. There must have been 30 kids my age there. There were many fun events that day, including a piñata-bashing. Because of our proximity to Mexico, piñatas were often sold by the side of the road. Piñatas are colored animals and characters made from papier-mâché, with hollow bodies. Ours that day was a donkey. The animal is filled with small candies, and party-goers are blindfolded one at a time and get to take three swings at the piñata. Eventually it breaks and the candy is strewn to the ground. At that point it is every boy and girl for themselves. It's probably been outlawed for safety reasons in this day and age. More than one party-goer has been cracked in the head by the blindfolded boy or girl. But we managed to burst open the donkey without incident that day.

However, the more memorable event was an old-fashioned scavenger hunt. We were divided into about six teams and sent out with a long list of items to bring back. I only remember two of the items on the list that day: a 1955 Lincoln Wheat Ears Penny – a coin – and a red thumbtack. At the second house we stopped at, a very nice elderly lady, who was probably all of 35 years old, helped us gather the complete list. We were amazed. We were six. She had everything for us, and she helped us gladly at a time when a group of five six-year old kids could still knock on people's doors in the daytime and have someone answer, with a Barbara Billingsley, "Leave it to Beaver" smile on her face – no pearls.

She had everything, I should say, except for one item – the red thumbtack. She apologized, saying she only had white ones. We were so happy to only need one more item to complete our list that we started to head off to the next house. But before we were able to go she said, "Wait a minute, I have an idea." And she disappeared for a moment, up the stairs – the kind where Wally and the Beaver had their bedroom at the top. When she returned she had a white thumbtack in one hand and a bottle of red nail polish in the other. She took out the nail polish and expertly painted the white thumbtack ruby red. Then she blew on it a few times, as if we weren't excited enough already, pronounced it dry, put the now-red thumbtack in the goodie bag and it was off to the races for us, back to the house to see if we had won. We won that day alright, by a good 45 minutes over the next placed team. And the lesson that woman taught me has stuck with me for 50 years.

The other memory has to do with those friends I mentioned – Johnny Miles, Bill Powers and Paul Connerty. It was a hot early June, if memory serves. The year was 1962 or 1963, making us about seven or eight years old. Late October and Halloween were still a long way off. Now Balboa Island, as you might imagine, was a trick or treater's paradise. Among the residents was the actor Buddy Ebsen, who was in his *Beverly Hillbillies* TV show heyday at the time. It was not unusual to see Buddy – shirtless, belly protruding – at the corner market, next to the ferryboat landing, like any other local. Buddy was the only resident on the island with a diving board on his private pier, where he also kept his boat and racing yacht. But unlike all the other residents who locked their private piers, Buddy left his open and let all the kids on the island use the diving board. Buddy was as cool as Jed Clampett, his character in *The Beverly Hillbillies*. At Halloween time the rule at Buddy's house was two handfuls. You got to stick your hands into a huge bowl and take away as much candy as two handfuls would allow.

But now we are back to that day in June over 50 years ago. It's a Saturday and it's hot. Bill has a bunch of Halloween costumes in his garage. One of us, I am sure it was not me, said: "Why don't we go trick or treating today?" And nobody could think of a good reason why we shouldn't. So we did. We got dressed up on that hot June Saturday, in four different Halloween costumes, and went trick or treating door to door on Balboa Island. Now we were not exactly sure how we were going to be received. But I know I was a lot cuter when I was eight than I am now, and my friends must have been too. Because you would have thought we had just made the day of everyone whose door we knocked on. And we knocked on a lot of doors that day. If they didn't have candy, we got cookies, cake, or apples and oranges. They all gave us smiles. One took our picture with a camera that used real film. It was a good day for us. I am sure of it because I remember it over 50 years later.

So what is the point of this story, you may be thinking? What does it have to do with this book, *Bangkok Beat*? For me, it's about self-limiting beliefs. My mom raised her three kids in the early 60s on Balboa Island, by herself, on less than $500 a month because she believed she could. Because she knew it was a good idea. Not an easy idea, but a good idea.

The nice lady who helped five six-year-old boys refused to believe that she didn't have any red thumbtacks in her house. And because she refused to limit her beliefs, the world of possibilities became larger for her and a group of boys who won a birthday party contest, fair and square, that day.

My three good friends, blood brothers, and I could not think of one good reason why we had to wait until October to go trick or treating. So we didn't.

The question I pose for you, the reader, and myself, is what self-limiting beliefs – if any – do you have today? What is out there in the world of possibilities that your belief system may be holding you from? The older I get the more convinced I am that the answers to the questions don't matter quite so much. What's important, I think, is that we keep asking ourselves good questions.

One of my favorite spots, where I spend my summers when I am not in Thailand, is Steamer Lane in Santa Cruz, California. It is a good

10-hour drive from Newport Beach. Is it a coincidence that I ended up living in a beach community, or did the footprints left behind from those early childhood years have a lifelong impact? It's good to live in the moment. It's also good, as the sailor Buddy Ebsen suggests, to look back at our wakes to determine the course we have steered that got us to where we are. I know the answer to my question, but it's the asking of the question that's important. And when I am not in California, I live in Bangkok, Thailand, walking the Bangkok beat. Because life is not always about white thumbtacks or waiting for the one day a year you are allowed to wear a costume. Sometimes you need to add a little color to your life on your own. And it's usually a lot more possible than you realize.

[VI]

The Checkinn99 Story

THIS STRANGE BUT true tale about the cabaret nightclub Checkinn99 begins on Sunday, December 14, 2014. Located for what seems like an eternity on Sukhumvit Road, between Soi 5 and Soi 7, Checkinn99 has weathered many a monsoon and more than a few floods. But that day will live on with memories of astonishment. The current owners of Checkinn99, Australian Chris Catto-Smith and his wife, Jiraporn Srihahach, known as Mook to her friends, were informed that they had lost their bureaucratic battle with a Thai Wattana police officer. The club's iconic and familiar sign, easily spotted as one strolled down Sukhumvit Road, was therefore taken down from the entryway. The club's infamous tunnel was thereby separated from its soul-mate thoroughfare.

Chris and Mook, you see, had been threatened with a summons for weeks if the sign was not removed on that date. It created such a stir that noted Bangkok blogger Stickman gave periodic updates on his weekly blog regarding the battle. "It was that serious. The regulars were on edge", the blogger wrote. Chris put up a vociferous defense to try to save the sign. While face-to-face on the footpath with a government official, asking why the sign had to go, Chris thought he heard the Thai man repeatedly say "psychopath, psychopath". Had he finally found an ally? No. The Thai official was actually saying "cycle path, cycle path," in broken English. Mournfully, Chris and Mook knew the game was up and the sign would soon be down. It did come down that day, so that cyclists (bikes and motorcycles, no doubt) would have more headroom to ride down the Bangkok sidewalk. As everyone knows, cycling is one of the great recreational activities that Sukhumvit Road and downtown Bangkok are famous for. Checkinn99 remains. The sign depicted on the cover of this book is now gone. Welcome to the Land of Smiles and 7ft 2" urban cyclists.

For two years running, Checkinn99 has been ranked as one of the Top Twenty Hidden Gems in the World by TripAdvisor. Clearly, 2013 and 2014 were banner years. But how did Chris and Mook do it? Stick around, there's a lot to tell.

Originally known as the Copacabana, Checkinn99 has the unique distinction of being Bangkok's oldest bar and nightclub. Established in 1957, it predates the start of the Vietnam War, and was a popular haunt of local expats, Peace Corps personnel and intelligence officers.

The Copa, as it was known to regulars, was located on the site of the original Bangkok Ice works on lower Sukhumvit – far away at the time from Bangkok's comparatively conservative downtown. It quickly gained a bawdy reputation. As Chris Catto-Smith says, it was "a naughty out-of-town entertainment place that wasn't in anyone's way".

That out-of-town destination might be difficult to imagine for Trip Advisor users using smartphones with built-in GPS systems to guide them to their hidden gem. The location is now part of what Christopher G. Moore, over 20 years ago, dubbed the Comfort Zone or the Zone for short. The Zone is a strip along lower Sukhumvit Road and other

The Copa in its early days and a rare picture of the neon sign at night

entertainment areas where tourists and expats alike feel most comfortable. It is an exotic oasis in a city which breathes in and out from nine million to 12 million residents and visitors on any given day, some of whom get chewed up and spat out by the Zone when it is is through with them.

The Copa had 35 or more short-time rooms available for nocturnal pursuits on the two floors above. Its sultry reputation was well-earned. You could call it a bordello or a brothel, depending on your native tongue – people were not going there to listen to the band in those days. Those rooms still exist and are very much in their original condition. But the access door located inconveniently behind the stage area has been locked since Chris and Mook took over the ownership and management of the place on April 1, 2011. The rooms now lie vacant, but, oh, if those walls could talk – and some of Checkinn99's more superstitious staff say they still do.

The Copa had live music, even in those days, but it was nothing special. A kitchen was added in the early 1960s. The club soon became popular with United Service Organization entertainers such as Bob Hope, Raquel Welch, Bing Crosby, Dean Martin and many others who were also headliners at the Starlight Ballroom and wanted somewhere discreet to enjoy themselves. Checkinn99 was a safe haven for these Hollywood stars, and it was out of the spotlight. Senior US military officers, including CIA spooks, were also known to use the infamous haunt for their clandestine meetings … as Chris knows, not much has changed to this day.

In those early days, the club operated as a live music venue and was

The beautiful Noi pictured with Bob Hope at the Copa in the late 1960s.

very popular during the Vietnam War. The bands came and went, and the hostesses were regular features of the club.

To get to the music and the ladies, one had to go through an initiation rite of sorts – the infamous tunnel entry. The narrow passageway harbors dark memories. Late one night in 1978, amidst one of Thailand's frequent political coups, the Copa's owner was beaten to death in the tunnel as he was locking up. The boss was dead! It was front page news at the time. Money appears to be one possible motive. Business disputes are reason enough for murder in Thailand. The circumstances remain murky but this may well have been a classic instance of a Bangkok business deal gone wrong, with the military coup used as a diversion for the investigation. No one was ever arrested for the crime. Like many Bangkok murders, it remains unsolved. The Copa closed for a short time after the murder, and then a Danish man opened the space as a traditional Copenhagen-style restaurant under at least two different names during this interim period.

Around 1980, the club was purchased by a consortium of Danish entrepreneurs, all young men with a plan. They merged the Copa with the equally famous Club99, which was located in the Silom area and which they already had an interest in. The new club became known as Checkinn99. After about 10 years, for legal reasons, the name was changed to Checkinn Garden. The two dozen shareholders operated the facility as a Scandinavian men's club, selling shares in it. What evolved was a rather odd and transparent Ponzi scheme membership. Members knew, up front, that the best way to get back some of their investment was to bring in new members and splitting the profit based on how much money they spent each quarter. The club was very much a private, word-of-mouth bar at that time and among its notable characters was a dwarf doorman among those who worked out front over the years. One of the doorman's principal duties was to screen and refuse certain demographic groups from entering through the tunnel. Nordic bloodlines and blue eyes were a plus. Dark skin and brown eyes not so much, unless they belonged to the female workers. The back door to the rear alley remained locked at all times, and unless you got the nod from the doorman you didn't gain entry at the front.

Longtime Bangkok visitor Kevin Conroy is shown in this 1980s photo taken at Checkinn99 — note old style doorman uniform

There has always been a bit of mystery and intrigue when it comes to Sumai, the dwarf doorman. He was a living landmark working across the street from the Landmark Hotel. Sumai was well-known and someone to know. Need something or someone in particular to get you through the night? Talk to Sumai. Talk to the man in a belittling way and you might bring on a big problem – he had many friends. Regulars of that time will tell you it only took two beers for Sumai to get drunk. The legend of Sumai, the dwarf doorman, grew under the Checkinn99 sign. Sumai and the overhead sign were often mentioned when directions were given to Checkinn99. "Look for the dwarf doorman working out front. You can't miss him."

Sumai working on Sukhumvit 16

Sumai had worked for a number of Bangkok clubs. He was a known personality and a man of the street. Before working at Checkinn99 he had worked at the long-since closed Nipa Hut Mexican restaurant on Sukhumvit 16. The best information available suggests Sumai worked at Checkinn99 for some fifteen years. Then one day he was gone, never to be seen again. Some say in his earlier days he appeared in movies. One local punter claimed he saw Sumai working the door of an Irish pub in Kathmandu. Others worried about his health – he wasn't much taller than exhaust pipe level and there was always plenty of pollution on Sukhumvit Road, even in those days. His later history may never be known. But even today, the mere mention of the Bangkok legend will elicit a smile and most likely a story from an old Asia hand beginning with: "I remember when the dwarf was working the door and …"

Around 1990 the club began to employ Philippine house bands as part of the entertainment package. The staff included the memorable Godang, a bar manager who ran everything Thai-Chinese style. He was tough, a habitual drinker and chain smoker. The staff included Uncle Wat, who along with Mama Noi has worked at Checkinn99 ever since the merger of the two clubs. The business model was slightly adrift, but the foundations had been laid.

These were wild and crazy times, and the club for all practical purposes was still private. Chris Catto-Smith was introduced to Checkinn99, at a time when Bangkok never slept, by a Thai business associate working for an Australian logistics company. Chris reports that it was not unusual to see a single customer drop US$1,000 worth of tips in those days, causing a scene among the hostesses similar to a flock of seagulls going after a loaf of bread. There was a bell, and patrons were not shy about ringing it. That meant a free drink for everyone – male or female – in the house, paid for by the bell-ringer. It was the mid-1990s and the internet hadn't impacted the entertainment industry yet. It didn't matter that this was a place for the shareholders to use as they wished. It was not uncommon to be asked to move to make way for a Danish shareholder who liked to sit in his own favourite bar chair. Chris took to the Club right away as, comparatively speaking, it was a comfortable oasis from the Patpong entertainment scene, which was going hot and heavy at the time. Even then Chris was drawn to the hominess and comfort of the place. It was a wild home but there were plenty of wilder places and that was the initial appeal. It was a respite from the craziness of Bangkok.

The current house band, Music of the Heart, also from the Philippines, perform seven nights a week and have been there for the past 16 years. The band is composed of four female singers – Cherry, Donna, Grace and newest addition April. They are led by an able and versatile manager, Kiko, an excellent singer and fearless bass guitar and sax player who also takes on the role of sound director. Kiko's brother

Jesse on guitar and keyboards fills out the band with some incredible guitar solos. As the lead singer and greeter of Checkinn99 customers, Cherry likes to say, when asked a common question: "Yes. We are family." Music of the Heart is indeed a family band – the six bandmates share three surnames among them. Kiko and Cherry have seen all the pitfalls that the music industry entails and it was their goal to form a clean, drug-free band able to perform at one place regularly. That place is Checkinn99 – it is their home. Chris and Mook have built a sustainable business around them.

Left to Right: Cherry, April, Kiko, Jesse, Grace and Donna — Music of the Heart

Prior to Chris and Mook taking over the establishment, the club was known to local expats and visiting celebrities alike. David Bowie visited during his 1983 Serious Moonlight tour. There is a picture of him in Bangkok where the setting looks remarkably like Mama Noi's kitchen. But all the classy Noi will say on that subject is "He was a nice boy". That's it.

Checkinn99 in its early days was not a place for couples. Up to 35 hostesses were available for the male clientele's every whim, and many

were taken out by customers for extended periods of time, seven days to
a month not being uncommon. Now a more casual atmosphere is on
tap but the celebrities still stop by for a drink or three. Sammy Hagar
was there at least twice in 2014 – he keeps a low profile. During one of
his visits, Sammy got on the phone to Jimmy Page of Led Zeppelin and
Stairway to Heaven fame while Music of the Heart were performing a
Led Zeppelin tune. Jimmy liked what he heard and told Sammy so.
There have been talks of Jimmy and Sammy dropping into Checkinn99
for some unannounced musical fun. Dan Ackroyd has been in talks
with Chris about a possible role in a future Blues Brothers event. Why
not? Checkinn99 is one of a few select venues that stock Ackroyd's
Crystal Head vodka. Sammy Hagar's Cabo Wabo tequila could well be
next. Chris is very discreet as to who visits the bar. Diplomats come
incognito and mix it with both active and retired three-star generals of
all nationalities. Undercover agents on stakeouts have been seen rocking
to Music of the Heart along with their targets. Bar girls are equally as
welcome as expat wives and even female airline captains.

That Checkinn99 is still in existence and didn't meet the same fate
as the sign that was located out front is a minor miracle. Or Thai
business as usual, depending on who you talk to. A house of cards had
been assembled among the private members, and the club seemed
doomed to closure in 2011. It was not only close to having the shutters
pulled down for good, but close to demolition. These were troubling
days for many of the staff. You wouldn't have considered it a family
atmosphere before Chris and Mook took over, or if you did, it would be
quite the dysfunctional family, with no shortage of black sheep in the
herd employed there at the time.

There were too many squabbling shareholders and they were not
seeing a profit. There were even rumors about there being two sets of
books. So on March 31, 2011, the Thai staff did what only Thai staff
would do in that situation: they invited three Buddhist Monks from
Wat That Thong to pray for a life. The life of Checkinn99. The outlook
was bleak. A miraculous intervention was needed.

Unknown to the staff, later that day – at around 3pm , Chris Catto-
Smith, one of the 24 existing shareholders, was approached directly by

the owner of the building, with a possible solution. Chris was a minority shareholder at that time, and one lacking political power among the group. As Chris put it, there was a voting bloc that enjoyed vetoing the many suggestions he made to improve the club, almost as a form of sport. Chris was an unlikely savior, but a savior he became.

Chris had flown jet planes for the Australian Royal Air Force and been a Pinkerton private investigator, complete with badge, but he had zero experience running a bar, little money, and was due to start a new job in Vietnam within 48 hours. The bar at this point was rundown, in a lowdown part of town, and had acquired a bad reputation as a place to avoid. At a meeting with a Thai lawyer, Chris was presented with a lease printed in Thai, which not even his Thai wife could understand. Neither-could he. Checkinn99 at that point was basically a shabby popular private party club, with hard drinking regulars. It employed lots of hostesses, some of them hardcore, with little good will or even liquor stock left to pass on. So much for its glorious history. Rather than going down in a blaze of glory, it looked like the Checkinn's colorful history would end abruptly.

What is the price of a business seemingly doomed from the start, you might ask? The Thai contract presented to Chris involved paying 15 months' rent in advance and 72,000 baht (about US$2,200) to pay out the old shareholders and transfer ownership of the club, including all the broken down bamboo furniture and remaining liquor bottles – but not before the Danish shareholders and guests had one last liquor-fueled send-off. The deal was done with a half a book of floated checks, the quality of which would depend a lot on when they were deposited. The Checkinn99 now belonged to Chris and Mook. Late that afternoon, Chris went across the street to inform the crew. The staff, upon hearing the news, took it in knowingly. They knew their prayers would work, as the Buddhist monks had assured them, after the ceremony, that all would be well in the Checkinn99 garden. Phra maa prode as the Thais like to say or "the god has come to the rescue". The staff were no longer worried – that burden had shifted to Chris and Mook.

What has happened to the Checkinn99 since Chris and Mook took over on April 1, 2011 – yes, April Fool's Day – is nothing short of

An interior Shot of Checkinn99 before the good times roll

remarkable. The history continues. The background Chris has as a logistics man came in quite useful, but even he admits today that taking over the bar was quite illogical. Where there were conflicts in the workplace, he and Mook eliminated them as soon as possible. One of the biggest conflicts was that he had a bar that provided live entertainment in the form of Music of the Heart and also employed 32 "hostesses" – working girls in Bangkok's competitive pay-for-play scene. In addition he had 60 bargirls living, partition-style, on the two upstairs floors, which contributed to leaks above the area where the band took their break. These were cheap digs with no windows, no air-conditioning and only four community bathrooms on the two floors, which supporting evidence indicated was also contributing to the leakage. Cherry never complained, but she did point out to Chris the mushrooms growing on the downstairs ceiling. Not surprisingly, nearly all the customers complained about the smell.

"It was the whole girlie scene that kept a lot of people out," says Chris. "Having live music and hostesses together was a conflict. People couldn't talk to the girls because the band was too noisy, and people who came for the band didn't want to be around girls hustling for drinks and other services. Couples don't come in if there are hostesses." The decision to make a change in the business model definitely went against a strong current in Bangkok, but it was a concerted, if not unanimous effort by Chris, Mook and the long-serving staff to turn around the reputation of the club. That and a set of odd circumstances.

The first night after the take-over, three bartenders failed to return for their duties, after Chris had called for a liquor inventory – another change in Checkinn99 policy. In that first month, the hardcore hostesses staged a walkout, gathering on the sidewalk in front of the club in protest against the new way of doing things and their loss of power. Mook handled that swiftly by calling the Lumpini police department. Mook, as you will learn in more detail later, is a captain with the Royal Thai Police. That alone didn't necessarily give the new owners a get-out–of-jail-free card, but it did make it easier to put people in jail if they caused trouble. The paddy-wagon was on its way when Mook told the working girls that they had sixty seconds to disperse. They did. The club's employees had been intimidated with gang-like tactics by a hardcore group of five manipulative hostesses. The good ones who had been bullied were allowed to come back, and remain on the payroll. The others were summarily let go. Chris looks back on the walkout as a blessing in disguise. Although it took more than a year to de-stigmatize the bar, by the end of his first year of ownership the Checkinn99 was headed in an entirely new direction. When Chris held a meeting to inform staff that it was no longer a hostess bar, everyone thought Chris had gone mad – including Mook. The consensus among the staff was that Checkinn99 had to remain a hostess club because that was what the longtime customers wanted. "They're not the customers I want," Chris replied.

Chris went with a business plan that had no cover charges, affordable drinks, a relaxed atmosphere, 99-baht snacks and a good restaurant menu,. This now can boast Chateaubriand steaks as well as enough Thai dishes to keep everybody happy. Customers were no longer to be greeted with "Where you come from?" and "I no see you long time." The transition took a while, but once the girls on the game could see the game had changed they left one by one, which provided the opportunity necessary to make such a bold change. In the early days, as the transition occurred, there was no profit. Chris put a lot of the money he was making as a logistics consultant in Vietnam back into the club. Some nights there were only four customers, and on a busy night there might be 10. The ace in the hole Chris had was a loyal team of remaining staff – waiters, cooks and servers anchored by their drawing card, the Music of the Heart band. There are currently around 20 employees, or about half the number there were when Chris first took over. This illustrates the advantages Chris and Mook created, by changing the club to a profit-sharing business model. In economic terms, all staff were now on the same page, for the first time.

Music of the Heart became more of the focus for Checkinn99. It wasn't always rock n' roll, but people liked it. Their eclectic song list and energetic performances left everybody happy. Well, almost everybody. Some customers did ask Chris where the girls were, but since the metamorphosis the bread and butter customers are tourists and locally based couples from the baby boomer set. They are looking for alternative forms of entertainment to the tawdry go-go bars blaring loud techno music around the corner. The backpacker crowd still comes in occasionally and they are still welcome, but the clientele has shifted to a loyal local expat following. It's a place you want to go, "where everybody knows your name". Customers also include the curious who walk in off the street, the knowledgeable TripAdvisor crowd and those keyed in to social media. In fact, social media, smartphones and special events have been a boon to Checkinn99's recent renaissance. Chris uses social media to its maximum effect, creating a stream of news and images that keep everyone up-to-date on what's been happening. There's also an ongoing stream of humor, and notes on the history of the place, all of which entertains, and keeps everyone connected.

When TripAdvisor ranked Checkinn99 as one of its Top Twenty Hidden Gems in the World in 2013, it was a big deal, and an increasing number of the website's users could be seen in the club. When it was listed for a second consecutive year in 2014 – a remarkable achievement considering the number of businesses it was up against – traffic increased again. As Bangkok Beat went to press in mid-2015 Checkinn99 was still holding its position.

Naturally, success breeds copycats. A ladyboy bar, full of glamorous transvestites, a complicated assortment of service providers legally recognized as the third sex in Thailand, and a common sight in Bangkok – has recently sprouted up nearby, sporting the name of

Check-In Bar. Thailand is the mecca of knock-offs, so this should come as no surprise. Because of the density of Sukhumvit Road, the GPS location finder for Checkinn99 was not entirely accurate for the Trip Advisor app. People kept being misdirected into the back lane and going up to the ladyboy bar and asking: "Is this the Check Inn?" It didn't take too many lost tourists to ask that question before a lightbulb went on in someone's head and they made the name change. As Lou Reed would have put it, a walk down Sukhumvit Road can be a "walk on the wild side". If you're planning a trip to see Chris and Mook's establishment you'll need more than GPS coordinates, especially now that the sign is gone and no one works the door. It's best that you make sure the numeral 99 is in sight, unless the Check-In Bar is your destination of choice – which it is, for many.

The tunnel leading from Checkinn99 to Sukhumvit Road — Photograph by Alasdair McLeod

Back to the original Checkinn99. Take a walk down the killer tunnel and you enter a club where a boss can now take his employees, husbands can take their wives, and girlfriends arrive as a group to have fun, drink and listen to live music. The atmosphere is not unlike being in a timewarp or a movie. Not a movie set, but an actual movie. As Chris likes to say: "All of life is a stage, and so is Checkinn99." Everyone has their part to play, and everyone is happy with their lines. Birthday celebrations are part of a typical evening and very much part of the marketing engine Chris has created, averaging two to three per night. Birthday celebrants get a small cake with a candle, a stuffed bear and a party hat, while Music of the Heart sing the traditional Happy Birthday song along with the entire room of customers. Very soon after, their photos are posted on Facebook, so that, soon all the friends of the birthday celebrant know where the fun has been. As the club's mastermind remarks,: "Everybody wants to wear the hat." Somehow it works, and birthday celebrations have increased, indicating that Checkinn99 is a birthday destination of choice in Bangkok.

Music of the Heart celebrating another special birthday at Checkinn99

Chris also went against the grain when he decided to keep the club open seven days a week. The previous Danish owners always had always closed on Sundays, considering it a money-losing day. Chris implemented a new concept. He decided to start a Sunday jazz jam session, starting at around 2.30pm, with the music flowing until 6pm, followed by another seven hours of live entertainment from Music of the Heart.

For the Jazz on Sukhumvit concept, Chris turned over the reins to two exceptionally talented musicians – saxophone player William Wait, and keyboard player Keith Nolan. Chris had first met Keith when he saw a Blues Brothers performance in Ho Chi Minh City. Both Keith and William are brilliant in their own way, and committed to their music. William has his regular players: Khun Torr on drums and Khun Tico on keys. Keith Nolan, when he is not on stage playing and singing, assumes the role of Chris on Sundays, by managing the floor greeting, and chatting with customers and being the social media coordinator, taking pictures and videos and uploading them to the popular Jazz on Sukhumvit Facebook page.

William Wait on saxophone and Keith Nolan on keyboard during Sunday jazz at Checkinn99

William has a difficult task. Like a good player-coach on a talented basketball team, he has to distribute the ball evenly among the many players, making sure the precious minutes on stage are properly distributed among the talent that floats in and out every Sunday. The level of play can be mind-blowing, whether you are a hardcore jazz enthusiast or just a casual fan. As I write in another chapter, you never know when greatness will appear. One week it can be a trombone player traveling through Bangkok from New York City; the next week it's Gerry Brown, the drummer for Stevie Wonder. Steve Cannon often pops in with his trumpet, before his five-star hotel appearances.

Jazz artists from around the globe, playing at a world-class level, can be found on any given Sunday at Checkinn99. One example was a Sunday in May, 2014, when Jafar Idris was in the house. You didn't talk when Jafar was playing his saxophone alongside William Wait, although many mouths fell open, that afternoon.

William Wait far left and Jafar Idris front and center during a Sunday jazz session at Checkinn99

Listen to Jafar on YouTube or download his high quality audio recordings. You won't be disappointed. Jafar has traveled, played and been well paid to play his saxophone all over the world, yet his Facebook cover picture shows him playing at the Checkinn99. What are the odds of that? Pretty good, actually.

Sunday Jazz at Checkinn99 started slowly. It had been going on for four months by the time I checked it out for the first time. Customers were sparse despite the level of play, often numbering 20 or fewer in those early days. Now, under the leadership of William, Keith and

Chris, it does a good trade. Sometimes seats are hard to find. Another reason I like Sundays is that Chris Catto-Smith considers it his "day off" from the two full-time jobs he has. So where does he like to spend his Sundays? Often, at Jazz on Sukhumvit at Checkinn99, hanging out with his many friends. And Chris has made a lot of friends during his time in Bangkok, for he knows well, you can have a thousand friends in Bangkok, but one enemy is too many.

The success of Checkinn99 today is directly related to the entrepreneurial ability, risk-taking and innovations brought in by Chris and Mook. In addition to turning a non-revenue producing Sunday into the profitable and entertaining Sunday jazz jams, Checkinn99 became known as a safe haven for artists, a place where they can relax and perform. The Bangkok Fiction Night of Noir events have become increasingly popular with each year, spearheaded by James A. Newman and Chris Coles. Author signings by Dean Barrett are fun and festive evenings. One of the most popular nights was the performance of Eve Ensler's episodic play The Vagina Monologues. Other special events have included the Moulin Rouge musical, Blues Brothers nights and Christmas pantomime. In addition the popular Rocky Horror Show (the full Samuel French production), starring Chris Wegoda and a dozen others, was brought to Bangkok for the very first time, and will return in 2015. The musicals are all possible through the participation of the Music of the Heart band, who sometimes make up over half the cast.

Chris Wegoda as Dr Frank-N-Furter

The second annual Jazz Dayfest was a success and will be brought back every December. Among the musicians at Jazzfest, as it is commonly referred to, were soulful singer Clifton Hardy, a regular performer at Sunday Sukhumvit Jazz at Checkinn99 and at Above Eleven on Sukumvit 11; Peter Montalbano, a world-class trumpet player who originally came to Thailand in the 1960s as a member of the Peace Corps, can also be heard blowing in the club. If you catch Peter in the right mood, he does a great Louis Armstrong imitation, and he blows like Satchmo too.

Warren Fryar at Jazz Fest 2014

Warren Fryar is another regular at Checkinn99 as a singer and trumpet player. You can catch Warren playing with his band Mother Funky at Bangkok clubs such as Brown Sugar and Saxophone. Vocalist Keithin Carter is another Checkinn99 Sunday Jazz favorite. Keithin gives an emotional, 100 per cent effort, every time he's at the microphone, and is a regular performer at Maggie Choo's. That's another club that should be on everyone's list of places to go in Bangkok.

Clifton Hardy [L] Ted Lewand [seated] Peter Montalbano on trumpet

As singer, musician, actor, and author Kevin Wood puts it, "Chris Catto-Smith has a pig-headed determination to give a voice to the often unheard talents of writers, poets, actors, singers, musicians and artists. Checkinn99 is a highly refreshing venue." Kevin Wood, as the official musical director for Check Inn99 special events and musicals, has been instrumental in improving the routines put on by Music of the Heart. This is an important role, as Music of the Heart have become the main drawing card for Checkinn99 under the new format.

Not only has Chris Catto-Smith given new life to artists in Bangkok, allowing them to relax, perform and support each other, but the artists have breathed new life into Chris. It's a classic win-win for the community and for the entertainment business in Bangkok. One of the highlights of 2014 for the customers and staff of Checkinn99 was learning that Chris would be eligible for the Big Chilli Entrepreneur of the Year Award. A number of customers and many of the staff turned out for the awards ceremony, hosted by popular Thailand TV personality

Kevin Wood performing at Checkinn99 before the Bangkok Fiction Night of Noir II —
Photograph by Alasdair McLeod

and newspaper columnist Andrew Biggs, another Australian. Awards ceremonies tend to be dry, stodgy affairs in the best of circumstances. The Big Chilli Awards were business-oriented and Chris was nominated in the entertainment category. How best to provide entertainment for such an event? Problem solved by logistics man Chris Catto-Smith. Music of the Heart members Kiko, Cherry, Donna, Grace and April performed a very rare live event away from their Checkinn99 home for one of only a very few times in the past 16 years. They turned what could have been a boring evening into another memorable Bangkok night. There is a great YouTube video shot by Alasdair McLeod showing Music of the Heart performing that night, which is worth seeking out.

Music of the Heart after performing the Boogie Woogie Bugle Boy of Company B.
On the far right is MC Andrew Biggs.

The fact that Chris won the Big Chilli Entrepreneur of the Year Award for 2014 was a bonus. Just being nominated was an honour, he told a group of friends before the winners were announced. "By just being here, I've already won."

It is this combination of generosity, humility and quiet confidence that endears Chris to his customers and staff. He has a good time when he sees other people having a good time. It's a rare quality. Checkinn99 is set up as a legacy business, which is unique in Bangkok. Qualified employees will get a retirement income.

As regular customer Christopher G. Moore, author of The Comfort Zone, The Big Weird, and Fear and Loathing in Bangkok puts it so well, "Checkinn99 is a modern Silk Road oasis where painters, poets, writers, and musicians converge to relax, chill and share a creative zone." Checkinn99 is a creative zone located in the midst of the red light zone. That's part of the appeal.

Chris Catto-Smith was interviewed by the Bangkok Post for an article headlined 'Checkinn to a bygone Bangkok', which was published in February 2015 – on Friday the 13th . Regarding the infamous nearby

Chris Catto-Smith(R) receiving his Big Chilli Entrepreneur of the Year Award

entertainment zones, he said: "It would sanitize Bangkok if these places closed down, but you would lose the edge of Bangkok. The thing about Bangkok is it's crazy and mixed up. If people want to go to easy places, we all could just book into a Club Med resort."

Christopher G. Moore echoed those sentiments: "If Checkinn99 wasn't in a sketchy neighborhood, artists wouldn't feel at home. Art emerges not from HiSo penthouses but from the back alley."

To learn about the modern Checkinn99 story one needs to understand the yin behind the yang – the good woman behind the successful man – Jiraporn Sriharach, or Mook. As I have already mentioned, Chris' wife is an officer in the Royal Thai Police Force. Her personal story reveals a woman with great character. In 2004 Mook, entered the police academy under a special scheme open to the wives or children of policemen killed on duty. Mook is the daughter of a slain police officer. Through this program, Mook sought and found an opportunity to become the one family member allowed to fill her father's shoes. Although she had already undertaken Thai army officer courses and graduated as a lieutenant in 1999, she decided to join the police force instead. Her father had been killed several years earlier during a drug-related arrest in the Northeast of Thailand, where Mook hails from. Then, taking over the role of family breadwinner, Mook, as a newly qualified industrial engineer, moved to Bangkok to look for work. She was met with a biased, prejudiced world. Fortunately, she met Chris in her first weeks in Bangkok, and an immediate and fiery bond was formed. The volatile element remains, as Chris and Mook do not always agree on how best to run the Checkinn99. But the combination of the two very different personalities has been crucial for the revival of the club.

After selling her red 750cc motorcycle, Mook was ready to settle down, joining the police after the birth of their daughter Anny. Chris and Mook were married and have lived together for more than 16 years, raising Anny and son Charlie while holding down full-time jobs.

Mook's first assignment was with the royal protocol department in police headquarters. This was a high-profile role, and she was soon promoted as an administrator and planner for the general staff. After transferring to the Immigration Bureau, Mook passed her inspector's course in 2010. Being a Thai police inspector is something Mook likes to keep quiet, preferring not to advertise the fact – unless there are times you need some leverage, as you might, from time to time, when owning a bar and nightclub on lower Sukhumvit Road.

In the first six months after taking over Checkinn99, Chris and Mook were faced with a raft of petty gangsters, minor extortionists, thugs, opportunists and local officials, along with some enterprising local police officers. All took the time to come and pay their respects to the new owners, and find out what they were offering.

With confidence, Mook was able to deal with these situations in the way Thais love – no confrontation, but with a clear understanding of power and hierarchy sorted out. These types of minor extortionist practices are not uncommon or surprising in Thailand. One night, with a bar full of customers, eight theatrically dressed gangsters came into Checkinn99. They were ridiculously overdressed and could have come straight out of a Thai soap drama or central casting in Hollywood – moustaches, black jackets, Elvis hairdos, sunglasses and chewed up faces. They moved quickly to all exits of the bar, and at the door was another stereotypical character wearing what most Thais would recognize as a policeman's uniform – brown trousers, black shiny shoes with steel instep, and black jacket. No rank shown; none needed. Mook immediately saw what was going on, and told Chris to sit tight. She went up to the obvious spokesman, right up into his space, and looked down at his hands waiting for him to wai her. In Thailand, the junior person immediately proffers the wai – a polite bow with the hands pressed together – to the senior person in status. Instinctively, Thais know what to do. They rarely get it wrong – except when they make the effort to dress as gangsters, and bring their mates along similarly dressed, plus a patsy policemen you would naturally expect to be wai-ed first. Not so with Mook – anyone who comes into her bar needs to show her respect first. Thailand has a hierarchical society that is often referred to as a patronage system. Mook, understanding full well the patron card she was holding, handled herself with her accustomed grace (along with a touch of coolness, under pressure). After a long standoff and all the cards were played – as if a game of poker – the outcome became clear. The stakes for the loser were high. There would be no protection payments paid by Checkinn99. Word hit the streets – a new sheriff was in town.

Chris Catto-Smith may have been inspired by the many artists that frequent his establishment, but the artists have been inspired in return. Film-makers have used Checkinn99 for location shoots, including nightlub scenes for the recently released Thai movie The Last Executioner. Christopher G. Moore has his protagonist, Vincent Calvino, walk down the Checkinn99 tunnel musing about the dwarf doorman in *Missing in Rangoon*. Author T. Hunt Locke, in his historical mystery *Jim Thompson is Alive!* has his sleuth Sam Collins visit Checkinn99 to have a talk with Mama Noi and gather clues regarding the whereabouts of the former CIA man Jim Thompson. Author Alan Mehew has written a thriller called *Lethal Legacy*, loosely based on a cast from Checkinn99. It includes the character of a resourceful weapons and demolition expert, based on a real-life character and past partner of Checkinn99 in the old Danish days. John Gartland's poem *The Eye*, about the Mambo Hotel and Bangkok personalities, was inspired by Checkinn99. The title and

Mook and Chris Catto-Smith on the evening of a Dean Barrett book launch at Checkinn99

inspiration for some scenes of James A. Newman's novel *The White Flamingo* came directly from the cast-iron white flamingoes standing below the now iconic painting of Soi Cowboy by expressionist painter Chris Coles. And the book you are reading, *Bangkok Beat*, was inspired in large part by Checkinn99, its customers and the events that occur in what singer and special patron Bernard Servello refers to as "a special place".

It is impossible to tell the whole story of Checkinn99 in one chapter of any one book. I have barely scratched the surface of what went on and what goes on at the club to this very day. My abilities as a writer are modest and this chapter has tested their limits. I have done my best.

Left to Right: James A. Newman, John Gartland, Chris Catto-Smith, Kevin Cummings, Chris Coles and Christopher G. Moore gather for a group shot during a break in the Sunday jazz jam at Checkinn99

The best way for you to explore the history of Checkinn99 is to visit for yourself, if possible, and make some history of your own. Even after being a regular customer of Checkinn99 for the past three years and writing this chapter, I don't understand exactly, how Chris and Mook are able to do what they do. I'm just very glad they do it, as are their legions of fans and customers from around the globe. It's not such a hidden gem any more but it's still, to those in know, a very special place.

Legendary Checkinn99 singer and special patron Bernard Servello

[VII]

The Beauty of Isaan
by Thom H. Locke

JUMPED ON THE skytrain. "Exit at Nana, directly opposite the Landmark Hotel, you can't miss us. Look for the sign, *Checkinn99.*"

The *'you can't miss us'* comment I later understood as Aussie humor. A glance at my watch showed I was early. I grabbed a beer and retreated back to the long entranceway I had just passed through. A Marlboro was torched. The photos lining the tunnel had not been missed. I now gave them the attention they deserved. A story, somewhat haunting, was on display.

The story of my appearance is worth noting. Stuck at a crossroads in my book, 450 pages in yet no ending in sight. Actually, the ending was clear, but how to get there? I'm a sleuth. No stranger to the labor of historical research, the answer lay close. A day or two, perhaps, and an article, an interview was found. The blog was titled 'Stickman

Bangkok'. I had never read it but the name was not unfamiliar. A name came to my attention. Mama Noi.

It would have been easy to walk into the bar, call her over, ply her with drinks, and get the information I was seeking. But, I had come down to the Big Smoke from up north. I needed to make sure the elderly mamasan would be on the premises. I needed to make sure she'd talk. Plus, an introduction to the owner seemed the polite course of action. My characters are often brusque. I am not.

Luckily I acted prudently. A friendship was born. The owner, Chris Catto-Smith, enthusiastically approved my request and encouraged Mama Noi to sit for the interview. A certain photo caught my eye. My mug was refilled. I lit up another stick. Bob Hope, a half-smirk caught in time, a stunning lady on his lap with an ample cleavage on display, acknowledged my presence. "This is a Sam Collins' type of joint," I murmured. An idea clicked in my mind. The ending to *Jim Thompson Is Alive!* crept ever closer.

The butt stubbed out, I was ushered to a shabby chic lounge chair and settled in. I had conducted several interviews to try to develop a sense of the times within which Jim Thompson maneuvered. One such interview, with a former US State Department official, had been quite helpful. Another, with a person prominent in the Thai art world, much less so. Both had been engaged with significant preparation. Mama Noi I would wing.

The interview actually began as I followed her movements around the club. The lady known as the Beauty of Isaan glided from one corner of the club to the next, four pillars observed, at each one a Buddhist ritual conducted. Strangely, I was taken back to my altar boy days at St Agatha's. The thought then struck me, wryly, that back in her day Noi had likely taken many a lad not far removed from the frock. My mind was clicking. Sam Collins too was a Boston boy. Would a part of his past emerge leading him to Jim Thompson?

"Sir, would you like a drink?"

I noted Mama Noi walk past. "Sure, a jug of Heineken please. And what does the mamasan prefer?"

The comely young waitress smiled with a wink. A hint of Kampuchea

(Cambodia) shone through her Thai eyes. My order arrived with my interview subject.

"Can I help you, darling?"

Dark tantalizing eyes bore into me. They seemed so familiar. Had I come across her before? Indeed I had. I was looking at the sexy young lady who had occupied Bob Hope's lap those many years ago. Beauty fades. It does not desert. I was sitting with one of the most beautiful women I had ever encountered. My heart skipped. I fumbled with my words, an awestruck kid trying to find just the right tone of seduction. A shot of Crystal Head Vodka made its way to me.

"Chris, boss, sorry he late. Here, drink up, on the house."

The shot of courage helped me find my groove. Mama Noi was funny, a fountain of information, and so at ease with her place in life.

"I came down to Bangkok from Ubon Ratchatani. Only 17, maybe 1960, and I found my way into this life." She waved her arms around the room. "It was different then," she said. Her voice was resigned yet not sad.

"Different how?" I asked.

"The name in those days was the Copa. The club I mean," she clarified. "My name always Noi." Mama flipped her head back in a deep laugh. She then squeezed her breasts. "Noi mean little. But the boys liked these, big." I joined her revelry.

"Tell me about Bing," I prodded. It was time to dig deep. Mama Noi was legend. She had seduced and been swept away by Hollywood royalty. When I exited out of the tunnel of memories, I wanted to know the story. I wanted to feel 60s Bangkok. Noi wasn't just some girl in some club. The Isaan beauty was *the girl* in *the club*.

"We Thai do not, cannot, talk about people from a higher status. And it was so long ago..." Her voice faded away. "My memory is not so good."

The waitress came to tend to our drinks. She refilled my mug. Another lady drink was ordered for Noi. The Crystal Head was smooth and quickly washed down.

"Where are you from?" she asked, her eyes beaming back to life.

"Boston," I replied.

"Ah," she laughed. "I remember the snow! The Boston Park Plaza. Bing loved to spend time there – '66 or '67, not too long before I returned."

She seemed to relax into her reminiscence, and events of another era came flowing back to life. And it was quite a whirlwind adventure she had enjoyed with her Hollywood icon. Atlantic to Pacific, trips to Mexico and a bit of mischief in Paris. A lifetime in a fling. I let her go, us both enjoying the ride.

She finally, abruptly even, stopped. "You're writing a book." Her voice contained a dash of suspicion.

"I am."

"Surely not about me."

"No. I am writing a novel around the disappearance of Jim Thompson. Did you know him?"

"Oh no. But Bing and Bob would visit him at his house, you know, now a museum, from time to time."

"And you never joined?"

"I was the *mia noi*, the second wife. I knew my place. But, even if I had, Thompson, from what I heard, wasn't the type you *got to know*."

I was puzzled at what she said. Cryptic. I tried to get her to elaborate but she danced easily away. Finally she held up her hand. "You see, every night I visit the four corners of our home. It is to keep the spirits happy so they will keep the ghosts away. Darling, you talk of a ghost."

Mama Noi looked deeply in my eyes, then leaned over the table and kissed me gently on the cheek. "I hope you find what you are looking for. He is not here." With that she was off.

In that respect Mama Noi was wrong. In that evening, within that moment, Noi led Sam Collins exactly where he needed to go. My voila moment had arrived.

Mama is now a friend. I always look forward, on my trips to the Big Smoke, to a night at Checkinn99. My first order of business is to buy the Beauty of Isaan a drink and sit for a chat. There is no talk of ghosts, just two acquaintances catching up. But, on your next trip, or if it is your first walk down the tunnel, buy a drink for the lovely lady from Ubon Ratchatani and let yourself be escorted into yesteryear.

[VIII]

Bangkok Fiction Night of Noir I

I WAS ONE OF the lucky ones in attendance at the first Bangkok Fiction Night of Noir, held at the Checkinn99 in April 2013. It was a night of music, poetry, art, literature readings and a sense of community. A village formed, however briefly, in a city of 12 million souls. The evening started off with British author James A. Newman, the organizer of the event, reading from the works of American author and essayist William S. Burroughs and also from his own novel, *Bangkok Express*, in an emotional and appropriate kick-off. Bangkok is a city where anything is possible, and that evening had become possible because of James A. Newman. One of three Bangkok Fiction Night of Noir readings he is responsible for, so far. Good on him.

Poet John Gartland, from England, whose poetry you'll read later in the book, was next with readings from his very dark and noir poetry. Of the entire line-up I was least familiar with John's work and I came away thoroughly entertained. It was a thoughtful and at times brutally accurate read. I found myself nodding in agreement many times with his dark assessment of Bangkok, and often smiling wryly at the accuracy of it all. Next up was a Bangkok legend, playwright, poet and author Dean Barrett, with a flawless and insightful reading from his novel *Identity Theft: Alzheimer's In America, Sex in Thailand, Tangles of the Mind*. Dean is multi-talented, and if my 58-year-old eyes were not lying there were times the 70-year-old Barrett did not have to depend on his glasses. Amazing. Dean is a role model and mentor to many in Bangkok, and not just writers. Always witty, always gracious. My only nit with Dean is he carries his very good quality of self-deprecation a little too far. I have a theory that sometimes there is a direct relationship between talent and self-deprecation, and the example set by Dean supports my theory. Next up was writer and Crime Wave Press publisher Tom Vater. I was much more familiar with how Tom has lived his life than his books, before that evening. The man knows how to live. Do yourself a favor and Google Tom Vater or Crime Wave Press if you are not familiar with either. You will not be bored. He is a very interesting man leading a very interesting life, and that night I had the pleasure of meeting him for the first time.

Bangkok artist and fellow American Chris Coles was up next. Coles is never boring. He is a former film-maker, and is a student and master of the visual arts. Chris never disappoints with his presentations. A slideshow of his many colorful and vibrant paintings was shown as he was at the microphone. He spoke of the noir movement in Bangkok and summed it up brilliantly in two words: density and velocity. As a professional summarizer of written documents, I don't think you can do any better in summarizing the attraction of the Bangkok night. They are worth repeating: density and velocity. That is the Bangkok night. That is what brings 14-22 million people on airplanes to Thailand every year. And the number continues to grow.

Chris had the pleasure of introducing another well-known Bangkok author, Christopher G. Moore. Christopher read an excerpt from his short story *Reunion*, from the anthology *Phnom Penh Noir*, about helping a Cambodian refugee get to America. Christopher relayed to the audience that there are times when an author meets a character he wrote about – sometimes they were real, sometimes they had been a work of fiction that became real. An interesting and entirely believable admission. The story concluded with these powerful words: "I don't believe in capital punishment except for one offense: fucking with people's hopes and dreams. Put those bastards against the nearest wall and shoot them."

And so this was how the first Bangkok Fiction Night of Noir concluded. But not really. It was just the beginning of more memorable moments as Chris Catto-Smith, the owner/manager of Checkinn99, came to the microphone and gave a brief history of the historic cabaret club. A seed was planted that night, which has grown into *Bangkok Beat*. Books were bought, books were signed, many pictures were taken and then Music of the Heart came on. They have been performing there for more than 15 years, and they were great. James A. Newman was also great for conceiving the night. It was a night to remember. As Dean Barrett so eloquently said when he thanked the audience for coming out, in Bangkok you have a lot of choices. For anybody who attended the initial Bangkok Fiction Night of Noir, it was a very good choice. People drifted out around midnight. The night was still young on the Bangkok beat.

[IX]

Cara Black Interview – Welcome Back to Thailand

CARA BLACK IS one of a number of talented authors published by Soho Crime, an imprint of Soho Publishing. They include none other than Colin Cotterill, creator of the Dr Siri series set in Laos; Timothy Hallinan, author of six Poke Rafferty novels set in Thailand; and Lisa Brackmann, author of the critically acclaimed *Rock Paper Tiger* and *Hour of the Rat*, set in China. Coincidentally or not, all of the above authors have been extremely nice to me and very cooperative.

It was my pleasure to welcome Cara Black back to Thailand and interview her for Bangkok Beat.

KC: I found it interesting to learn that you spent some time in Thailand in the 1970s. What are your recollections of Thailand and Thai people from that time? How has the country changed and how have the people changed, if they have?

CB: I lived in Bangkok for five months – way past my visa – when the Vietnam War was in full swing. After traveling from India and running short of cash, a fellow traveler – also staying at the Atlanta Hotel – advised me to "go to Patpong and look for a hostess job". The second bar I tried, a large Chinese one, hired me on the spot as the only foreign hostess. Bangkok then had few high rises, no BTS, and the tuk-tuks were bicycle powered. Every morning on the soi the monks came with their bowls for alms – that hasn't changed – and I remember in the evening before work everyone putting offerings before the shrine at the next corner. Bangkok was such a quiet place – apart from the adrenalin charged GIs on R+R from battle duty in Vietnam. One evening everyone on the soi was excited – my Thai was very limited – something about a boat and offering. Finally the lady on the soi from whom I bought my *som tum* and sticky rice every day explained with laughter and sign language that I should take a tuk-tuk to the Chao Praya. The river was full of lantern boats with candles for Loy Kratong. Amazing. People prayed before launching them into the water. I've never forgotten the glittering lighted lanterns floating by the thousands past the temples. The warmth and gracefulness of the Thai people stayed with me, and I've found it again.

KC: Those are wonderful recollections, Cara. They will help explain the attraction Thailand still holds today for many. I've just finished reading my first Aimee Leduc Investigation novel, *Murder Below Montparnase*. But it is your 13th in the series. And the 14th, *Murder In Pigalle*, is due to hit the book shops in March of 2014. Raymond Chandler wrote a total of seven Philip Marlowe novels, I believe, back in another era and another time as far as publishing goes. Your goal is to write 20 Aimee Leduc Investigation novels. What do you like about writing a long series of novels involving Aimee? What difficulties, if any, does it pose writing a lengthy series?

CB: I never intended to write a series, much less set in Paris. I was thrilled to get published. That still feels incredible, and I count myself lucky. In *Murder in the Marais*, my first book, I was passionate to write about the story I'd heard from my friend's mother who was a hidden Jewish girl during the German occupation. Using that theme to explore the less-known side of collaboration, the gray areas, I needed a detective. She needed to be half-American because I couldn't write as a French woman – I can't even tie my scarf the right way – but Aimée in the detective mold made famous by Chandler is a lone wolf, neither fish nor fowl, an outsider, yet part of a Paris I saw. Every book in the series – at its core – explores social issues, mores, traces of old colonialism and often the ethnic areas I stumble upon in Paris. Paris has twenty arrondissements, each with a distinctive flavor and ambience, which still excites me. I feel fortunate to have the chance to write stories of the places, the people who inhabit these particular slices of Paris and research the history that pervades the cobblestones. To keep a series fresh and yet familiar to readers who want to spend time again with the characters, who must grow and change, is a challenge I never envisioned, but I love it.

KC: Your energy comes across in your writing and also here. A younger Aimee Leduc reminds me of the cool girl I would have been attracted to but afraid to ask to dance in high school. Aimee likes the bad boys and may have a tattoo or three. Tell me about Aimée's romantic interests in the past and from which novel(s) readers can find them?

CB: In the first three books, Aimée's gotten involved in an on-again off-again affair with Yves, a French journalist who she keeps saying goodbye to on the boulevard Saint Germain or on Cairo street corners. She's drawn to him like metal filings to a magnet – the traveling foreign correspondent, a bad boy and unavailable, as her best friend Martine keeps telling her. In *Murder on the Rue de Paradis*, set in the tenth arrondissement, their relationship takes a turn on the Canal Saint-Martin. I can't reveal much, but decisive and heart-rending come to mind. In *Murder in the Bastille*, she's treated by Guy, an eye surgeon with whom she develops a relationship in later books (*Murder in Clichy*, *Murder in Montmartre*). But he's the type who wants her to settle down, become a doctor's wife, give luncheons and live in Neuilly. Not Aimée's style at all. Aimée's vowed never to become involved with a 'flic', a French cop (she knows it's a hard life and killer on relationships – her father was a former flic) but Melac, a detective in the elite Brigade Criminelle, homicide squad in Paris treats her as a suspect in *Murder on the Ile Saint-Louis* (where she lives) and becomes more than she bargained for. Things get complicated from there on. She's got an air of *je ne sais quoi*, handles a Beretta, finds haute couture at the flea market – all the things I've experienced and some I'd like to. And along with it Aimée's personal life – her boyfriends, the sense of belonging she's always looking for which reflects the young Parisiennes I know who, even though chic, slim and with cheekbones that could slice paper, have relationship trouble.

KC: Can you tell me when your love of Paris began? What is the attraction for you, if you can explain it to me?

CB: My Father was a Francophile – loved good food and wine and Jacques Tati movies. He sent me to a French school in California with old French nuns, back in the day when they wore headgear like the Flying Nun. We learned what I later found out to be an archaic form of French. I had so many expectations and ideas of what France would be like that the first time I arrived in Paris it felt familiar yet different. Hitting Paris with a backpack to find the wafting scents of butter from the boulangerie, the apricot sunset painting the roof tiles, the quais with bookstalls lining the Seine, the narrow cobbled streets with women clattering on high heels, sealed it for me. I fell in love with the City of Light, which has turned into a long-running affair. I love the Parisians – cynical one minute, caring the next, passionate over everything and full of contradictions. That keeps me coming back hoping someday I'll understand them ... but mystery and elusiveness like any good affair keeps it alive.

KC: When was the last time you smoked a cigar?

CB: Last October in Paris, outside a café – a Cuban Cohibo.

KC: That trumps my Wolf Brothers Crook after the 49ers Super Bowl XVI victory. And I doubt you'd be impressed that it was rum soaked, so let's change the subject. Anais Nin has one of my favorite quotes on writing: "We write to taste life twice, in the moment and in retrospect." She and Henry Miller get a mention in *Murder Below Montparnasse*. I like many of the quotes Henry has on writing. Feel free to comment on either of those two writers, if you'd like, but I'd like to know how you would complete the sentence: We write …

CB: We write to give a voice to those who aren't heard. PS: That's funny, Kevin, I have that saying above my computer!

KC: I like your sentence. It ties right in with the best advice I ever got from Henry Miller: "Forget yourself." Tell me the best reason I should go back and read the first in the Aimee Leduc Series, where it all began for you, *Murder in the Marais*.

CB: If you like to start at the beginning of a series and meet Aimée Leduc and her dog Miles Davis, a bichon frise, who live in a frayed-around-the-edges 17th century townhouse on the Ile Saint-Louis, and René Friant, a dwarf, her partner, it's a good place to launch. As I mentioned above, this story was inspired by the experiences of my friend's mother – a young hidden Jewish girl during WWII. Her experiences haunted me for years after I heard them. The book took me three-and-a-half years to write – of course I was learning and discovering the process of writing. I think in writing, I tried to make sense of that past time, that world at war on everyday people, the dichotomies and the choices between right and wrong. But what if right and wrong weren't clear when one's trying to survive and live to the next day? And what if that choice to survive comes back to haunt you 50 years later in the City of Light?

KC: You've made a good case for me. And those Miles Davis references in *Murder Below Montparnasse* take on a whole new context. Thank you Cara Black, again, for doing this interview.

[X]

Bangkok Fiction Night of Noir II

NINE MONTHS AFTER Night of Noir I, author James A. Newman, artist Chris Coles and company decided it would be a good idea to hold a Bangkok Night of Noir II. It was. The purpose was to have an evening of music, readings, art and photography depicting the numerous sources of noir found in Bangkok. The Checkinn99 is the perfect venue for such an event – a place where Bob Hope, Dean Martin, Bing Crosby and Raquel Welch relaxed after United Service Organizations shows during the Vietnam War. To say the club has a colorful history is certainly an understatement! It's a place where, Christopher G. Moore reminded us in a finale reading, about the infamous dwarf named Sumai who worked as the doorman for years. And then one day he disappeared. How does a dwarf go missing? It's Bangkok, that's how.

The day of Bangkok's second Night of Noir – Sunday, January 5, 2014 – there was a film crew shooting a karaoke scene in the morning inside the Checkinn99 for the recently released movie about Thailand's infamous last executioner, Chaovaret Jaruboon, a drinking buddy of

Bangkok author Jim Algie and a living noir legend until he died in 2012. If you were looking for a setting to read dark fiction and show the neon noir world of Bangkok's nightlife, you were in the right place. There was a full house, and the club was much more crowded than it had been for the previous event.

The readings kicked off later than anticipated, but the Music of the Heart Band came to the rescue as people were still buying books and getting them signed. Highlights for me, before the readings began, were talking with the visiting American mystery writer Cara Black about some of her colleagues at the publisher Soho Crime, such as Lisa Brackmann, Timothy Hallinan and Martin Limon. It was also a pleasure to meet John Burdett, author of the Bangkok crime series starring Detective Sonchai Jitpleecheep of the Royal Thai Police, which started with *Bangkok 8*. Just when I was getting impatient, the Music of the Heart Band broke out into a song in French, known for its dedication to the fighters of the French Foreign Legion – *Non, je ne regrette rien*, which caused Cara Black, a *New York Times* best-selling author and Francophile, to smile broadly and sing along.

The readings started shortly thereafter with screenwriter, actor and presentation coach John Marengo reading from James A. Newman's latest, *The White Flamingo*. Marengo has decades of acting and voice-over credits. Newman's fictional Fun City, AKA Pattaya never sounded better or bleaker, depending on your perspective, coming from Marengo's microphone. That was followed by his reading of the Charles Bukowski poem *Dinosauria, We* – a dark Bukowski special about death, decay and pessimism for mankind.

Writer and publisher Tom Vater, author of *Devil's Road to Kathmandu* and *The Cambodian Book of the Dead*, read next. When Vater talks, I listen. He always has something interesting to say. He prefaced his reading with some fascinating history regarding the world's busiest airport up until 1975, run by the CIA in Long Cheng in Laos. Tom is the co-author of the screenplay for the documentary *The Most Secret Place on Earth – The CIA's Covert War in Laos*. Tom read from his novel *The Man With The Golden Mind*, which has since been published. It was a riveting read.

The Dean of Bangkok Fiction was up next to read from a book I am proud to say is in my library: *The Go Go Dancer Who Stole My Viagra and other Poetic Tragedies of Thailand.* I am a fan of Dean Barrett's writing and poetry. I am also a Dean Barrett fan. The world needs more authors like Dean Barrett, a lot more. He is always entertaining, gracious and humorous. All of Dean's readings are very good, but it's tough to beat the classic *No One Wants to Boom Boom Anymore.*

John Burdett was also in the house, and he was a pleasure to see and listen to as well. He read from his latest in his Sonchai Jitpleecheep series, *Vulture Peak*, which is about organ trafficking. You'll read much more about *Vulture Peak* in this book. He started off by juxtaposing these two quotations from the beginning of the novel, which gets one thinking about morality and unintended consequences:

What you do to yourself, you do to the world. What you do to the world, you do to yourself. – Buddhist proverb.

If a living donor can do without an organ, why shouldn't the donor profit and medical science benefit? – Janet Radcliffe-Richards, *Lancet* 352 (1998).

John then read a wonderful passage on the murder investigation from *Vulture Peak*. I include only the last part of the brilliant conclusion here:

"Really? That will be helpful. By the way, what genders are the victims?"

"Two men and a woman."

Now I notice something else. "No blood?"

"Somebody cleaned up meticulously. They even used some chemical that neutralizes our tests. I tell you, whoever did it were professionals. There were certainly more than one." I nod.

"Any ideas?" the doctor asks when we have replaced the sheet.

"You mean whodunit? Only in the more general sense." She raises her eyes. "Ronald Reagan, Milton Friedman, Margaret Thatcher, Adam Smith. Capitalism dunit. Those organs are being worn by somebody else right now."

Cara Black was the guest of honor for the evening, and when he had finished, Burdett handed her the copy of *Vulture Peak* from which he had read. Cara seemed genuinely thrilled to receive it. Chris Coles also presented her with a copy of his book *Navigating The Bangkok Noir*. I learned later that the copy of *The Marriage Tree* which Christopher G. Moore read from last also now resides with Cara in San Francisco. Charles Bukowski got it all wrong. This was a congenial, generous and optimistic group of noir scribes.

Ms. Black, dubbed 'Madam Noir' by MC James A. Newman, was next up. Her protagonist is Aimee Leduc – half-French, half-American. Aimee is a computer fraud expert who can dress fashionably in Paris or in disguise for the job. She can also handle a Beretta when need be. Her partner is a 4-foot dwarf and computer genius named Rene. Together they could probably team up with Moore's protagonist, Vincent Calvino, and solve the mystery of the missing Checkinn99 doorman in a couple of weeks. But that was not the task at hand. Cara Black read from her first of 13 Aimee Leduc novels, *Murder in the Marais*, but she did need the assistance of Calvino's creator, as she wore Moore's spectacles to get the job done. I find her writing style eloquent and tense where it needs to be. Cara lives in San Francisco with her husband and son, and visits Paris frequently. Paris, the City of Light, is always a central character in her novels. I got the feeling Cara likes a good adventure and she got one at Night of Noir II. She seemed to appreciate every moment, and to be in the moment.

A Night of Noir is incomplete without a Chris Coles' presentation and Chris Coles' art. Coles is very enthusiastic about the where and when of Bangkok, and what lies beneath the city. The where being almost anywhere after dark, and the when being now. Chris also had the honor of introducing the final author of the evening, Christopher G. Moore, well known for his more than two dozen novels including the *Vincent Calvino Crime Series* and *The Thai Smile Trilogy*, and his books of essays on Thai politics and culture.

Moore read from his latest Calvino caper – *The Marriage Tree*, the 14th in the popular series, which has Calvino dealing with some cumulative trauma issues regarding the deaths of close friends in

Rangoon and Bangkok. Moore's reading was appropriate as he chose a scene where the fictional Calvino walks down the real-life tunnel of the Checkinn99 to find Colonel Pratt playing the saxophone near some white flamingos. It was art imitating life, and it was fun. Even Uncle Wat, a waiter who has worked at Check Inn for over four decades, was smiling.

Longtime Checkinn99 employees Uncle Wat and Pi Long
take a break before the start of Night of Noir II

Club owner Chris Catto-Smith was coaxed onto the main floor one more time to recount the colorful history of the Checkinn99. I never tire of listening to Chris speak about the old days, or seeing the old black-and-white photos of the club and Bangkok in an earlier time, flashed onto the big screen. Among the things I learned is that those white flamingos may like to hang out around plastic flowers but they are made of cast iron, and Chris even hammered the point home for the audience. The Music of the Heart Band came back on to perform. Some stayed but it was late and many headed for home or wherever they were going in the Bangkok night.

Could the readings have started a little earlier for Night of Noir II? Jerry Hopkins, the biographer for Elvis Presley and Jim Morrison would probably tell you that they could have. But for one night some of the top noir stars from Bangkok and San Francisco aligned just as they were meant to align – perfectly. Newman, Coles, Catto-Smith and the rest of the authors are to be commended, once again, for pulling it off. Anyone who plans to live or stay in Bangkok for any length of time would be well served by the words of the philosopher Alan Watts: "Things are as they are." Since the group picture was taken late some of the authors had already left due to commitments the next day. When asked to join in for the group photo, no one had to ask me twice. I'm not a noir writer or a noir artist, but the world still needs them. And as Chris Coles stated more than once, enthusiastically, during his presentation, this is a city with an almost infinite source of inspiration for noir. It was a memorable evening.

John Marengo, Dean Barrett, Christopher G. Moore, Kevin Cummings, James A. Newman, Cara Black, Chris Coles

As I was heading up in the elevator to my condo around 1.15am, my telephone vibrated. It was Cara Black messaging me: "Back at the bar!" it read. I smiled as the doors opened to my floor. The beat goes on in Bangkok city.

[XI]

Never Go To Thailand,
and the Reasons I Love It

IN 2013, A VIDEO titled *Never Go To Thailand* was making the rounds on the social networking sites. It was a very professional production and a lot of people chose to comment without actually viewing the video – making incorrect assumptions, as we all do in life at times. Not surprising, given that we live in a society that has book reviews written by people who never actually read the book. Why let the small details of living a good life get in the way of our desired end result? The video is worth seeking out on YouTube.

The video's title is tongue-in-cheek. The video itself is the antithesis of the title – at least for most people, I would hope. It shows all the many and varied good things about a country I have spent well over half my time in since 2001.

It got me thinking about why I like Thailand, why I even love it, warts and all. And make no mistake, we are talking about one ugly, wart-covered frog, living in a cracked, upside-down coconut shell, in the dark, at times. Life may be a beach but in Thailand, double murders happen on those beaches, rapes happen on those beaches, yachts are pirated and people are kidnapped not far from those beaches. Tsunamis even happen on those beaches.

I've always believed that, whether it is in business or in life, the little things matter. Little things add up to great sums over time.

"A jug fills drop by drop." – Buddha.

And just as a jug will indisputably fill one drop at a time our lives are filled up one moment at a time. The one common denominator we all share is that we know we are going to die. Unlike the happy and content dog that has no idea he's being measured for a grave, we humans do. We know we may have a choice between ashes or mahogany, small, medium or extra-large containers, but we will all die, one day.

I came to Thailand to die. I needed to be surprised. I wanted to be shocked. Bangkok is unpredictable and it delivers if you give it a chance. Even the small adventures are memorable. – Stirling Silliphant.

The above quote by Oscar-winning Hollywood television and screenplay writer Stirling Silliphant is from Jerry Hopkins' excellent book *Bangkok Babylon: The Real Life Exploits of Bangkok's Legendary Expatriates.* If you want to look at one of the most impressive writing resumés ever, go to Stirling Silliphant's Wikipedia page. If Bangkok was good enough for Stirling, a man who could choose to live anywhere in the world, it sure seems like a great choice for this former Auburn, California boy. Among the advice one receives from reading Hopkins' book is the quote I mention earlier, which I have practiced as much as is practical: "When in Bangkok, do what your mama told you never to do – talk to a stranger."

One of my favorite restaurants on the Gulf of Thailand is Deutsches Haus on Beach Road Soi 4 in Pattaya City. I've been eating there for 15 years. I've eaten there with my wife and daughter; I've eaten there many times with a friend and fellow tennis aficionado, who passed away of a heart attack at the age of 61, a few years ago now. The last time I saw him, before I went to his Buddhist funeral, was at a breakfast we enjoyed at Deutsches Haus on the last day of a trip to see the Pattaya Women's Tennis Tournament, among other things.

The waitress who works there is named Mook. She has served my food many times. Mook is not a stranger but she once was, until I began talking to her, as Jerry advises. Mook is skinny, appears shy, cross-eyed, makes about $8 a day plus tips and has one of the most beautiful smiles you will ever see. And her crossed eyes always sparkle when she smiles. I asked Mook yesterday what her name meant, because most Thai nicknames have an English meaning. *Nok* means bird and *Lek* means small, for example. She just waved her hands, said: "No meaning, Mook *mai suay*." Translated, that means Mook is not beautiful. I don't concur with Mook. I think she is one of the beautiful souls that Henry Miller talks about in the quote that inspired the creation of my blog, Thailand Footprint, and this book, *Bangkok Beat*. This is the quote you'll see at the beginning of the book and it expresses my own personal philosophy:

> *"Develop an interest in life as you see it; the people, things, literature, music – the world is so rich, simply throbbing with rich treasures, beautiful souls and interesting people. Forget yourself."* – Henry Miller

If you can forget yourself long enough, the Mooks of the world are everywhere. I was told later by her waitress friend, Da, that Mook may mean a small seashell, like those you would find in the sand at the beach. The grace, humility, positive attitude towards work and inner beauty of people like Mook is just one reason I love Thailand.

One time I told Mook about how someone had snatched the gold chain off my neck at that very restaurant, two days before – it had been Mook's day off, and she wanted to hear all about the big story she had missed out on. So I told her: as I sat at my table alone, drinking coffee, somewhat lost in thought, a man had approached me and in the blink of an eye yanked off the gold chain I wore around my neck. A chain purchased for $100 in a Kalgoorlie, Australia, gold shop after an eight-hour train ride from Perth, 15 years ago. It had great sentimental value as that purchase came just one day before I met my wife, Ratree, for the first time. I chased my assailant as quickly as I could, repeatedly yelling "Thief! Police!" The calls did not go unanswered. Four good Samaritans, three of whom were Thai motorcycle taxi drivers, answered the calls. One of those three was a large, strong Thai man with five Buddhist amulets dangling on his chest. He was most responsible for pursuing, capturing and holding the man for the police who arrived shortly after, as a crowd gathered round.

One small, very Thai detail: the man who stole my gold chain was a cross-dressing ladyboy or *kathoey* as they are known in Thailand. The *kathoey* that Jerry Hopkins plans to write a book about. There are many in Thailand. And some steal often. The amazing thing was, the transvestite thief could sense the jig was up as the police arrived so he tossed the gold chain on the restaurant floor and then pointed at it, pretending he had helped find it. It was a good ploy on his part as the man in brown who talked to me in English soon after said it would be difficult to press charges with the evidence not found on him. I was so relieved to regain my object of sentimentality that I was okay with that. They did take his picture – 5ft. 8", 150lbs, red lipstick, real shoulder-length black hair and common yellow house-dress. This is Thailand too. Did I mention the restaurant is located just 25 yards from the beach?

As I told Mook the story, which was still very fresh in my mind, she smiled the whole time and seemed genuinely happy, which made me happy. Mook repeated in English several times: "You lucky. You very lucky." On that point, I had to agree with Mook. I am lucky. Lucky to have lived for as many months and years in Thailand as I have. Lucky to have had so many small moments fill my jug. If I am really lucky, that jug is only two-thirds full.

Mook the smiling waitress

Because I cannot think of a better place to fill the last third of life's jug than Thailand. A country where lucky is defined as having a man wearing lipstick and a dress snatch and break your cherished gold necklace. Stirling Silliphant got it right: "Even the small adventures are memorable." Just another day of collecting seashells (and an occasional pearl, for the lucky) at the beach, in Thailand.

[XII]

Artist Chris Coles -
Bringing It to the Bangkok Night

Kevin Cummings (L) James A. Newman (R) Painting by Chris Coles —
Photograph by Alasdair McLeod at Baccara Bar

PULP FICTION WRITER James A. Newman, photographer, poet and videographer Alasdair McLeod and I were granted access to Baccara Bar on Soi Cowboy in Bangkok, for the purpose of photographing the art of Chris Coles and hanging out with the artist during our time there. Four of his paintings had recently been purchased by the owner, a Frenchman named Patrick.

Patrick gave us just one caveat – "No photographing the girls". We complied. In addition to owning Baccara, which most consider the premier go-go bar on Soi Cowboy and in all of Bangkok, he also owns the former Insomnia Disco (now called Insanity), a nightclub called Bangkok Beat (no relation to the book of the same name), Baccara A-Go Go and four other popular venues in Pattaya. Patrick is the exception to the expat bar-owner scene; he is very successful.

As *Bangkok 8* author John Burdett has pointed out in an excellent video interview with the Thai Law Forum, prostitution in Bangkok benefits from being illegal. It remains by and large a cottage industry, run much like a mom-and-pop store. Patrick runs things quite differently, however. He would be the equivalent to the owner of the mansion on the hill. Baccara sees around a thousand customers come in and out of its doors almost every night of the year. That's not an exaggeration. The numbers add up.

Patrick is creative, in a big way, paying attention to lighting, layout, costumes, audio systems and the rules of engagement, or what I would call the art of the deal. The women working there earn large sums of money each month – 200,000 baht a month and up, for the elite – over US$70,000 a year. That is more money in one month than their fathers might make in decades.

Patrick is a collector of Chris Coles' paintings. The businessman showcases the original artworks depicting the Bangkok nightlife, along with 200-plus dancing girls, every night at Baccara, which has distinguished itself from the crowd. High season or low season, the good times roll every night at Baccara – for a price.

The 1994 $5 milkshake in the movie *Pulp Fiction* has been replaced with the 2015 $6 Coke at Baccara. We'll now take an inside look at Baccara Bar and the paintings in the neon world of the artist Chris Coles.

Before we begin our journey into Baccara Bar here is some personal history about Chris Coles, the artist and the man. It's been more than 10 years since Chris and I met, less than the length of a football field away from Baccara Bar. That first meeting occurred because I had stumbled upon his art on one of his websites – Chris Coles Gallery Expressionist Art. I found the art interesting a decade ago. I still do, today. I surmised that the man painting the bright lights and big city of Bangkok might be equally interesting. We arranged to meet. When Chris arrived for that initial meeting I was sitting with a group of five or six guys around a table. I introduced Chris to the others and conversation ensued. Some of it was interesting, some of it mundane. It was always lively, to me, when Chris spoke. I remember thinking: "This guy is the smartest guy in the room."

The fact that the 'room' was the outdoor bar at Tilac on Soi Cowboy, which had 50 or more people scattered about, drinking fluids under a polluted Bangkok night sky didn't matter. Chris talked about his time in California and the movie business. The big-budget 1995 romantic comedy *Cutthroat Island* brought him to Phuket and eventually Bangkok, which the former Maine resident now calls home. Chris is like the carriage horse of a different color in *The Wizard of Oz*. He pulls his own weight. There is only one of him, and he is it.

Meetings with Chris are always memorable. There was a lunch at Suda restaurant years ago when Chris told me that I had to buy *Very Thai*, a book by Philip Cornwel-Smith. After we finished eating we walked to the Times Square Building on Sukhumvit 12 and went up the escalator to Asia Books on the second floor. That Asia Books store is now gone, but I still own *Very Thai* thanks to Chris Coles. It is a great book about everyday popular culture in Thailand.

In 2011, Chris had his art shown at Koi Gallery on Sukhumvit 31, as part of an exhibition titled Color of Day/Color of Night. One half of the gallery was filled with traditional impressionist paintings of trees and flowers by an artist called Anita Suputipong. The other side was filled with the large and loud expressionist art of Chris Coles, in the self-described style of Emil Nolde, Otto Dix and George Grosz. Chris' art made the more favorable impression on this observer. Chris was spread pretty thin that evening but still made time for me, and I met some interesting people on a hot Bangkok night.

Another time I took my wife to hear a talk by Father Joe Maier, the American Catholic priest who lives and works in Bangkok's Klong Toey slums. We had a dinner table reservation. Chris was sitting at the bar in the packed Foreign Correspondents Club of Thailand. After Father Maier finished his very entertaining talk, Chris came over to our table, despite the fact he probably knew over half of the people in the room. He spent half an hour talking to my wife about painting, colors, medium, style and art. My wife appreciated it, and so did I. She had begun taking art classes at our community college in California. Chris had seen some of her work and shared his experiences and enthusiasm. Another memorable table conversation.

More recently, I was about to leave the Checkinn99 in the early hours of the evening on a Sunday, after listening to jazz for many hours, when Chris walked in carrying one of his large acrylic paintings. He stood for a while, holding the painting and looking for the owner, Chris Catto-Smith. They went and hung the painting and Chris eventually came back and joined our table.

That prompted a call to my wife. "Honey, I'll be home later than I said. Chris Coles just arrived." She understood. She likes Chris Coles and so do I. Chris is the kind of friend who will let you know when you have put on an extra 10 pounds. He's also encouraging – to my wife, to me and to others. As he puts it in the video interview with James A. Newman that Alasdair McLeod shot that night: "You need to bring something to the Bangkok night. And then make something out of it." I appreciate Chris Coles. I also like and appreciate the fact that he has some critics. Show me a man with critics and I will show you a man with accomplishments.

Fast forward to Friday the 14th in 2014. Our group of four had just finished eating our dinners at the Queen Victoria Pub. Big dinners. Bangers and mash kind of dinners. We were to meet Chris at Baccara on Soi Cowboy, one of three infamous 'entertainment zones' catering to foreign tourists and expats in Bangkok. Someone joked that no one had ever seen Chris eat dinner, which may explain how he maintains his weight better than most in the City of Angels. Chris is not a starving artist, by any means. But he certainly knows how to paint the overweight, contrary and even the ugly side of life. Bangkok noir. Chris Coles paints Bangkok realities, not American fantasy. Thomas Kinkade he is not. The art made by the Ivy League graduate, and father of an M.I.T grad daughter, has been exhibited in at least four countries. His clientele is diverse, ranging from Baccara owner Patrick to people close to the royal family, Chris Catto-Smith, well known authors, art collectors, and even a blogger or two.

"I like using distortion, sharply contrasting often rather ugly images, disharmonious colors and a rough technique." Chris Coles, artist and author of *Navigating the Bangkok Noir.* (Black and White conversion of a color self-portrait of the artist, Chris Coles).

Chris was waiting outside when we arrived, at a table in front of Baccara Bar, wearing Levi 501 jeans and one of his trademark plaid shirts. We had permission from Patrick to photograph inside and videotape outside. We had Chris Coles for a tour guide, he had agreed to a video interview and it was Friday night in Bangkok city. No one was talking politics and no one was complaining.

We went to the second floor of Baccara, where three of Coles' paintings are showcased. The first floor and second floor of Baccara are quite different in atmosphere. If you have trouble making up your mind where to spend your time, you need only look through the glass ceiling or glass floor, depending on your point of view. To get to the second floor one must climb up a spiral staircase. A fire ravaged Baccara Bar in 2014, destroying three of the four paintings that had been purchased. So Patrick bought three more. Baccara Bar is worth a trip, at least once, for the tourist and expat alike, to see the atmosphere and the Chris Coles paintings. There is no place quite like it. There is no cover charge. Just be prepared for those $6 cokes.

James A. Newman, who writes about the entertainment zones in entertaining fashion, interviewed Chris Coles for a YouTube video,, that evening, which can easily be found. It's a revealing interview put together by Alasdair McLeod. You'll learn what motivates Chris Coles to paint the Bangkok night. Does he go looking for real subjects or does he sometimes make them up? What thought lies behind the atmosphere at Baccara and whether a pulp fiction writer prefers to drink white wine or red?

The Bangkok night can be a big nightmare or a big party. But like any good party you are invited to, as Chris Coles suggests, it's never a bad idea to bring something to it.

[XIII]

Jerry Hopkins - Blue Suede Shoes

"I HOPE I SEE you today, I'm meeting Jerry Hopkins there at 3pm." The message came from Will Yaryan, another former Northern California resident and Bangkok expat. It was all the motivation I needed to get to the Sunday jazz at Checkinn99. I had never met Jerry before but I had heard a lot about him, in addition to reading some of his books and knowing about many others. A passage he wrote in one of those books, *Bangkok Babylon*, had altered the course of many an afternoon and evening for me in Bangkok. I wanted to thank him. I grabbed the book as I headed out the door.

When I arrived at Checkinn99, Dr Will and Jerry Hopkins were already there, listening to the sounds of William Wait on saxophone, Keith Nolan on keyboards and other talented musicians. Dr Will Yaryan is a former record company public relations man with Atlantic Records. His friendship with Jerry Hopkins goes back 40 years. Will introduced me straight away and I learned that Jerry and I have at least one thing in common, which didn't make the conversation easy although it was always interesting. Jerry and I are both deaf in one ear, and the good ears don't always align well. During a break in the jam session, Keith Nolan joined in on the conversation. The subject was music and everybody there liked it. At one point Keith told me the batteries were dead on his camera and asked if I would mind taking a picture of him with Jerry using my camera phone. Done. You can see that picture on Keith's Facebook page where he adds the words, "Jerry Hopkins – A gracious legend."

I agree with Keith Nolan's assessment of Jerry Hopkins. What makes a man a legend? That's a difficult question to answer. For starters, Jerry Hopkins has published best-selling biographies of Jim Morrison of The Doors, Elvis Presley and Jimi Hendrix. In addition he's penned biographies of David Bowie, Don Ho, Yoko Ono and, almost, Raquel Welch. Hopkins is the author of 40 books, including a definitive book on the Hula. He is also the author of an unpublished work, *The History of The Condom*. The most recent of Jerry's books I have purchased is *Romancing The East: A Literary Odyssey from the Heart of Darkness to the River Kwai*. (Tuttle Publishing, Singapore, 2012). It's a wonderful read, spanning 150 years of literature in Asia and featuring the intrepid authors who have travelled here during that time.

But it takes more than books to make a legend. Jerry also had two stints as a correspondent for *Rolling Stone* – one in London and one in Los Angeles – and served as contributing editor for the iconic magazine for 20 years. His stories are legendary and enchanting. On that first day I heard about his time as chief "kook booker" for *The Steve Allen Show*, where he met Frank Zappa for the first time. Jerry's job was to book the talent for *The Steve Allen Show* and the kookier the talent the better. About 30 minutes into the conversation I handed Jerry my copy of *Bangkok Babylon*. Rather than have him sign in the standard place, I asked him if he would read a passage on page 16, which had meant so much to me since I first read it almost 10 years ago. He did. And as he did he chuckled and signed the page, still smiling. "It's true. It's good advice," he said. The passage reads:

"When in Bangkok, do what your mama told you never to do. Talk to a stranger." – Bangkok Babylon

I next saw Jerry Hopkins one week later. It was the evening of the second Bangkok Night of Noir, Sunday, January 5, 2014. I was at a table that included Collin Piprell, author of *Kicking Dogs* and many other books, and a longtime acquaintance of Jerry's. There was an open chair next to me. Jerry sat down and ordered some food and drink. Christopher G. Moore, one of the featured authors for the evening, saw Jerry and came over to shake his hand and tell him how pleased he was to see him at the event. "Kevin told me about it last week," said the man whose books have sold in the millions. I got a kick out of Jerry's reply on a couple of levels. One, I was glad Jerry remembered my name from a week ago. Two, I couldn't remember telling him about Night of Noir, although I am sure I did. Jerry may need a hearing aid but his memory, short term and long term, is just fine. If you read *Bangkok Babylon*, which is about the real-life exploits of Bangkok's legendary expatriates, you will learn that Jerry Hopkins likes to have a good time. So I wasn't completely surprised when at a little after 9pm for a scheduled 7.30pm start, Jerry stood up. "You leaving, Jerry?" I asked. "Yeah. I hate Filipina cover bands."

And just like that, the man who has been described as a real-life Forrest Gump for his knack of being in the right place at the right time went up the tunnel leading to Sukhumvit Road. Unlike the Forrest in the movie, Jerry didn't seem tired and I didn't think he was going home, just yet.

After those two meetings at Checkinn99, I wrote to Will Yaryan telling him I'd very much like to interview Jerry, and suggested that the three of us get together for a lunch meeting. I wanted Will to come along because I thought it would be fun, and suggested a restaurant where we could meet. Will wrote back: "Jerry says the food there is no good." Jerry has appeared on Anthony Bourdain's popular cooking and travel shows, not once but twice. The first time he was responsible for the footage that shows Tony on the second floor of Nana Plaza as the show's credits roll. The second time, Tony and Jerry pull up to a restaurant in a longboat – again Jerry's idea. Jerry has written books titled *Strange Foods* and *Extreme Cuisine*, and on his website there is a picture of him eating a deep-fried baby frog. I figured he was entitled to call the dining shots. We settled on Hemingway's Bangkok on Sukhumvit 14, outdoors by the fountain.

Jerry and Will arrived on time, Jerry looking fit in his trademark Hawaiian shirt, well-groomed beard, large spectacles and sparkling blue eyes. For a man of 78 years, with four wives, two grown children, triple bypass heart surgery, a heart attack and pacemaker in his bio, he looked damn good.

All my previous interviews had been via email, so I felt a bit like a fish out of water in the company of a career journalist and distinguished author, even if he has described himself as a whoremonger and bottom-feeder at times. Jerry always maintains a comfortable, if not joyful, manner and soon apologized for leaving early on the Night of Noir, explaining that a friend of his had opened a bar nearby and reiterating his feelings for Pinay singers. Jerry Hopkins likes all kinds of music, but not all music. My temptation, when in the company of a rock n' roll legend, was to talk about sex, drugs and rock n' roll, and I told Jerry so. But I thought I'd be clever, so I asked Jerry: "Since you are the journalist, what would you talk about with Jerry Hopkins if you were interviewing Jerry?"

"Sex, drugs and rock n' roll, of course," Jerry said, somewhat incredulously. Now I was feeling better.

Curiosity may have killed the cat but it has helped Jerry Hopkins see the world. There is a quote attributed to Yogi Berra that goes, "When you see a fork in the road, take it!" Jerry struck me as the kind of guy who would take that fork, every time. In addition, when he comes to the same fork a second time, he would go left if he'd previously gone right. Jerry Hopkins would be a fascinating person even without his fascination for transsexuals, or ladyboys as they are known in Thailand. I was curious about where and when that interest first began. As Jerry tells it, he was in Hawaii around 1989 when he saw what he described as a vision walking on the other side of the street. Jerry did what Jerry does – he crossed that street and made an introduction to a very "beautiful creature". They went to a nearby bar. Jerry wanted to know her story.

"Well, I was born a boy," she told him. Jerry sat up straight to demonstrate how she thrust out her artificial but perfect breasts and told him: "And now I'm a man!" That relationship remained platonic only. But the meeting led to an introduction to another transsexual, Vanessa, whom Jerry unashamedly admits to falling in love with and sharing his bed with during those Hawaii years. And oh, by the way, she was a hooker to boot, working the Chinatown beat on the island of Oahu. Jerry told a story about his live-in lover hitch-hiking home and arriving with a large box of donuts in one hand, received from a grateful bakery truck driver as a tip for services rendered, and a pair of high heels in the other. It was 6am and Jerry was sipping his morning coffee. If you were looking for Ward and June Cleaver, you'd have been in the wrong neighborhood or perhaps the wrong galaxy. The whole time Jerry spoke, he had a gleam in his blue eyes.

There was pretty much no subject Jerry was unwilling to get into, except perhaps wife talk, but I didn't really press him on that subject since there was so much else to talk about. Even his bad experiences, if you can call them that, are memorable. The originally authorized biography of Raquel Welch didn't get written, after a terse letter arrived from an attorney representing the sex symbol. It was never written, but you cannot take away all the memories Jerry has of being in Rio de Janeiro with Raquel, having his picture taken frequently with her at public events and being treated like royalty. Another time, Jerry was hit while crossing the road in Hawaii, and left with serious injuries. But it was during his convalescence that he decided that when he could ambulate again he would go to the divorce court, as he had already been to the bankruptcy court, and start the next chapter in his life – which led to Bangkok, Thailand.

"Jerry Hopkins' No One Here Gets Out Alive sets the standards for rock biographies and Jerry's just as good in person." Timothy Hallinan, author of *Little Elvises*.

Hopkins' rock biography *No One Here Gets Out Alive,* about the iconic lead singer of The Doors, Jim Morrison, has been translated into at least 16 languages. It was the first rock biography that made it to #1 on the New York Times Best Sellers List. It made the list again when the Oliver

Stone movie *The Doors* was released in 1991. Those facts are pretty well established. I found it more interesting to learn from Jerry that the first topless bar he ever went to was with Morrison in Los Angeles. Hopkins told me Morrison was nothing like the person the press portrayed him as: "Jim had read more books than any rock star I had ever met." It was Morrison who was a fan of Elvis Presley, more than Jerry, and encouraged him to write the biography – one reason the first Elvis biography has a dedication to Jim Morrison, who never lived long enough to see it published. Dead of a heroin overdose in Paris at the age of 27.

When you get three hours of Jerry's time, which is what I got at Hemingway's Bangkok, it's not a matter of getting enough material suitable for print. It's a question of what the hell am I going to leave out? Trust me, I am leaving out plenty, and it is not your typical cutting room floor stuff. It would make most people's highlight reel. The "Groucho meet Lenny" story, when Jerry introduced the famous Marx brother to Lenny Bruce, has been written about before. But perhaps lesser known is Jerry being in the audience when Harpo, the Marx brother who never spoke, grabbed a microphone on stage and said to the crowd: "As I was saying..."

"What was the response?" I asked Jerry. "The place just erupted," the legend said. Among the biographies discussed but not written by Jerry, in addition to the one of Raquel Welch, is one of the famous rock concert promoter Bill Graham, who Jerry spoke with about the possibility more than once. Bill died many years later, in a 1991 helicopter crash.

In the course of the interview I noticed that Jerry Hopkins, the legend, was wearing the same pair of shoes he wore the first two times I saw him at Checkinn99. They were blue suede shoes, like those immortalized in the rock n' roll standard written by Carl Perkins and recorded by Elvis Presley, among many other rock legends. Hopkins' biographies of Elvis Presley are so closely linked to the musician that he has been flown in by the Presley estate to participate in Elvis activities at Graceland in Memphis, and in Honolulu. The shoes Jerry was wearing could not be a coincidence. How many people do you know who wear blue suede shoes? I mentioned them to Jerry about two hours into our lunch. "I've got the title for this interview already," and said, pointing under the table. "A Conversation with the Man in the Blue Suede Shoes." Jerry smiled for the hundredth or so time that day and said, "You're the first one to notice in quite a while. I like it."

If you look up, "Sex Drugs and Rock n' Roll" in your Urban Dictionary, you'll read the term is a nickname for the lifestyle of rock stars. You'll also see that of the three rock examples used, Elvis Presley is #1: Died of a drug overdose. I learned from Jerry Hopkins that Jim Morrison's drug of choice was alcohol. Jim told Jerry once: "It's suicide, one drink at a time." As for Jerry's own lifestyle, it has been comfortable. When I alluded to his 2013 interview 'When You're Strange' in the *South China Post Magazine* and asked him how much money he had put up his nose over the years, Jerry peered at me over his glasses and said: "Not that much."

Jerry also told me about the time he went to a Billy Preston concert at a club on Sunset Boulevard. The concert was to be filmed, and it was decided to bus in some of the residents of nearby Watts, California. The date was August 3, 1966, just over one year after the famous Watts race riots. On the way to the concert Jerry heard, on his car radio, that the comedian Lenny Bruce had died. He took that fork in the road again, to Lenny's house on Hollywood Boulevard. When he arrived, Lenny's naked body was in the bathroom and the police were letting people have a look-see, two at a time. The crowd began to grow. "It's time to go to Billy's concert," Jerry thought. And he went.

What is Jerry Hopkins working on now, you may be wondering? He is researching a book in which he will profile 25 *kathoey* (ladyboy) sex workers. That should bring a whole new context to the Joe Friday line, "Just the facts, ma'am."

[XIV]

Bangkok Taxi Drivers

BANGKOK, IF MY opinion counts, is a great taxi city. I have no idea how many taxi cabs and taxi drivers there are in Bangkok city. If anyone knows, let me know. I would like to know. One can read just about anything happening either in or near a Bangkok taxi cab.

Acts of kindness, births, rapes, murder and theft are just a few that come to mind. My experience with Bangkok taxicabs and their drivers has been mostly positive. Mostly, as in 90 per cent positive.

Bangkok taxi cabs come in many colors – orange, pink, yellow, blue, white, and my personal favorite, the green and yellow.

Many of the Bangkok taxi drivers are poor, Buddhist, from Isaan and in my experience friendly. I have my prejudices about them. I'm not keen on the pink taxis – not because of the color, rather because of the attitude of the drivers. Bad attitude. I don't mind older taxi cabs and I prefer older taxi drivers, anytime. Older taxi drivers, in my experience, are far less likely to turn down your request for a ride and, if I had to wager, less likely to pull a four-foot sword out of their trunk when provoked. The fact that taxi drivers in Thailand can and do turn you down took some getting used to. It used to bother me. Bother me as in, it would get me royally pissed off 10 years or more ago, when they did just that all the time. Now I have adapted to the Thai *may pen rai, jai yen yen* attitude. My life expectancy in Thailand has gone up accordingly.

I had a favorite taxi driver in Bangkok, from the hundreds I have ridden with. His name was Mr Khemsak. His business card is one of the few I keep in my wallet. I used him many, many times over the years – more than 50, I would estimate. As a lone passenger, with my wife, my family and sometimes with visiting friends from America. Short trips and long ones. Fares that were 40 baht ($1.25) and 2,000 baht ($65.00). On his card are the words: "Service Mind". He had that. He also smiled a lot, was helpful and spoke pretty good English. He was a driver during the Vietnam War era, and shared many interesting stories. He had a daughter who received a university degree, and he was very proud of her. She owned her own condo.

One time, he took my wife and I to Khao Yai National Park, where we spent a night in a fancy tent. The next day was our 10th wedding anniversary, a special day, as is every day we are alive. My wife and I ate a bowl of noodles at an outdoor restaurant surrounded by greenery, with Mr Khemsak at the same table. He often wanted to eat away from us, thinking perhaps – incorrectly – that he would be intruding on our privacy. On that day, our anniversary, I insisted he eat with us. Later, we saw three elephants in the wild – a male, a female and their one offspring. I had seen elephants and ridden elephants in Thailand many times. But seeing wild elephants in a national park is different. It's better. Way better. I will always remember that day, and I hope I always remember Mr Khemsak and think about him from time to time.

The last time my wife and I rode together with Mr Khemsak was to Bang Saen, a beach resort 85km south of Bangkok, and back. There was always a comfort level anytime he drove us. Not long after that, he fell ill. I felt bad about this but was comforted by the fact that he had a caring daughter in his life and a wife of his own of many years. I spoke with him on the phone a few times after he became ill. And then I learned of his death. It was something I had feared. It became a reality for him, and is a reality we will all face one day. Mr Khemsak faced his reality in his mid-60s. He wasn't famous. He was far from rich. He owned some land outside Bangkok and he lived modestly within the city. He was humble and happy, from what I saw. He liked his job as a Bangkok taxi driver, and I believe the people he drove liked him.

Mr Khemsak left only favorable impressions upon me. How many people can you say that about? Not enough, to be sure. I am thankful for having known him on this magical mystery tour called life. Rest in peace, Mr Khemsak. You left the world you touched a little better than you found it. We can all aspire to do that.

[XV]

A Trumpet Player at Checkinn99 – Steve Cannon

O NE SUNDAY AFTERNOON at Check-inn99, I had a 1970s flashback – of the good kind. In 1979 I was living in San Francisco, and one Sunday my best friend left after spending the weekend there. After he left, on a whim, I went into a comedy club called  Holy City Zoo in the Richmond district. On that Sunday there was an improvisational comedy group doing their thing, and they were doing it well. I commented to the guy next to me, in the not-particularly-crowded bar: "That guy looks like Robin Williams." The response was: "That's because it is Robin Williams." The rest of the evening was spent watching greatness, and it wasn't all Robin. They were all great, and improvisational comedy is a tough nut to be great at.

There is another art form that requires improvisation, talent, teamwork and unselfishness. It's called jazz. Listening to jazz was the goal that Sunday when I met a friend to check out the Sunday Jazz on

Sukhumvit at Checkinn99.

Whether it is comedy, basketball or music, when you are in the presence of greatness it's evident. It's obvious. So it was that Sunday. Among the talented group of jazz performers rotating in and out, just like a winning basketball team, was leading scorer and trumpet player Steve Cannon, who played every minute.

You never forget being in an uncrowded, intimate setting at a historic venue, as I was at the now-defunct Holy City Zoo when I saw Robin Williams perform. Likewise, to find a trumpet player of the caliber of Steve Cannon playing on a Sunday afternoon at a place Bob Hope used to frequent is also memorable.

Steve's musical credits are too numerous to list in this chapter but a partial list of the artists he has played with includes piano-playing comedian Steve Allen, The Clarence "Gatemouth" Brown Big Band, Mary Wilson and the Supremes, The Temptations, The Four Tops, The Spinners, Frankie Valli and the Four Seasons and The 5th Dimension. Steve produced his debut album, *Nowhere Man,* in 1999. His 2006 album, the award-winning *Full Blown* by Steve Cannon and the Blow Hard Big Band, was named best album of the year by *All About Jazz* magazine. Steve is also among an elite group of jazz musicians who performed at a command performance for His Majesty the King of Thailand – and anyone who lives in Thailand knows full well the high regard King Bhumibol has for jazz. The Jazzy King, as he has been referred to, once played side-by-side with Benny Goodman.

I love living in Bangkok for many reasons. The diversity and talent of the expat community is just one. After two long stints in Los Angeles and Portland, Steve Cannon now calls Bangkok his home. Steve can be found performing regularly with his piano-playing brother Randy at the internationally acclaimed Living Room jazz club in the Sheraton Grande Sukhumvit Hotel. I write about the Living Room experience in the next chapter.

In the meantime, anyone who appreciates good jazz music and the somewhat limited options that exist in Bangkok should make a visit to the Jazz on Sukhumvit series at Checkinn99 on Sunday afternoons. You never know when greatness will decide to make an appearance.

[XVI]

Earning the Couch – Jazz at The Living Room

"**Y**OU'VE GOT TO earn the couch," one university mountain biker said to his biking buddy as I stood behind them, preparing for the big event in my day – ordering a sandwich at my local deli. Bush Senior was president at the time. It's an expression I liked immediately and haven't heard much since, but thought about a lot one weekend recently: earning the couch.

My wife has only two speeds – stop and go. It's difficult to get her to downshift. I'm more like a Waring 12-speed blender: no need to work at ice-crushing speed when the task at hand only involves blending peanut butter into your yogurt. But this particular weekend, we both got a lot of stuff done. My wife and I had earned the couch. I'm an American. We're trained, some might say brainwashed, to get stuff done so we can get more stuff. And like the instructions on a shampoo bottle there are those out there who want you to "repeat process" until you hit the grave. Most of the time I ignore them. Sometimes they have a point. My wife had earned the couch and a nice night out. The choice was the Living Room located on Sukhumvit Soi 12, inside the Sheraton

Hotel. I had never been before and neither had she. Time for a new experience.

The Living Room is known for its world-class jazz. That night the Steve Cannon Group was playing. Steve's four man jazz combo features the man himself on trumpet, along with a trio on piano, drums and double bass. Most jazz aficionados agree that without the trumpet, jazz is just not the same. It's been an integral part of jazz from the beginning, long before the piano got on board. The combo was great that night, the acoustics lively and Steve was the leader on the stage and in The Living Room, coming over to our cozy couch a few times during the evening. It was a weeknight but they still pulled in a nice, comfortable crowd as Steve worked the audience with tunes by Grover Washington Jr, Dizzy Gillespie, Chet Baker, Lee Morgan and others. As jobs go, it seems like a great one to me.

Although it was my first visit to the Living Room, I had a sensation of deja vu when I arrived, like I had been there before. And then I remembered – I had. One of the many pleasures of reading fiction is not just the characters we meet, it's the places we get to go. It turns out that I had read a novel about another duo who had gotten a lot of stuff done and decided to reward themselves with a night at the Living Room. The duo were fictional detective Vincent Calvino and his fictional saxophone-playing friend, Colonel Pratt of the Thai Royal Police. The novel is *Missing In Rangoon*, one of my favorites in the Vincent Calvino Crime Series by Bangkok author Christopher G. Moore. The last chapter in the book is titled 'Bangkok: The Living Room'.

I won't bore you with all the details of the chores that earned my wife and I a visit to the Living Room, but Calvino and Pratt had gone to Rangoon, Burma to locate a missing person and break up a gang smuggling amphetamines into Thailand. Vincent even worked in a couple of 10k runs while he was there. In the process, guns were fired, people were killed and rich people had to find new ways of getting richer. In short, Vinny and Colonel Pratt had earned the couch.

The chapter begins:

It was closing night at the upscale nightclub, located at a five-star Sukhumvit Road hotel. Yadamar wore a newly tailored tan suit, a purple silk shirt and alligator shoes with shiny soles. He sat behind a grand piano, smiling at the audience, hands dancing across the keyboard as Colonel Pratt finished John Coltrane's My Favorite Things — which he dedicated to Manee, his wife, who was sitting at a front row table. — From *Missing in Rangoon*, by Christopher G. Moore

It's not in the book but my guess is that Pratt's wife, Manee, also earned the couch. The music always sounds better when you do. Given the choice between being a couch potato or earning the couch, go for the latter as much as you can. Get out and watch some live music, comedy or theatre performance wherever you live. Appreciate the talented musicians, actors and artists who ply their trade all over town in every town, almost every night. Read a good book by one of your favorite authors — preferably a paperback or, better yet, splurge on a hardcover. Get some stuff done. Be nice to your partner if you have one. Earn the couch.

[XVII]

William Wait -
The Saxophone-Playing Psychologist

ONE OF THE great things about the Sunday jazz sessions at Checkinn99, as I have touched on previously in another chapter, is that no two Sundays are ever quite the same. Quite the contrary. What does remain a constant, though, is the steady hand of experience – saxophone player and floor leader William Wait along with the friendly countenance of keyboard player Keith Nolan, who fills in for Chris Catto-Smith as general manager while still contributing on the musical side at Checkinn99 on Sundays.

The focus will be on William today, as I was able to get some one-on-one time with him, away from Checkinn99, at Hemingway's Bangkok recently. Nolan is on my interview wish list. William is one of the cornerstones of a winning Checkinn99 formula, having turned a day that was previously closed, under the old ownership model, into a fun day for all concerned. Reservations for large groups at the Checkinn99 restaurant on a Sunday at 3pm are now common.

William, by the Chinese calendar, has completed six cycles of life. His life has been interesting and full in those first six cycles, and remains interesting and full in his active seventh cycle. In addition to his musical ability, William is a licensed psychologist, having practiced at Fort Help Counseling Center, among other places. Fort Help was one of the first alternative counseling centers arising from the humanistic psychology revolution taking place in California, in particular, at the time. Just as William played and plays alongside many great musicians to this day, he also trained and was a colleague of many pioneering psychologists in the 1970s and beyond.

I have long believed that Dr Wait, as a wise and elderly saxophone player, is one of a composite of real-life people that led to the Colonel Pratt character – the saxophone-playing, wise colonel in the Thai Royal Police, found in the Vincent Calvino crime series written by Christopher G. Moore. Neither Christopher nor William will confirm my belief, but I will hang onto it just the same.

William Wait (L) and Christopher G. Moore reflect during a break at Sunday jazz in Checkinn99

William grew up in a musical family. His mother was a pianist and his earliest memories are of having a piano in the home. He began hitting the keyboards as early as four years old, and was soon on to lessons. As a young boy, music became a transforming experience. It still is. How nice is that? When the music of the March King, John Philip Sousa, would come on more than five cycles ago, young William would feel compelled to march around the house. That sounds like fun to me, at any age.

By the age of 12 he had learned to play the trumpet, clarinet and saxophone. By the age of 15 he was a working musician in a rhythm and blues band. It was the mid-50s, and although racial segregation was still in place in many parts of the US, it wasn't in the central valley area of California where William was raised. William was often in the audience watching black musicians play at the black clubs. Soon William began playing in a blues band. He was often the lone white musician playing the blues in the band back then, and frequently the only white person in the audience as well. His youth worked in his favor in both circumstances, as he was looked after by others, as an adopted little brother of sorts.

Having never been a musician, I can guess that one would never forget your first paid gig. William's was a memorable one, playing Rose Lee's Chicken Shack in Fresno. His pay came in the form of chicken and beer. When you're a teenager, that's about as good as it gets. William's mother encouraged his musical pursuits but not so much that William shared that particular payment on that particular night with his mom.

In the summer of 1959, soon after finishing high school, he headed to San Francisco, for more in-the-moment experiences. He later received his undergraduate degree at Sonoma State University, after a brief one-and-a-half year stint at the Berkeley school of music.

There was then a long stint working as a musician on the East Coast with many musicians of note. Mostly blues clubs at that point. It was a golden era for rhythm and blues. From the early 60s up until 1967, he was a regular working musician for the Hacienda Hotel and Casino in Las Vegas, working alongside and interacting with many of the great entertainment acts that rotated through there regularly in those years. William quit his job at the Hacienda in 1967 and returned to San Francisco, simply because he had had enough of Las Vegas and was ready for a new set of present experiences. His neighborhood was North Beach on Montgomery Street, walking distance to Broadway and the

San Francisco scene that was then happening. It was quite a scene in those days. The Haight-Ashbury district and Golden Gate Park weren't far away. Neither was the summer of love. More transforming experiences followed. A lifetime of experiences for many, some of whom never made it past their second cycle of life.

William originally came to Thailand with a Buddhist monk to study Buddhism and meditation and tour different monasteries after spending time in India, where he had played in a meditation group. He was carrying around his saxophone in Bangkok, with the intention of returning to India, when he was spotted with the musical instrument case and asked to jam at a club with some Thai musicians. After the jam he was offered a job playing saxophone. That was more than 20 years ago, and he still lives and plays saxophone in Thailand. You can catch William on Sundays at Checkinn99 and also at Apoteka on Sukhumvit 11. He has played all the prominent jazz and blues clubs in Thailand over the past 20-plus years, including two straight decades of New Year's Eve celebrations, but now finds that playing two days a week allows him the freedom to take frequent upcountry trips to the Isaan area of Thailand.

In an interview with Keith Nolan's Access All Areas music show, he spoke of the relationship between the human experience and what jazz teaches, specifically areas of creativity, spontaneity and openness. Music is vibration at its essence, and William cannot imagine a life without music and all of the many therapeutic benefits those vibrations bring.

William Wait on saxophone at Checkinn99

William has a pleasant and peaceful temperament both on and off the bandstand area, although more than one person has told me he knows how and when to take control of the reins as he choreographs the playing time for as many as two dozen singers and musicians who can show up for the jam session on any given Sunday. As all good coaches know, dividing up the playing time minutes among a talented team is not always easy.

Stop by and say hi to William at Checkinn99 or Apoteka on a Sunday afternoon or Thursday or Friday evening. They are both great environments for any jazz or blues enthusiast – counseling sessions may run extra when Dr Wait is in the house.

Crazy Hour at Checkinn99

[XVIII]

Forget Yourself – What did Henry Miller mean?

T THE BEGINNING of this book, a Henry Miller quote concludes with the words: "Forget yourself." What did Henry mean by that? Only he would know for sure. In my interview with Malcolm Gault-Williams – author of *Legendary Surfers*, which you'll read later in this book – I asked him if he agreed with the entire quote. Malcolm did agree, except for those two commanding words.

It was a good answer but it was not the answer I expected. Not the one I wanted. How often do we ask a question with our answer already in mind? Too often, for me. People can be like the guy at the race track who has already decided which horse he will bet on because of the name of the horse or the color of the jockey's silks, but then goes to the racing form for information to back up his unwavering choice. Malcolm is right – when you write you cannot forget yourself entirely. You need to add that special ingredient, as he puts it, to make the writing unique. But the best story, in my opinion, is almost always elsewhere. The quote again:

"Develop an interest in life as you see it; the people, things, literature, music – the world is so rich, simply throbbing with rich treasures, beautiful souls and interesting people. Forget yourself." – Henry Miller.

Years ago I met someone for the first time at my Bangkok gym. We would later become friends. On that initial meeting I was on a weights machine. Dick, the name of my future friend, was on the machine next to me. As he rested, he struck up a conversation with me. My first impression of Dick was that he was a "fat cat". He was older than me by a good 20 years, heavy but in good shape and very tanned, which made his blue eyes look even bluer. He wore a singlet and had a thick gold chain around his neck – a lot thicker than the $100 string I was wearing. Circumference does matter to some, I'm told, when it comes to gold. He was friendly enough but I was probably terse with him as I have this peculiar idea that gyms are for exercising and not so much for socializing. In short, I was thinking about myself at the time, as we humans tend to do, rather than thinking about the opportunity to meet a new friend who didn't fit the mold of my friends back in California.

Over the next few years I would share many meals, and a few beers, with Dick and my circle of friends in Thailand. Dick was always fun to be around. I would also tend to run into him from time to time, even when I was out of town. He always made room for a bit of conversation and sometimes those bits would lead to a few more beers. He came to our family Christmas party one year with a video camera running as he entered the front door, and was very entertaining all evening, yet always polite. We shared some things in common, Dick and I. He also split his time between Thailand and the USA – in his case, Maine. Our schedules were similar: winter and spring in Thailand. I always enjoyed catching up after not seeing each other for six months. Dick was generous, with his time and with his compliments. He was the opposite of a balloon chaser. In Thailand, if a free meal or a great deal is being offered by a bar they will often put balloons outside to let potential customers know of that fact. Dick was the type of guy who would be a regular at a pub and then stay away when they had a free meal promotion, figuring someone else could use the seat and the meal that day more than him. One year he came back and his thick, heavy gold chain was missing. "Where's your gold chain, Dick?" I asked right away when I noticed. "Oh, I gave it to my nephew. He always liked it and he's a senior on his Florida high school football team this year," he replied with his trademark smile. Dick was always proud of his family members back in the USA. It turned out that Dick wasn't really a fat cat at all. He was a retired accountant who was more of a cool cat, even at 70-plus years old. Dick was one of those guys you were always happy to see, and when you left you always felt a little better. And I was never exactly sure why that was.

After about five years of friendship and good memories, I learned from a mutual friend while I was in California that Dick had died of a heart attack, suddenly, during a visit to family members in Florida at the age of 76. His funeral was to be held in Maine. I didn't go, and like most regrets I have it is the things I didn't do which I regret most. But I did get a chance to communicate with his son, a few times via e-mail and once on the telephone. During the course of that conversation I told his son that Dick was a friend and I liked him very much. I told him I used to tell his dad that he reminded me of my Uncle Al, a very important man in my life. I also told him how Dick had a way of making everybody around him feel good. His son responded: "My dad was the kind of guy that was always interested in what you were interested in."

And he was. And that was it – that's what I couldn't put my finger on. Henry Miller, I suspect, would have liked Dick a lot. Because Dick understood what Henry meant. Dick was confident in who he was, just as I believe Henry Miller was confident, on most occasions, with who he was. They both knew, more often than not, that the best story, the best moments in life, were not about them.

When you are interested in what other people are interested in, you find what Henry Miller found: interesting people. Will it happen every time? No, but often enough that I would bet on it.

[XIX]

The Rocky Horror Show comes to Bangkok

BANGKOK IS A CITY with a lot of entertainment choices. People here are spoiled for choice, I have heard it said. But there are certain entertainment choices that people still talk about years later. Such is the case with the first ever Bangkok musical production of *The Rocky Horror Show*, which was shown at the perfect venue. Years from now, I am sure of it, people will be asking the question: "Were you at the Checkinn99 when they did *The Rocky Horror Show?*"

If you are not already aware, *The Rocky Horror Show* is a comedy-horror musical about a newly engaged couple who must pay a call to the bizarre residence of Dr Frank N. Furter after their car breaks down in an isolated area. It was first shown in the mid-1970s and became a popular midnight movie for the young at heart, complete with participatory moments which took on cult status.

There's no business like show business and there is no show quite like *The Rocky Horror Show*. The performance at the Checkinn99 featured 13 professional performers in the cast, including the entire Music of the Heart Band. I had the good fortune to be invited to see a rehearsal.

The narration was done through the character of The Criminologist, played by performance poet, and former dramatist, John Gartland. You'll read John's poems in this book. Well-known Bangkok singer and musician Kevin Wood played the role of Riff Raff, who reminds us that time is fleeting and madness takes its toll. No argument here. Kevin Wood has some world-class pipes to go along with his stage presence earned over the last 45 years of performing to live audiences. It is always pure pleasure to listen to Kevin Wood sing, and he got to sing some Rocky classics.

You could not pull off a production of The Rocky Horror Show without the right man cast as Dr Frank-N-Furter. Checkinn99 owner Chris Catto-Smith personally recruited Bangkok actor and comedian Chris Wegoda, and it was an inspired choice. Dr Frank N. Furter is the straw that stirs the drink, and *The Rocky Horror Show* was one bloody good drink – at rehearsal that day and when I saw it later that week, live, at Checkinn99 before a sold-out crowd.

The Rocky Horror Show director was Jonathan Samson. Apologies for not listing the names of all the actors and their roles. There were no weak links in this chain. It wasn't a flawless production, but all the flubs, prop accidents and wardrobe malfunctions only added to the fun. One would hope this becomes a Halloween tradition in Bangkok. But there are no certainties in life. It was evident this production took a lot of time and energy by a lot of talented people. It may be back – it may not. Time is indeed fleeting. Years from now, when people ask, "Were you at the Checkinn99 when they did the Rocky Horror Show?" I'll be able to answer: "I was. And I smiled so much, my face ached."

[XX]

A Trip Around the Sun for James A. Newman

"YOU CAN'T GET there, from here." It's an old line but one I still like, said to private investigator Nick Danger in an old LP by the comedy troupe Firesign Theatre that I spent too many hours listening to in the early 70s. But James A. Newman is doing his level best to do just that. The here is Bangkok. And the there is great literary success.

The former is much easier to define than the latter. Newman was Master of Ceremonies for an event I enjoyed immensely, the Bangkok Night of Noir II held on January 5, 2014. That date is oddly significant, and is the source of inspiration for this chapter.

On January 5, 2013 – one year prior to the event – I had never met James A. Newman, but I had recently read a book he wrote called *Lizard City*. A most peculiar book, unlike anything I had ever read before and anything I have read since. My first thought was that I must be outside the intended audience demographic. It was a weird book for me. And yet, lurking in there was a good writer, I was pretty sure.

So I decided to do something I rarely do. I wrote a review of a book where I liked the writing but not the book so much – a first for me.

Here is that review, originally posted on Amazon.com on January 5,
2013:

Lizard City by James A. Newman – A Book Review by Kevin
Cummings

*If James A. Newman's writing was music and he was a musician
instead of a writer, I would tell you he can flat out play for long
stretches but occasionally hits the wrong notes, for me. The problem is
I feel like I have been thrown into the mosh pit at a grunge concert,
where everybody around me is having a great time, but I am feeling
like the Lone Ranger because my tastes run closer to the William Tell
Overture. What I liked about Lizard City is the character, Kat. I
was curious about her and my curiosities got answered. Good one.
Johnny Coca Cola (Love the name change) was also a good character.
But a match made in hell is sometimes better than a match made in
purgatory. When in doubt an old fart like me asks: WWHD? What
would Hemingway do? Save the $5 words for where they are needed.
Hell can do without them, in my opinion. There was a line akin to:
"An obese tourist sat outside." I want that tourist described to me. I
want him described to me in such a way that I go on a diet
tomorrow. Bangkok's full of great writers and I have started more
than one diet based on the accurate description of a fat tourist that
hit a little too close to home. The Buddhist stuff, great. Rama
references I liked. I am never keen on characters that are writers. The
only thing the world has more of than writers is critics – so if I am
going to read something, I'd like the writer to use his imagination
more. And my bias goes all the way to the top. As beautiful a writer
as Tim Hallinan is, I am not that keen on his protagonist, because
he is a travel writer. Give me a shoe salesman, a Buddhist cop, a
man named Sue, anything but not another writer. All in all, there
was much to like. But the music was a little too loud for my tastes
and the style not quite to my liking. That doesn't mean the composer
isn't talented. Keep on playing. The rain drops have stopped.*

Then of course, coincidentally, one year to that date, the Bangkok Night of Noir was held with James A. Newman as MC and a line-up featuring John Marengo, Tom Vater, Dean Barrett, John Burdett, Cara Black, Chris Coles and Christopher G. Moore. We sometimes forget, or at least I do, that in the course of getting one year older it is another orbit around the sun in what is sure to be a finite number of trips. Baby James had come a long way in one year.

But this is where, I think, it gets interesting for James' journey. Because Bangkok is 14 hours ahead of Los Angeles, on that same day, January 5, 2014, the very same beautiful writer, Timothy Hallinan, who I referenced in my review, wrote a review of Newman's third Joe Dylan book, *The White Flamingo*.

I really enjoy reading book reviews by great writers. And make no mistake about it, Timothy Hallinan is a great writer. Pick your pleasure – the Simeon Grist Mysteries, Poke Rafferty Bangkok Thrillers or Junior Bender Burglar/P.I. series. If you've not read any Timothy Hallinan, buy anything he's written, in paperback. If you don't like it, send me the book and I'll send you a full refund.

Some things in life are priceless and thus you cannot buy. If you are a young author or an old author or somewhere in-between, a favorable Tim Hallinan book review is one of those things. Here is Tim's review of *The White Flamingo*:

Noir with a Capital N

James Newman writes with a flamethrower. He's terrifically gifted, enormously energetic, and in The White Flamingo he builds up, layer by layer, like lacquer, the everyday reality of "Fun City" – a/k/a Pattaya – with such intensity that he creates a nightmare town so terrible that even the advent of a modern-day Jack the Ripper can only make it a tiny bit worse. Newman has serious talent, devoted (in this case, anyway) almost entirely to the noir side of life in a city that has more than its share of noir. If I have two quibbles, it's that he has so much energy and eloquence at his command that he gives us more than we need on occasion, and that I would have liked to have seen more of his detective's inner deductive processes, but nonetheless I ripped through the book in about seven hours. If Newman reminds me of anyone, it's early Ken Bruen, which is high praise in itself. A warning, however, to people who have read my books to be prepared for something very different: the darkest scenes I've ever written are like an air kiss compared to what Newman can do when he gets going.

Tom Vater started in Germany, writing screenplays. Dean Barrett started in New York City, writing plays off Broadway. John Burdett started in Hong Kong with *The Last Six Million Seconds*. Cara Black started in San Francisco with multiple airplane rides to Paris. Timothy Hallinan started in Los Angeles with Simeon Grist. Christopher G. Moore started in Vancouver, Canada, in radio and then New York City with *His Lordship's Arsenal*. James A. Newman, for the most part, has cut his teeth in Bangkok. Can he make it "there"? Newman is still young. The Charles Bukowski and William S. Burroughs fan appreciates the history of the Checkinn99 in Bangkok and the Beat Hotel in Paris. A lot of people feel he has a chance. What more can you ask for as one takes another trip around the sun?

[XXI]

A Spirit House for Stirling Silliphant

Black and white photo of a Chris Coles watercolor, Spirit House
[The color original may be seen at Checkinn99]

AT THE BEGINNING of this book is a chapter titled 'What is a Writer?'
If you had to choose a picture of someone to put next to the
definition of writer in a dictionary, one choice could very well be
Stirling Silliphant, who won an Oscar for his screenplay for *In The Heat
Of The Night*. Stirling was, in a word, prolific.

In television he wrote for shows including *The Mickey Mouse Club*,
Alfred Hitchcock Presents, *Route 66* and *The Naked City*, to name just

some. He worked with dozens of Hollywood legends, including Bruce Lee.

Stirling was also the creator of *Longstreet*, which I remember watching as a kid. It was unusual in that it featured a blind detective played by James Franciscus.

His movie credits are equally impressive. My favorite Hollywood story about Stirling concerns the time he was the screen writer on *Route 66*. The television series was being shot in San Antonio, Texas, and the producers told Stirling that if he could come up with another episode set in San Antonio, they could save $100,000 instead of returning the whole crew back to Dallas. In short order – hours that never reached three figures – Stirling wrote a new episode of *Route 66*. They flew in the guest star, shot the episode where they were and saved a huge sum of money, at the time, in the process. Stirling to the rescue.

Stirling Silliphant left large footprints wherever he lived and he chose to live in Bangkok, Thailand for the Third Act of his life. A quote by Stirling Silliphant is featured in the *Bangkok Beat* story 'Never Go To Thailand ... And The Reasons I Love It'. The quote comes from *Bangkok Babylon*, the excellent book by Jerry Hopkins about legendary Bangkok expatriates. It's a great quote and it is worth repeating here:

> *I came to Thailand to die. I needed to be surprised. I wanted to be shocked. Bangkok is unpredictable and it delivers if you give it a chance. Even the small adventures are memorable.* – Stirling Silliphant (1918-1996)

Stirling died, in a Bangkok hospital, of prostate cancer. There are many things I love about Thailand and Thai people. One of them is their beliefs about death and spirits. It is not my desire to make an argument for or against those beliefs, I choose only to celebrate them. My own personal belief is that Stirling Silliphant had a spirit, and it is plainly evident to me that his spirit lives on.

It got me thinking about what kind of spirit house Stirling should have. He earned a classy one if my opinion matters, like the one in

Chris Coles' painting of a spirit house. Everyone dies, but not everyone lives like Stirling did.

> *Whether a spirit house is seen as containing the actual spirit of a loved one or as a nook for honoring the still-fresh memories of the family is just a matter of vantage point.* – Alasdair McLeod, Bangkok writer, photographer and videographer.

These are some of the things I would place in my imaginary spirit house for the spirit of Stirling Silliphant to enjoy for eternity:

1. A miniature Smith Corona typewriter and a mini-pallet of typing paper.

2. A mini stretch limousine to represent his Hollywood days, with a fully stocked mini-bar in the back.

3. A small notepad and a good pen. One that can handle the heat of Bangkok city.

4. A miniature statue of an Oscar. Why not?

5. A memento of the Little Oscar mobile, a car driven by a dwarf named Little Oscar, which Stirling must have seen often in his Southern California days in the 1960s, as I did growing up there at that time.

6. His own personal 7-Eleven convenience store, because I want eternity to be convenient for Stirling's spirit.

7. A bottle of good drinking water and a Coca-Cola placed out front every day. It's important to keep hydrated, even for spirits. None of that red Fanta stuff for Stirling.

8. A good neighborhood bar for Stirling to meet up at. Something like Checkinn99. And we'll leave a replica of the old Checkinn99 sign, to make it easier to find the entrance.

9. A mini tuk-tuk to navigate the Bangkok noir scene on Sukhumvit Road.

10. Figurines of Thai ladies from all classes – upper, middle and lower. This will create a little tension from time to time, and perhaps some conflict, which is good for any writer living forever in the Big Weird.

11. A mini pool table. I don't know if Stirling played pool, but I bet he had friends who did, and the spirits of Stirling's friends will no doubt drop in from time to time.

12. A box of matches. The good kind with the wooden sticks, to represent the creative flame of Stirling that still burns on.

13. A good book to read, *For the Dead* by Timothy Hallinan, which he couldn't have read before, since it came out after his death, to remind him a bit of *The Naked City* on those hot Bangkok nights.

So that's my baker's dozen items and thoughts on the life and spirit of former Bangkok expatriate Stirling Silliphant. Space is still available in the spirit house. And eternity is a long time. What would you add?

[XXII]

A Sense of Where You Are -

A Conversation with Muay Thai Champion Melissa Ray

Far better is it to dare mighty things, to win glorious triumphs, even though checkered by failure... than to rank with those poor spirits who neither enjoy nor suffer much, because they live in a gray twilight that knows not victory nor defeat. – Theodore Roosevelt

Melissa Ray wins her first of four Championships
in a rematch against Praewa Sor Penprapa

IT WAS MY DISTINCT pleasure to spend an afternoon in July 2013 at the Eminent Air Boxing Gym in Bangkok talking with former Muay Thai champion Melissa Ray, from Great Britain, in the best possible environment I could imagine. We had a wide-ranging, back-and-forth conversation – in person and later by email – on many topics. Melissa held four different championship belts during her career and retired due to injuries in 2011, although she has recently taken up training again. Where it will lead is uncertain, but she is healthy enough to reconnect with her passion, which is Muay Thai. Her CV includes a PhD in neuroscience as well as professional Muay Thai fights in seven different countries. Her blog, *Muay Thai on the Brain,* is a must read for any fan of the sport.

Melissa and I talked about winning and losing, rivals, the psychology of a rematch, the East vs West way of looking at competition, athletic careers and what makes a good one, and the *wai kru* ceremony at the beginning of each match where the fighters pay respect to their teachers. We also talked about living in Thailand as a farang (white foreigner), what it is like to choose the road less traveled and how, sometimes, not everyone back in your home country is understanding and supportive when you take that road. During the course of our conversation I was reminded of one of the most influential books I have ever read – at the age of 11 years old – about one of my favorite athletes. It was written in 1965 about Rhodes Scholar and Princeton All-American basketball player Bill Bradley, by the author John McPhee. Its title: *A Sense of Where You Are.* I left with a belief that Melissa Ray has an awareness and an appreciation of where she has been, where she is, and who she has become, due to the competitive sport of professional Muay Thai. I would later learn that

Muay Thai Champion Melissa Ray —
Photograph by Eric Nelson

her favorite book when growing up was another from the 1960s, *To Kill A Mockingbird*, by a female literary champion, Harper Lee. What follows is my interview with Melissa:

KC: Thank you, Melissa, for agreeing to be interviewed. Where did you study for your PhD and what is it in?

MR: I studied for my PhD in neuroscience – the study of the brain – at Newcastle University, UK. During my research project I used various laboratory techniques to analyze human brain sections for the levels of the neuronal nicotinic acetylcholine receptor, comparing normal healthy cases with patients with Alzheimer's disease, dementia with Lewy bodies, Parkinson's disease and autism.

KC: When did you first come to Thailand? How long was it before you stepped into a Muay Thai gym and what was it, exactly, that hooked you on the sport?

MR: My first ever visit to Thailand was a short trip in 2005, when I competed in the WMF World Amateur Championships in Bangkok. I first came to Thailand on a longer-term basis in May 2006. I first tried out Muay Thai in my early twenties. It was a Muay Thai class held at a sports centre rather than in an actual Muay Thai gym. As a sufferer of polycystic ovary syndrome (PCOS), I have always had some issues with my weight (as described in my blog post 'Hormones and Muay Thai"). A typical unhealthy student lifestyle during my first degree had not helped my condition. I decided to try out Muay Thai after resolving to lose some pounds, and was hooked from day one. I was never particularly interested in sports as a child or teenager, but somehow Muay Thai captured my imagination. I loved the endorphin rush I got from the vigorous exercise and the release of aggression when hitting the pads. And sparring appealed to my competitive side, I suppose. I was also fascinated by the cultural aspects of the sport, including the *wai kru* – a ritual dance performed before a fight to pay respect to one's teachers and family members.

KC: I heard that females are not allowed to compete at some of the big arenas, like Lumpini. If true, why is that? Is it politics? Will that change in the future do you think?

MR: Women are not allowed to compete (or even touch the ring) at stadiums such as Lumpini, Rajadamnoen, Channel 7 and Omnoi because of age-old superstitions and beliefs that women are unlucky. Apparently, these beliefs were reinforced in the 60s or 70s, when a female journalist stepped into the ring at Rajadamnoen and several boxers were seriously injured that night. I do think there will eventually be change, and that women will be allowed to compete in the major stadiums in Thailand, but that could be some years away. The current Lumpini Boxing Stadium is scheduled to be demolished in 2014 [it closed in February that year] and a new stadium is under construction in Ramintra Road. My hope is that women might, at some point, be allowed to fight at the new venue. Such a change would really symbolize progress for women's Muay Thai.

KC: Tell me about competing on the King and Queen's birthdays – that must have been quite an honor. Tell us about the atmosphere, the environment.

MR: Considering the restrictions placed on where we are allowed to compete in Thailand, I believe that for a female Muay Thai fighter, to fight on a King or Queen's birthday event at Sanam Luang is the highest honor, and there is no better venue for atmosphere and exposure. On these dates, the entire Rattanakosin area would be swarming with people paying respects to their monarchs, with the streets adorned with light displays, and various stages set up for musical and dance performances. The area where the Muay Thai fights were held would tend to be rather chaotic, and there would often be last-minute changes to the program order, but the disorganization kind of added to the energy. The crowd would always provide an enthusiastic reception to a spirited fighting display, regardless of a fighter's sex or nationality.

KC: How long did you compete, what titles did you hold and why did you retire and to where?

MR: I think I competed for about eight years in total (from my first amateur bout to my last bout in June 2011). I won the WPMF 126lb title, the S-1 126lb title, the WMA 57kg title and another WPMF title at 126lb. I also won silver medals in the amateur European and World WMF championships. I stopped fighting because of two relatively serious injuries. First I tore a group of tendons in my arm (requiring surgery), then I tore a posterior cruciate ligament (no surgery but a long rehabilitation). The knee injury sent me back to the UK for five months last year, but fortunately I was able to return "home" in December 2012.

KC: What question do you most hate being asked, and why?

MR: I have always hated answering questions about my record. My record is not perfect (41 professional fights with 27W, 13L, 1D, by the way) – I can admit to having had good and bad days in the ring. In the West, people can be quite judgmental about records; however, I don't believe a boxer's fight record necessarily provides an accurate reflection of their fighting abilities. For example, a friend of mine has had a few losses in a row against top Thais in his weight division. Another fighter might have had a string of easy KO wins against lesser opponents but – according to his record – looks the better fighter on paper. People say you learn more from a loss than from a win and that's certainly true. I've also heard people say that if you're only winning fights, you're not fighting good enough opponents. That also can be true in some cases.

Another aspect a record doesn't reflect is when a boxer may have had to take fights when he/she was carrying an injury or suffering/ recovering from an illness. It's not always easy to pull out of fights because of the hassle it creates for the promoters and the gym. For the Thais, financial obligations might also come into it – no fight means no purse for the boxer, and no income for the gym.

KC: With your educational background, I am going to guess that reading was important to you at an early age. Tell me about your earliest memories of reading and what books stand out among the ones you have read? Do you have time for reading now?

MR: Very much so. I can remember that every Saturday during my childhood my mum, siblings and I would catch the bus into the town centre to visit the library, and I would take out the maximum five books to read within the week. I was extremely studious at school and my parents would encourage (bribe?!) me to do well in my end-of-year exams by paying me some money for every A grade. When I was growing up, my favorite book was *To Kill a Mockingbird*. Now I rarely have time for reading for pleasure – maybe only when travelling, when I don't want anything too demanding on the brain. The last book that made a lasting impression on me and I would highly recommend reading was *Bounce: the Myth of Talent and the Power of Practice*, which includes personal experiences from the author (an ex-table tennis player), as well as elements of sports science and psychology.

KC: What did you do to fill the void of Muay Thai when your injuries occurred – when you couldn't go to the gym and get that endorphin rush?

MR: When I had my knee injury I started my blog Muay Thai on the Brain. I think writing about Muay Thai helped me to deal with not being able to participate in the sport. Now my knee has much improved and I take every opportunity I can to train, so my writing has been rather neglected of late! Although I have not fought in two years, Muay Thai very much remains a major part of my life and I can't imagine ever choosing not to be involved in it.

KC: Professional writers often use the boxing ring as a metaphor for life. Everyone admires and respects people who do the hard work, which is necessary to get into the ring; those who take their swings and can take a hit, and those participants who get knocked down but keep getting up. We cheer our champions and we root for the underdog. You've actually done and been all those things, and I commend you for it. Thank you, Melissa, for sharing your world of Muay Thai with me here at Eminent Air Boxing Gym. It is such an important part of the culture in Thailand. It will remain a memorable day for me. I wish you well with your training and good luck in avoiding any future injuries.

MR: Thank you, Kevin.

[XXIII]

A Rematch with Champions at Eminent Air Boxing Gym in Bangkok

SOMETIMES IT IS better to be lucky than good. Shortly after starting my blog, I had a lot of good luck. A friend introduced me to professional photographer Eric Nelson, from Chicago. Eric became the second interview I did for this book, which you can read in the next chapter.

I liked Eric's style as a photographer and a person. He is an explorer and Bangkok presents the perfect environment for exploration. My luck continued when after those photographs and interview with Eric ran, a comment came in with an interesting avatar and the words: "Great interview with Eric! I am privileged to have been photographed by him on his wanders to the area of my Muay Thai gym. A talented photographer and a lovely guy too."

Five minutes of Google research told me the comment came from Melissa Ray, a champion *muay ying* – female Muay Thai fighter – with a PhD from England (see previous chapter). The holder of four championship belts until injuries forced her retirement. I now knew I had a female, expat, Muay Thai champ leaving nice comments about my interview with Eric. When luck presents itself, as the late soul singer Sista

Monica said back in California, "sometimes you gotta move". Arrangements were made to conduct an interview with Melissa Ray and watch her train at the Eminent Air Boxing Gym. She had only recently recovered from her injuries enough to allow her to return to training at an elite level.

A few months after that, I asked Eric Nelson if he would like to go back to the Eminent Air Boxing Gym, where he had photographed Melissa, to see her again and take some more photographs. Some decisions are easier than others. We went.

The first thing I noticed about Melissa since I had last seen her was how much leaner, stronger and fitter she looked. As part of her training that day, she ran laps around the neighborhood where the gym is located with another champion, Australian Victor 'Hotchilli' Ntg.

Eminent Air is a gym of champions. It is like a scene out of a movie. It is where Apollo Creed would have taken Rocky Balboa to train seriously if Rocky had ever fought in Thailand. Victor was one of two champions Melissa introduced me to that day among the many elite fighters training. The other was a Thai champion named Chok. Muay Thai fighters frequently use the last name of the gym they train in as their fighting name or name found in promotions and newspaper stories. In this case, his full fighting name is Chok Eminent Air.

Before Chok and Victor got into the ring at Eminent Air Muay Thai Gym, I had the opportunity to speak with Victor at length. Victor is an Aussie bloke and a very friendly one at that. The smile on Hotchilli seemed so permanent that I asked him if he smiles during a match, as I had witnessed when I watched a live Muay Thai fight at Channel 7 Arena two months earlier. Victor said he has two personalities, and that he often felt like a completely different person

Victor Ntg [Photograph by Eric Nelson]

inside the ring. And when the stakes were higher, when the competition was greater, Victor became even more serious inside the fighter's ring.

In Thailand most Thais enjoy Muay Thai as a spectator sport, including monks on their way back to a nearby temple – as you can see in the Eric Nelson photograph. It is a tough, grueling sport to participate in. Victor Ntg is a gifted athlete. He also trains most every day and he works hard at his progress. In the past he has participated in Aussie Rules footy at a high level, been a top sprinter in track and field, and a point guard on the basketball court.

It was another fun afternoon spent at Eminent Air Boxing gym. It was great to see Melissa again, to meet Chok (Thai name: Sarawut Jaishorb) and to talk with Victor.

Eminent Air Boxing Gym has an intoxicating, addictive environment. Monks like it. Athletes from all over the world train there. Photographers are drawn there for the array of images to choose from. It is a unique place. As an old basketball gym rat I know how important gym camaraderie is. It was on full display that Saturday afternoon in Bangkok.

Thai Buddhist Monks enjoying Thailand's favorite spectator sport

Eminent Air is where champions train and are honored on the walls. It's a serious place and a fun place. It's a gym I have now been to twice. I know I will be back, and next time I hope to meet and speak with owner Somboon Niruttimetee, the founder of the gym and promoter of 'Suek Eminent Air' events at Lumpini Boxing Stadium. Somboon is a former corporate lawyer and currently owns multiple businesses in Bangkok.

Before Eric Nelson and I left Eminent Air Muay Thai gym that day, I wished Victor good luck for an upcoming champion's tournament in which he had made it to the final four. Sometimes it is better to be lucky than good. But nobody ever said you can't be both.

[XXIV]

Keeping Photography Alive with Bangkok Photographer Eric Nelson

Bangkok Photographer Eric Nelson ponders his next shot

KC: Eric, I am pleased to welcome you here at Bangkok Beat. I have just been looking at a file of your photographs, and I came away thoroughly impressed. I also have many questions for you, so here goes. Tell me about your interest in photography, how it started and how long you have been doing it. Has it been an avocation, a vocation or both?

EN: Thank you Kevin, I'm excited to talk with you today. My interest in photography came from an odd place. As a kid, I was an avid malacologist – a collector and studier of specimen sea shells and the animals in them, buying from dealers all over the world. I wanted to do a slide presentation using the specimens I had in my collection at the time. My dad had a 35mm camera and tripod so I did a simple set-up and photographed them. My interest in photography grew and the relationship between photography and shell collecting was a symbiotic one for a time until photography became my main interest. I no longer collect, and haven't for over 40 years as the ocean needs all its animals intact, but I still have an extensive collection.

Photography has been both a vocation and an avocation, but for the last 30 years it's mainly been a vocation and I've worked in many parts of the photo industry, from commercial labs to photo journalism to studio, location, and stock photography, and lastly owning and operating a custom black-and-white lab service in Chicago for 21 years, Archival Custom Printing (ACP).

KC: I was particularly struck by your photographs of Thailand and neighboring countries. I'd like to focus on three – Thailand, Myanmar and Cambodia. How are they similar and how are they different? How much time have you spent in Myanmar vs Cambodia?

EN: Of the three places you asked about, Myanmar is the most different from Thailand. I don't speak a word of Burmese but my Thai and English got me by somewhat. People will smile back at you here in Thailand, but in Myanmar they don't. They seemed more serious in some respects, 'seemed' being the operative word there.

There's something about the light there that's different from Cambodia and Thailand. Just like how in a place like New Mexico where the light has always been lauded, Myanmar's light is somehow different from other Southeast Asian countries. I liked shooting there a lot, but my trip was too short and insulated to make any more specific comparisons. I've spent a total of 2 weeks in Cambodia at this point.

Cambodia's light seemed a bit harsh, even in the morning with haze, but mornings and evenings here in Thailand are great for shooting. By getting shots with "window" light such as in the noodle shop image, one can escape the harsh look of midday sun here.

KC: Tell me about Chicago, where you lived for many years, from a photographer's perspective?

EN: When I was in Chicago, the city became old and ugly to me, and uninteresting photographically. Many others will disagree, and that's great as there are photo opportunities there for those who can see them. I just could not. I think that can happen if you live somewhere too long. I've always traveled to Southeast Asia just to shoot, for myself and

Noodle Shop Sukhumvit 101, Bangkok

for stock photography. I've always been drawn to Asia with my camera. Five months of the year in Chicago are inhospitable for shooting outside, whether it be rain, snow or the cold. I did a lot of studio shooting during my time there.

KC: What is it about Bangkok that makes it such a fertile place to take photographs? How would you explain it and help others understand what makes it so great?

EN: The key, I believe, is to get out each day, and see things with new eyes, like one newly arrived. I don't believe it is a bad thing at all as it keeps your vision fresh and one's self interested.

Bangkok, and Thailand for that matter, is a great shooting destination. Personally, I'm not that interested in shooting well-known spots. One should go to the Grand Palace and so on once in their life for sure, but I've no inclination to return to well-known "family vacation" destinations for my photography. I find that almost any street here will do nicely. There will be someone or something one can shoot.

People here are genuinely cooperative if not downright happy when I ask to take their photograph. All you have to do is just go for a walk in your neighborhood and you'll find fascinating things to shoot. I've just moved to a new neighborhood and I'm looking forward to getting out and shooting here as there's a large Muslim population and diverse groups of people living all around me.

Modes of transport here also fascinate me. The boats and *motocy* taxis aren't found in the US and where we have them (specifically boats) they are not utilitarian and geared more often to tourists. In Southeast Asia, it's just another way to get around and I love it. I don't drive here and hate even being a passenger in a car here. I much prefer any other method to get places if it's safe. Those are opportunities to see the streets and life in general in a different way instead of in an air-con car with tinted windows. That, and the fear-inducing traffic and driving styles here make the trains and boats and walking much more appealing to me.

I try to keep myself open to as many subjects as possible, whether it be people, places or things. I do enjoy photographing people as there are some unique looks folks have here and in other countries in Southeast Asia. People are much more approachable here than in the US, where they don't have time to stop for you or are just suspicious or irascible in general.

KC: How has the digital age impacted your profession, both positively and negatively?

EN: My lab, ACP, was where I was negatively affected by the change to digital. I had many clients up until the day I closed my doors who were trying to keep film alive, not just for its own sake but because it's the way they liked to work and they preferred the look film gave them.

One day back in Chicago, I needed a cheap digital print and I uploaded the file to Walgreens, the national drug store chain, and within 15 minutes I got an email saying the print was ready at the store around the corner from me. At that point I knew I could never compete with digital as handmade analog printing and processing takes time, and fewer and fewer people were willing to wait anymore.

I began offering drum scanning, digital to black-and-white film conversions via a 4×5 film recorder, and custom archival ink jet (digital) prints on rag paper, but even the cachet of the custom hands-on printing and scanning was not enough to bring in a large volume of work as many photographers were making those prints and scans in their own studios, and others were just sending their work to Walgreens or the like as the quality wasn't that important for a lot of work. Also, the need to go to print at all, all but disappeared in advertising and commercial photography.

KC: What is the best photography advice you have ever received?

EN: Best photography advice is my own as well, which is to keep shooting. Whatever it is you want to shoot, whether film or digital, just keep at it.

KC: Do you have any projects in the works? What is your ideal photography assignment? Do you prefer freelance work over model shoots, or is it a balance that you strive for?

EN: I have two teaching projects in their early stages right now, both requiring my darkroom and digital. The first is to teach some folks here how to do wet plate photography. The major stumbling block I've run into there is the chemistry. Shipping from my suppliers in the US is very expensive and its arrival is iffy at best. One supplier told me of a shipment he made to Singapore that took three months to arrive. So I'm in search of companies that have the needed chemistry here in Thailand.

The other project is to teach alternative photo-printing techniques such as cyanotypes or salted paper, using negatives made with a digital printer. These historical processes require the negative to be the size of the image you want as the negatives are printed in contact with the paper. Working from scans or digital files to print onto overhead transparency material allows one to easily make these large negatives.

Actually, still life and product shoots interest me more than model shoots, as those depend heavily on the talent and support people such as hair and make-up. I enjoy model shoots for a sideline as I can do pretty much whatever I want.

KC: If you had not been a professional photographer, can you imagine what other profession in the arts you might have liked to try?

EN: I'm really at a loss to think of any profession other than photography!

ERIC NELSON PHOTOGRAPHY
Website: ericnelsonphoto.tumblr.com

[XXV]

Verse by the Poet Noir,
John Gartland

John Gartland on Sukhumvit Road — Photo Eric Nelson

ENGLISHMAN, JOHN GARTLAND, has travelled widely, and has done dozens of jobs, from the menial to the executive, since his Honors degree in English, and Master's degree in Elizabethan and Shakespearian Drama .at Newcastle University. He's also been a lecturer and professor in four countries, recently returning to Bangkok, after posts as visiting Professor of English Writing at the Korea National University of Education, and lecturer at a University College in Muscat. Bangkok Beat is pleased to showcase some poems by this published novelist and performance poet.

THE COMPANY OF POETS

You've heard a kind of clown
dismissing poetry,
as rarefied and precious, not real life;
till, cut and sliced by love's
exquisite and inexorable knife,
he'll find the bottle comfortless enough,
and fumble in his misery for rhyme.

Still craving for some vanished stuff of rapture,
attempting to contain the heart's decline,
and learning there's no science that will capture
or can resurrect a passion. It's a sign that life
will seek out rhythms, incantations, dreams,
to celebrate its stature, and to wonder at itself.
Each dances, in his fashion, to that driving score it seems;
but poets live the fuller, by their nature, beating time.

And I'll seek out the company of poets,
the company of poets I'll make mine.
When poetry has bitten you you'll know it;
it's just an arc of words but in the overall design
of things, there's everything in life laid out below it;
from birth to love, and death, and celebration;
and before the robot reaper can consign
you to your headstone you will ride imagination's
launcher high above the milling cities,
be the Process speaking, for a time.

So I'll seek out the company of poets,
the company of poets I'll make mine.
They're taking passion's pulse
and they are signaling the future,
they've freedom for a mistress
and they've history for a tutor,
and they can image water into wine.
Each new day is their holy book,
and apparatchiks hate them
for scoffing at all priesthoods
while embracing the divine.
So give to me the company of poets,
the company of poets I'll make mine.

Those black flags of mourning, who better to fly them?
The tender intrigues of the aspirant heart,
that life-shaking love that you have for your children,
how better to tell them? Where better to start?
Where else but the company of poets?
whose alchemical pilgrimage sets them apart...
Where else but the company of poets?

Those ephemeral fires of the beacon lights,
on the century's headlands, glowing;
like poems, are markers we leave to rite
our passage and our going.
Bright seeds on the wind that flower despite
the perennial cloud of unknowing,
and they're sown by the company of poets,
the indelible company of poets.

ANNA JET

Anna glides among the drinkers
and her girls at Anna Jet.
The customers pay tribute with their eyes.

Her girls are young,
available and beautiful, and yet,
as she irradiates the storyline
of evening with her smile,
and lets her hand rest lightly
on some shoulder for a while,
her backless dress of silken gold's
as tight as gilt upon
an art collector's statuette.

Her girls are young,
available, and beautiful and yet,
it's Anna with her silken style
who dances in the memory
while we cross the floating world
to Anna Jet.

Hot night, the bar that's open
to the dealings of the street,
the techno music, short time girls,
a DJ who is seemingly determined
to defeat our death in this
sublime apotheosis of the dance.

I think of Wagner talking about Beethoven
and glance at strangers who
are dancing on their naked lives.
Here in the floating world, the dream survives;
drink deep, and dance, and banish sleep

for Anna shines among her girls
like some erotic statuette,
and it's always short time, you can bet,
golden short time.
And the bass is driving nails
into the past
in Anna Jet.

THE EYE: 1

Man, I'm an ex-Private Eye, I can strike a cool pose
while listening to others' production-line prose,
self-published wunderkinds who believe their own hype,
burned-out actors on valium bogarting the mike,
tales of drug-hauls and bar girls and crooked police,
and hard-drinking dicks who've adopted the east.

Look! I'm old-school detective, I've seen the whole bag,
Spillane-heads, in trench-coats, Dash Hammett in drag.
Just a crime-writers' gig, at the Mambo hotel,
but outside it's for real, and they're guilty as hell.

THE EYE: 2

It's a crime-writers' gig, at the Mambo hotel,
where whore-hounds had partied for fifty-odd years.
But life, like a crime scene, is not all it appears;
the old cathouse is cabaret, now; it's a fact,
and, under new management, the riskiest act,
would be squeezing the original Mamasan's hand,
which once, like the anthem, could make a room stand,
and left a broad smile on the girls in the band,
at the Mambo Hotel.

Two floors of short-time ghosts,
a locked-up beauty shop, and dust;
now pulp-writers rap about crime here,
and must shoot the fictional breeze on stage.
But, as the Eye on the case, I'll cut to the chase,
the major heist is on the street,
and there's fresh blood on the page.

THE EYE: 3

Bent judges and psychopaths, hustlers and has-beens,
professional liars, Bangkok is a crime scene.
Hey, I was an Eye, wrestled crime for a living,
and still have a hunch for who's making a killing.
The patriots and flag-sniffers, feeling the force,
play patsy for billionaires, hit men, and punks,
they've closed down the city and cheered themselves hoarse,
till the tourists and hookers are packing their trunks.

Man, the hacks know the issue, but no one dares say;
destabilization is sent from upstairs,
since they can't get Joe Public to vote the right way.
More generals than doormen, tear-gas everywhere,
there's gold braid enough here to carpet a whorehouse,
gridlock on the streets, and a coup in the air.

Look, I'm just an Eye, with an odd tale to tell,
at a pulp writers' gig at the Mambo Hotel.
But, outside? It's for real, pal.
They're guilty as hell.

You'd better believe it, they're guilty as hell.

THE NIGHT MARKET

A spring night in Cheongju.
A thousand mysteries
in the elixir of cold oranges.
Korean seamstress in the closing market,
floor littered with remnants of others' finery,
your head is bowed, machining quiet hours
into a wrap of restfulness we slip on
like a comfortable coat.
We stare, the dreaming needle flies,
and you, peace-working,
never lift your eyes.

These dark aisles draw us in;
down there, a couple in white smocks
and yellow gauntlets, by their silver trove
are ladling heaps of ice in bright
obeisance to the shuttered night.
We fly into the frozen moment,
seabirds through a sudden window.
Around us, shadows; doors
are slamming. Cries of watchmen
greet returning ghosts,
announce the close, and crash the iron bolts,
on the frozen moment
crash the iron bolts.

ENCOUNTERS WITH THE EXTRAORDINARY

In Battambang, Chris led the way,
from smoke-laced afternoon, a small café,
to find my reading gig that evening;
the Lotus Gallery's magic space.
I see us, with our bullet-proof dog,

he, marching through that intersection,
oven of a place, and spiked with motorcycles,
pick-ups, four-wheel drives. Me following,
face fixed upon Street Two point Five;
my head still in an elevator,
levitating effortlessly to the other side.

Khmer wedding-music, spilling from
anonymous marquee; immortal female voice
brings old Cambodia to haunt me.
Arcadian shadows frame the day; and sitting
by a sunlit chessboard, in the sainted hour,
Lao Tzu sips coffee, contemplating play.
I linger on that high street; as Life
mercifully turns, holds up a flower.
With wings upon his feet, Chris flies on, faster.

Unmasked,
Street Two point Five becomes the Way.
That Zen-rush of a bit-part poet,
stepping into Master.

BAR GIRLS GAMBLING

Like five little dice were boulders,
and this intense game
a tremor, changing landscape,
these bar girls, gambling,
slam a dice pot down so hard
the beers shake.
Bar girls, gambling
throwing exit routes to easy street,
an expertise of feline boredom,
shaking out of happy hour

good fortune as an earthquake
or a fracture line of freedom,
and the old game for its own sake.
Bar girls, gambling,
'till the beers shake.

BANGKOK NOCTURNE

Eight floors below, in the shadows,
a security man slides into the quiet pool.
Having seen him pace the poolside
in the afternoon heat
I wish him well,
stripped of his peaked cap
and paramilitary tunic, surrendering
to the night embrace of water.
Towards On Nut a hundred dogs
begin a howling competition,
hoping to dislodge the rainstorm
hanging like heavy fruit
over the towers.
Lightning barks an invocation
to the deluge;
a restless city, under sticky heaven
dreams cool consummation;
some naked assignation with
the night embrace of water.

[XXVI]

Timothy Hallinan - King of the Bangkok Fiction Hill?

THE POKE RAFFERTY series consists of six critically acclaimed thrillers set in Bangkok by author Timothy Hallinan, who divides his time between a Southern California beach community, Bangkok and a slightly less idyllic seaside town on the Gulf of Thailand, where he gets a lot of good writing done. Tim frequents other parts of Southeast Asia as well.

Tim is also the author of a six-novel mystery series featuring the erudite private eye Simeon Grist, and the more recent three-novel mystery series starring Junior Bender, a wise-cracking investigator who has a second job as a successful burglar. Both series are set in Los Angeles. Here are Tim's own words regarding the background for the Poke Rafferty series: "Poke Rafferty had written two rough travel books – *Looking for Trouble in the Philippines* and *Looking for Trouble in Indonesia* – when he arrived in Thailand to write the next one. And Thailand – especially Bangkok – changed his life forever.

"Now married to the former "queen" of the Patpong bars, Rose, with whom he's adopted a daughter off the sidewalks, Miaow, Rafferty finds family life in Bangkok to be more of an adventure than rough travel ever was. But, after years of travel, he's also in the process of finding his heart and his personal true North. The books are thrillers, but they're also the continuing story of a hand-made family trying to stay together against all the odds."

It is the patchwork nuclear family setting, for me, which sets the Poke Rafferty series apart from much of the other Bangkok-based fiction. That and the brilliant prose of Timothy Hallinan.

Timothy comes from a rock n' roll background. He wrote songs and played in a folk rock band while still a university student growing up in California. His songs were recorded by many well-known artists including the platinum-selling group Bread, which placed 13 songs on The Billboard 100 between 1970 and 1977. My sister owned every album Bread ever made.

You need not read the Poke Rafferty series in order. They stand alone perfectly well. I first read *The Queen of Patpong*, which is fourth in the sequence, followed by *Breathing Water* (third), *Fear Artist* (fifth), *A Nail Through the Heart* (first), and *The Fourth Watcher* (second), which I picked up periodically but never finished. Do not make anything of that fact. I can say the same about all series of novels by any of my favorite authors, and Timothy Hallinan is one of my favorite authors. I topped off the series by reading *For The Dead* last.

In *A Nail Through the Heart*, Poke wants to marry ex-bar girl Rose and adopt the eight-year-old and streetwise street girl Miaow. Hallinan gets across the bleakness of Bangkok with ample doses of humor. And it works.

In *Breathing Water*, the family unit is properly set. Poke, now married to Rose, and their daughter Miaow make a threesome you care about. Hallinan does first class antagonists – in this thriller it is Pan, once a two-bit thug who used his considerable skills, good and evil, to turn himself into a billionaire. Poke wins the right to pen Pan's biography in a poker game with the help of his friend, Thai policeman Arthit. Poke and his family always seem to be in jeopardy, and Poke loves his family. We know the drill by now, but it is a good drill with Hallinan's prose leading the way. The Thai power elite are after Poke because they don't want the book written. In a scene we've seen many times before, an abduction takes place and Rafferty wears a hood over his head in the back seat of a limo with heavies on each side of him. Only this time, it's Hallinan style:

> Rafferty says, "I'd be frightened if you hadn't put the hood on."
> "That just means we're not going to kill you. It doesn't mean we're not going to beat the shit out of you."
> "When I'm frightened, I shut up," Rafferty says.
> After a moment of silence, the man to his right chuckles.
> "You chuckled, too," Rafferty says. "Did somebody teach all you guys to chuckle?"
> "The chuckle," the man to his right says, "is a perfectly acceptable form of laughter."

Besides humor, Hallinan paints the desperation of the Bangkok street people and the perks of the privileged class in Thai society to perfection. *Queen of Patpong* was nominated for an Edgar Award by the Mystery Writers of America in 2011, and rightfully so. It is a great novel with great writing.

Anyone who characterizes *The Queen of Patpong* as a bar-girl book diminishes it, intentionally or unintentionally – it is not that. It is what astute readers look for, a good story with conflict all over the place and resolution where it is needed most. Rose is as strong a female character as you will find in any book, and she literally and figuratively takes center stage in this, my all-time favorite Bangkok thriller. For those who might think Hallinan glamorizes the Bangkok night, sample this as Poke listens to his wife speak among a group and think again:

> "I let one of the men rename me. A man gave me the name Rose – you didn't know that, did you, Poke? ... He said, this man, he said that Kwan was too hard to remember, even though it's a good name and it means 'spirit,' and that the rose was the queen of flowers and I was the queen of Patpong." She laughs, rough as a cough. "The queen of Patpong. A kingdom of whores and viruses. Death with a smile."

What makes *The Queen Of Patpong* unique is the second section, which is turned over to the female characters, completely, in a revealing and compulsive read. Hallinan does what all great writers do, he makes you want to turn the page to learn of the journey Rose took from the lanky, innocent girl teased in her village to the most coveted prostitute in all of the Patpong bars, before Poke walks into her life.

We also see Miaow's progress. She's smart, a good student, still ballsy in all the right ways and is preparing for her upcoming part in her school play, *The Tempest*. I am leery when authors throw Shakespeare in the back-story – not being a fan myself – but it worked. Once again, Poke's family is at risk – this time at the hands of a serial killer, a man from Rose's past. And once again Poke needs the help of his policeman friend, Arthit. The boat scene is more than good enough, it's brilliant, and the cinematic and entirely believable Thai justice ending is as satisfying as it gets for a reader.

The fifth in the series is *The Fear Artist*. It was published just nine months after the flood which hit Bangkok in 2011. Hallinan allows the deluge to soak in just enough as a perfect back-story, which impressed me because the original draft must have been dry.

The book opens with Poke backing out of a paint store with cans of paint in his hands. Apricot cream and urban decay are the colors of choice in a busy Bangkok neighborhood, when a bleeding man, shot, crumples into Poke's life, knocking them both to the ground. Before he dies he whispers: "Helene Ekersley. Cheyenne." Poke gets taken in for questioning, conveniently forgetting the dying utterance, which irks the wrong people in power. As a result, Poke is framed for a crime he couldn't possibly have done. But this is Thailand. As Poke states: "Bangkok may not be glamorous … but it's got lurid down cold." Poke must send Rose and Miaow up-country, make a rooftop escape from the police when they visit him a second time, and find the real killer. The absence of Rose and Miaow is filled in by the re-appearance of Poke's half-sister Ming Li, who is 17 years old going on 30.

There is some excellent writing in *The Fear Artist*. The characters and setting are superb. The evil and greedy antagonist, Murphy, is an ex-soldier who has to cover up past atrocities in a Vietnam War-era life by committing more atrocities in real time. But it's Murphy's daughter, Treasure, who is the mesmerizing one. Hallinan's cynical humor gets a perfect character to play with in Janos, an otherwise forgettable Russian spy left over from the Cold War, who Hallinan makes memorable for all of his forgettable qualities. Many say *The Fear Artist* is their favorite in the series, and for good reasons. Hallinan makes valid political commentary about the US Phoenix Program in Vietnam, the troubles in the south of Thailand, and good old American greed. But I still give the nod to *The Queen of Patpong*, because Rose and Miaow are absent so much here, and by now, let's face it, they are family to the reader.

In case you don't recall Bread or their songs, think of Hallinan as more of a Brian Wilson of The Beach Boys type of writer. Pick up anything written by Timothy Hallinan and the chances are you'll soon be pickin' up good vibrations. Read any of the Poke Rafferty series with the statuesque Rose and find out how she started working on the brain of Poke with just one look. Rose now runs a successful cleaning business, but the former go-go dancer and tall Thai beauty is capable of giving so much more than just excitations to any reader.

An inference can be drawn from the aforementioned quote by Rose, about how she earned her memorable moniker, that no one person should ever decree the title of King or Queen of anything on anyone. No attempt will be made to do so here. But if there was to be a contest for King of the Bangkok Fiction Hill, Timothy Hallinan would be on any respectable invitation list. Bangkok fiction has a diverse cast of authors and titles from which to choose. You may prefer the Rolling Stones' *19th Nervous Breakdown* over the Beatles' *She Came in Through the Bathroom Window*. Tom Waits' *The Piano Has Been Drinking* over Tom Petty's *Mary Jane's Last Dance*. Bob Dylan's *Lay, Lady Lay* or Sam the Sham's *Little Red Riding Hood?* Neil Young's *Cinnamon Girl* or Jackson Browne's *Redneck Friend?* I look for good writing, wherever I can find it.

And great writing is what you will find in the Poke Rafferty series by Timothy Hallinan, which just so happens to take place in Bangkok. And some of those moments are spent in bars. The Thais have an expression – they even have to use the English word when they say it, because they have no Thai equivalent. That's how *jai yen yen* (cool) they are. It is, "Don't be serious." Put another way...... it's only Bangkok fiction ... but I like it.

[XXVII]

Review: For the Dead
by Timothy Hallinan

ONCE YOU'VE READ any of the first five Poke Rafferty Bangkok thrillers by Timothy Hallinan, chances are you'll be a fan of the series. You do not get the Edgar Award, Macavity Award and Shamus Award nominations and have NBC develop your Junior Bender novels into a television series by tweeting. You do have to write at least sixteen novels, though. Tim Hallinan has also written a book of non-fiction on the works of Charles Dickens, as I mention in an earlier chapter.

In the previous chapter I discuss Tim's first five novels in the Poke series. They are, in order: *A Nail Through the Heart*, *The Fourth Watcher*, *Breathing Water*, *The Queen of Patpong* and *The Fear Artist*.

To recap, Poke Rafferty is an American travel writer. He is a family man with an improbable family blossoming in the mud of an even more improbable city – Bangkok. His wife Rose, the former lanky Isaan country girl, was once a Patpong dancing superstar until Poke rescued her or she rescued Poke. Love and marriage followed. They adopted a homeless street girl named Miaow.

In some ways, not much has changed in *For the Dead*, and yet a lot has changed. Miaow is now 13 years old. *For The Dead* is, for the first time in the Poke series, primarily Miaow's story. How best to describe Miaow to the unfamiliar reader? Hallinan does it superbly in the narrative thoughts of Rose:

> *"Miaow, she thinks. The throw-away child, tossed onto a side-walk. As tough as she tries to seem, Miaow worries about everything. She double-checks everything. If she were hanging over a cliff, held only by a knotted rope, she would try and improve the knot. She has no idea how remarkable she is, how smart, how decent, how much she's loved. Somewhere in the center of her being, Miaow is still the short, dirty, dark-skinned, frizzy-haired, unloved reject who tried to sell chewing gum to Rafferty on his second night in Bangkok."*

For The Dead opens with a wonderful up-country dream sequence. It concludes with heart-tugging laughter. What you get in between, besides a fast-paced thriller featuring technology, pulse-pounding chase scenes and contract killings conducted at the highest levels by a corrupt Thai police force, is what is missing in so many novels today – quality. Page after page of quality. What you read in a Timothy Hallinan novel has importance, it's useful and it's entertaining.

In *For The Dead*, Poke is happy, financially secure for once and learns that his family of three will in nine months' time become four. Miaow helps her nerdish Vietnamese boyfriend replace his second lost iPhone with a used model during a skillful negotiation with a Sikh merchant in India Town. They learn later that the phone contains pictures of some very dead policemen. Poke would normally be an early confidant, but news of Rose's pregnancy was relayed in an awkward manner, creating domestic strife. Serious jeopardy ensues and leads to the heaviest of hit men.

You could make a good case for saying that in the Poke Rafferty series the last three novels have been the best, although I very much enjoyed *Breathing Water*. For me, *The Queen of Patpong* had the perfect mix of thrills, antagonists and family. In *The Fear Artist*, I found myself missing the family at times, although again the thrills and antagonist were stellar, plus you got the intriguing character of Treasure, who we last saw disappearing into the fire and explosions of her abusive home. *For the Dead* puts Poke and family front and center, plus Treasure gets an encore along with two memorable Bangkok street kids. The thrills are still there, as is the terrific prose of Hallinan, detailing in great depth the best and worst of mankind. My criticism of For *the Dead* is that the antagonist didn't live up to the level of evil or consistency of the last two, but Hallinan can take the blame for that one, for setting the bar so high. My suspension of disbelief also had to be ratcheted up a notch for a rather conveniently timed plot solution, no matter how much I wanted it to happen.

The Queen of Patpong is a Bangkok thriller – my favorite Bangkok thriller of all time. The Poke series is a Bangkok series when looked at in totality. *For The Dead* is, first and foremost, a human story – a story about a family and the bonds that hold them together. A story that could play within the backdrop of a dozen cities throughout the world – the corrupt police department and poor rice farmers notwithstanding. And that is not a criticism; that is a compliment to Hallinan's storytelling ability and the multi-dimensional characters he constructs in his writing. The Poke Rafferty series is no longer confined to the genre of Bangkok fiction or a simple mystery – this is first-class literary fiction.

We are reminded often that we now live in a world where books, music, authors and musicians have all been devalued. But value is still out there if value matters to you. Smart and appreciative readers will always invest in reading good books by good authors. *For the Dead* is one such book and Timothy Hallinan has proven time and time again that he is one such author.

[XXVIII]

Interview with Bangkok Author
James A. Newman

I MET THE ARTIST James A. Newman under a starless sky over a basket of chicken livers washed down with pints of dark ale at an outdoor eatery, catty corner from Bangkok's Queen Victoria pub. The burned-out second-floor window at the bar across the soi had been replaced, and a cat was licking one of the paint chips left behind on the red awning. Leaded or unleaded, I wasn't sure. Foot traffic was picking up, and so were the green and yellows. Newman seemed more interested in a busty woman in long heels and short shorts, and a nerdy gal wearing white-framed glasses and eating deep-fried larvae than this interviewer. But this wasn't my first rodeo. No. On with it, as Christopher Minko of the Phnom Penh noir band Krom once told me.

KC: Someone, a long time ago, gave me some good advice about women. He said: "Tell the pretty woman she's smart and the smart woman she's pretty." It made sense to me at the time.

JN: That's pretty smart advice.

KC: You're a writer.

JN: Thanks. So are you.

KC: Well, I'm not expecting a call from New York literary agent Elyse Cheney anytime soon. Thanks, though. You, on the other hand, have written four novels in the Joe Dylan detective series, not to mention *Lizard City* with Johnny Coca Cola, have a screen option out on *The White Flamingo* and have published tons of short stories, which garnered you numerous rejection slips in the process – all years before your 40th birthday.

JN: I have. Rejection slips are my badges of honor.

KC: Your story *Pacific Coast Highway*, in Paul D. Brazill's *Exiles: An Outsider Anthology*, really hit home. And all the proceeds go to charity. Good on Paul and you. You've even published a book about Buddhism under a nom de plume, so that leads us, naturally, to music.

JN: Naturally.

KC: Can you be like Tom Petty and do some free fallin' about the musical influences in your life from the time you held your first Atari joystick to what you listened to with your eggs this morning?

JN: Okay. Let's see. I thank my parents for introducing me to The

Beatles, Stones, Squeeze, The Smiths, Neil Young, Leonard Cohen and many more bands and songwriters that I wouldn't have discovered so early otherwise. In fact, my grandparents are Beatles fans, God bless them. I discovered The Velvet Underground and Nico through my friend Scott, who bought the record after watching the Oliver Stone movie *The Doors* based on the book *No One Here Gets Out Alive*, written by none other than Jerry Hopkins who was at the last Night of Noir event in Bangkok, albeit fleetingly. So it all moves in circles.

As a teenager and during my early twenties, opening my CD cabinet was like opening an angry teenager's diary. There was a lot of dark stuff in there. *Music for a New Society* by John Cale. Early Jeff Beck, Sonic Youth and God Machine for a stateside trip to hell. The Auteurs and Pulp with their wonderfully British brand of fallen-actor-pop-star gloom. Suede with their glorious drugs-in-a-council-flat chic. Dinosaur Jr with their wee-inspired fuzzbox meltdown, and the Jesus and Mary Chain for an absolute nihilistic hit of the dark stuff. I took *Metal Machine Music* by Lou Reed seriously – it was just a record of noise and feedback. It almost ruined his career, yet Reed toured the album shortly before his death. So, there you go. I like risk takers with dangerous minds. On the back of the *Metal Machine Music* LP is that wonderfully spikey quote: "My week beats your year."

Early 90s in London I went to hundreds of gigs and a handful of festivals, and played in a band as a guitarist, singer and songwriter. We were lucky enough to have a studio and a producer (all on a government loan!) and I wish I still had some of those recordings. We practiced solidly and spent a lot of time recording and experimenting with samples and effects, and basically monkeying around with all the equipment at our disposal. Thousands of rehearsals over a number of years and we never even signed a record deal! We landed in the local paper, and our live shows were unmitigated disasters as I had chronic stage fright and a weakness for Russian vodka. I love rock and roll and back then, in my youthful naivety, I had the narrow belief that the only thing I was any good at was writing and recording songs. This was nonsense. I was actually quite good at other things too, like smoking, drinking beer, fumbling around in the dark reading Burroughs and watching *Easy Rider*, and generally acting the fool with my friends.

Right now I like Big Fat White Family. Tom Vater turned me onto them. *Touch the Leather* is an awesome track.

KC: I'll check it out. Vater is irreverent and informed, I've read. And a great comedian. Speaking of objectivity, can an artist be objective about his own work?

JN: Nah ... Shane McGowan said during a brief period of coherence that art is like throwing shit at the wall. Some of it sticks and some of it doesn't, and the thrower really doesn't know which way it will splat. I've struck out more than I've hit. A wise man realizes he's a fool just fumbling around in the dark. I don't cling to praise and I don't cling to criticism, and I am certainly not objective about my own work. Writing a novel is like bringing up a child. You love your child more than anything in the world but you know deep down inside you made more than a few mistakes along the way.

KC: Who decides whether someone is an apprentice, a craftsman or a true artist? Is it his peers, the public or the almighty sales figures?

JN: Peer acceptance is very important to me personally, although I reckon in the end the audience decides, word of mouth decides, the readers are the real story makers, writers just kind of lay out the path. A promotional push can get the ball rolling but if the ball is bad it won't sell after the first few months. Then there comes one who just breathes talent, and nothing can stop him or her. He or she needs no promotion, word of mouth spreads like wild fire. Very rare, but it happens.

KC: Give me an example.

JN: A good example would be (Henry) Miller.

KC: Isn't it possible that if Henry Miller had not hooked up with some well-heeled sponsors in Paris no-one would have ever heard of him? Did Henry get lucky or did he create his own luck?

JN: Miller was certainly not lucky for much of his life, if the books I've read are accurate. Miller published in France, and then Barney Rosset (the former owner of the publishing house Grove Press, and publisher and editor-in-chief of the magazine *Evergreen Review*, who died in 2012) took a risk and put his books out Stateside. Thus the circus began; scandal, court case, and huge sales. I can't see anything scandalous in Miller's writing personally. I just see good prose and wonderful flights of imagination. When he flows he really flows like some kind of possession is at play, you know? He would enjoy success if he started writing now. He was a good writer who followed the simple discipline that one word should follow the next as if it were supposed to be right there.

If you study the careers of successful writers in depth and read the biographies, you will see that they just kept plugging away until at least one person enjoyed what they were doing just enough to sustain the magic. Some of the great novelists were writing for just one person, normally a lover or a friend, or quite often themselves. It seems that financial success and critical recognition for any artist normally comes later in life, if at all. Some people luck it and some have talent, but usually it's just good old hard work over many, many years.

KC: A friend of mine said, as we discussed musicians: "There is more talent in the world than luck." Do you agree with that?

JN: An individual either has or doesn't have musical talent, although some do have better musical talent than others. Musical talent is easier to spot than writing talent, you can hear it, but when you see writing talent, you really see it. Bob Dylan, for example, is an average musician but an enormously talented writer who made a fortune in the music business owing to his use of words. The guitar was a prop to success and the Beats had blasted the barn door open in terms of what you could sing about at that time and place. I'm not saying that Dylan wasn't a rock and roller, or a folk musician, he was – but first and foremost, like Lou Reed, he was a writer who used the rock and roll platform to express himself. Is there a creative gene? I don't know. Perhaps it is a strain of autism. Musical talent has been proven to be genetic. Perfect pitch is passed on down generations. Anyone can play the guitar or the piano, but how many can reach that state where the instrument takes over the musician? When the musician is just a puppet on a stage guided by some strange higher power? Writing can be learned to a certain degree, yet a writer in full flow is like the piano player guided to that golden place by the muse. Burroughs wrote in a Tangerine letter to Ginsberg that "the writing is coming on like dictation; I can't keep up with it." Perhaps there is something supernatural at play. I don't know. I know only one thing. Talent and luck are less important than work. Work brings talent and luck. Warhol said work is the most important attribute any artist has in his toolkit, and many would say Warhol was untalented and lucky.

KC: Warhol critics are not hard to find. Warhol-like success is quite rare. He was a worker bee. Tell me about your book on Buddhism. Is Buddhism a mist, a lacquer, a veneer or a hardwood in your life? Expand on these things called thoughts? Should we pay them any attention? How does one unlock the great mystery of life, anyway?

JN: *Thai Meditations* was written after staying at several monasteries in Thailand. There is a short story or observation for each of the 77 provinces of Thailand. You would have to ask someone else about unlocking the mystery of life. I'm not qualified; I'm merely fumbling around in the dark. Thoughts shouldn't be held on to for too long in daily life. Living in the present moment is difficult, yet as writers we get to play with thoughts. Novelists rearrange thoughts and construct them into stories that allow the reader to become lost in the story and forget their own anxieties. Stories really are a magical gift in that respect. It all goes back to the hunter gatherer society and tales around the camp fire. I guess the storyteller was a lousy hunter.

KC: Sean Penn once said that one is either born with a resistance to cynicism or you're not. He went on to say that his friend Charles Bukowski was one of those guys who was given every opportunity in life to become a jaded, cynical prick. But Penn claims Buk was anything but. Sean Penn goes on to describe Charles as the sweetest, most vulnerable pussycat who disguised it wonderfully. Do you agree with Penn's assessment of Bukowski?

JN: I agree and disagree. I don't think a child is born a cynic nor born with a resistance to cynicism. I think a cynical person becomes one by way of parental or institutional belittlement – social conditioning – although some argue genetics are at play, I'm not so sure. I do agree that Bukowski was sensitive and vulnerable. Most poets are. Penn knew Bukowski after he had made some money and had gotten himself married to Linda and had the hot tub and the BMW. He was cynical as hell while claiming to ride box cars and living on skid row. But when Penn knew him he was living the high life, Santa Barbara, baby. It's difficult to be a cynic when you're sitting in a hot tub smoking a Honduran cigar with close to a million dollars growing in the bank and a nice BMW on the drive, and you're having Dennis Hopper and Madonna over for brunch.

KC: How do you avoid becoming cynical? How would you describe yourself? What, if anything, do you disguise?

JN: The best way to avoid becoming cynical is to remove yourself from the source of that cynicism. If Thailand or any country brings out these feelings of cynicism, take a trip somewhere else for a week or two. If your job sucks, change it. I describe myself as a humorist creative type, a loyal son of a bitch who has a drive to succeed, but could be a better family guy. Disguise? A writer disguises nothing at all; it is all in his work for anybody to read. Do you know how much bravery it takes a novelist to publish their first novel? First novels are generally terribly personal, and packed with the author's most awful secrets.

KC: Tell me about your writing process.

JN: It varies. *The White Flamingo* took a few sittings. After the notes were made and my outline was mapped out I hammered the novel out in a few weeks. I just deleted 25,000 words of my latest book *Fun City Blues* as I thought about a new science fiction direction. You know I was once asked by an attractive tall blonde, "What is a writer?" I replied: "Someone who can't stop writing." So perhaps it's an obsessive thing.

KC: That blonde sounds smart to me. Raymond Chandler wrote about Bay City in his seven Philip Marlow novels, which everyone pretty much knew was Santa Monica, California. You write about Fun City in your Joe Dylan series, which most, but not everyone, would recognize as Pattaya. Explain this literary technique if you can. What are the advantages of doing it the Chandler way? Is there a down side?

JN: First and foremost, I love Chandler's work and admire everything he has written apart from some of the very early work. Secondly, Fun City is a strange beast of a city, a product of my warped imagination but grounded in visits to Pattaya and Bangkok, where I've lived for 13 years. The series has become more popular than I ever imagined it would have. Fun City gives me the license to spill out any literary fantasies I may have without the geographical or cultural restrictions of actual place. I can push the fictional world further with the freedom of this make-believe city. In the current book I have the harbor, the beach, the Central Business District and the Red Night Zone all set together in the blade-running future. I have discovered my terrain after years of fumbling around with the concept and the formula of the series. The tourist zones of Thailand are so close to science fiction that it just makes sense to write in a cyber punk vein, and go all the way with it. Joe Dylan is of course a fedora-wearing gumshoe detective who navigates around this strange neon world by night. It's a nice concept. I'm content with Joe and Fun City. They mix together well, like red wine and cheese. I like writing the series and am happy that the series is being read.

I am very lucky and grateful to be here in this space and time with such wonderfully creative people. Including yourself, Kevin. Thanks for the time and the questions. I enjoyed it. Is it over? Do you mind if I hit Suzie Wong?

KC: The chicken livers are all gone. So, yes. Suzie Who?

JN: Exactly.

[XXIX]

Interview with Christopher Minko

Christopher Minko — Photo by Jonathan van Smit

I FIRST BECAME AWARE of Christopher Minko and the Khmer musicians who make up the band Krom when the lyrics to some of their songs appeared in *Phnom Penh Noir* (Heaven Lake Press, 2012) edited by Christopher G. Moore. The more you learn about the Minko and Krom story, the more you are drawn to it. Christopher Minko was born and raised in the land that has rightfully earned the moniker 'The Lucky County', Australia. Music was emphasized at an early age, his mother being a concert pianist. He now lives in what could easily be cast as one of the unluckiest countries, working with people who were not born into fortune but have found ways to make their lives a success, despite enormous obstacles.

I have long been a fan of lyrics as standalone works of art, so I was perfectly comfortable with the idea of musical lyrics appearing in a book of noir short stories. I was comfortable with the idea, but the actual lyrics created occasional discomfort. It never occurred to me, at the time, that it was part of the Krom message and the Minko plan. Christopher Minko screams what few dare to whisper, because to whisper his messages would be to acknowledge the existence of a dark abyss not occupying a fictional world but a real one. And that gets many of us, including me, out of our comfort zone. Here is an excerpt from the lyrics of one such song, which can be found on the last two pages of *Phnom Penh Noir*, titled *Tango Traffic Tango*:

The cattle class
Of ancient Men
Are greeted with open arms
Welcome to our daughters
We breed them on our farms

Ripe for human trafficking
We sell their innocent charms
Yea, air traffic
Rail traffic
Road traffic
And human trafficking
Where money and sex are king
Yea, human trafficking
Where money and sex are king

So welcome to our daughters
We breed them on our farms
Open up and take them
In your aging sagging arms
Yea, welcome to our daughters
We breed them on our farms

So thank goodness or badness or darkness, or whatever you wish to call it, because somebody or something needs to get us out of our comfort zone more often. One of those people is Christopher Minko, the lead man for the noir band with a Khmer edge, Krom, with whom I conducted a lengthy interview:

KC: I'm an old basketball junkie. And although my playing days are well behind me, I continue to think it is a great game and see the beauty in it. In basketball you have five starters. On the court, they need to get along, to be unselfish, to cooperate, and to acknowledge they are part of something bigger than themselves. To show poise under pressure. After the game is over, they can get along together or not. It doesn't really matter. At the professional level, these are referred to as a one taxi team or a five taxi team. My question to you, Christopher, is does the principle apply to bands? Is it necessary to get along with each other after you finish playing, or can you play well on stage and then go your separate ways after the gig? Have you played with mostly one taxi bands, five taxi bands or a combination in your career? And finally, how would you characterize Krom, on and off the stage?

CM: Kevin, firstly my appreciation along with thanks from Krom – we are honored at the interview. Your first question is a tough question indeed. I've been a professional musician a number of times in this rather twisted life of mine to date – the early 80s were spent playing with cult Australian Band The Bachelors from Prague, which was without doubt five different cabs combined with the folly of egoistical youth – great band but we split when one half wanted to go Tijuana Brass whilst personally I was along the lines of that gentleman deviant Chet Baker (at that time I played both trumpet and guitar). The split could be slightly compared to the current state of Thai politics insofar that friendships were certainly shattered (not all) – however, a violent break-up it wasn't.

Now Krom – that's a very different story, believe it or not, as I am nearing 60 years of age. I am now working in the most professional band I have ever worked with, in one way very much a one taxi band – tight, well-rehearsed, disciplined, cohesive and very professional. There are many that say the live shows are even better than the CDs. However, there are some very interesting points about Krom that create the unique signature Krom sound. It's also important to note that both Sophea Chamroeun (Krom co-founder/songwriter and lead vocals) and Sopheak Chamroeun (lead vocals) have studied Cambodian traditional dance and music under the best of masters since they were 12, through the internationally acclaimed Cambodian Living Arts Program, plus both are recent graduates of the Royal University of Fine Arts in Phnom Penh – they both have a very professional work ethic and approach to their work with Krom.

Hey – can't forget my good friend and musical colleague, multi-instrumentalist Jimmy B, who is the fourth member of Krom and understands my music better than most.

So, to Krom-things. Firstly – let me get this one out of the way before I start – I have little to no time for white-boy bands or musicians trying to play the music of another culture – for me the resulting sound of white boys playing Khmer music sounds clichéd and tacky, plus locals just do it better. That's just the way it is, and I have a deep love and respect for Khmer music. Therefore, I would never dare, out of respect, to tamper with this remarkable music created by Cambodians.

That now said, Krom is, and always will be, a Phnom Penh-based bilingual band (Khmer and English) playing original compositions – the key to the original music of Krom is the following formula which is not easy to do from a composer's viewpoint as you have to have your ego well under control to allow this to happen with your compositions. Noting also, once in a while remarkable musical partnerships of unique productivity evolve – such is the relationship between Sophea Chamroeun, the Krom lead vocalist, and me. Sophea seems to just totally understand where I am coming from with the Krom music. What I do is record the guitar foundations of a Krom song, put it on a memory stick and then hand it to Sophea without saying a word, or even humming a suggested melody riff (this is where one puts the ego in a box and closes the lid). Sophea goes away and totally on her own creates the Khmer lyrics and vocal melody without any influence whatsoever from me. All I can say is that she has never ever let me down in this regard and I am always so surprised (and usually very excited) at what sounds she builds around the delta blues picking of my guitar work and compositions. I use the same principle of respect with our Khmer producer, Sarin Chhuon, who then also adds his own unique Khmer interpretation of the master tapes, and at the end you have the rather unique signature sound that is Krom.

I should also mention the social issues that Krom touches on within many of the Krom lyrics, with a focus on the ever ongoing tragedy of sexual trafficking and sexual slavery, which is prolific in Southeast Asia along with being nurtured and developed as a major industry by the very corrupt ruling elites of the Southeast Asian nations who are willing, as I sing in the Krom song *Tango Traffic Tango*, "to sell their daughters". Sorry, but that's the harsh, brutal truth about these societies and it needs to be sung about. That's simply part of what Krom do.

Sophea and Sopheak, in their own way, are very courageous individuals and represent the first wave of protest singers or singers of songs of social justice to come out of Cambodia – interesting development indeed. Something also of great relevance to Krom are the ongoing noir-related themes [Krom's debut 2012 album is suitably titled *Songs from the Noir*] ... All Krom lyrics are very personal and there is a true (and often very dark) story or seven within all Krom songs. I should also acknowledge renowned Bangkok-based noir author Christopher G. Moore, and our ongoing friendship which has resulted in me using words from Christopher's novels in the Krom song *The Ying* and other songs. I believe Christopher Moore should be acknowledged for his lead role in the development of the now internationally recognized and growing creative movement known as Southeast Asia Noir. Many of us involved in the noir movement, including the second generation of Asian noir writers such as Tom Vater and other recent newcomers, are deeply indebted to Moore for his decades of effort to promote and develop Southeast Asian Noir as a recognized creative genre.

And noting your book's title, *Bangkok Beat*, allow me to make a personal reference to Thailand. My wife who came from Thailand and the mother of my now 20-year-old daughter passed away three years ago. As a result of her death and the associated personal grief, I returned to my musical roots. Out of something so sad came Krom – a remarkable woman from Bangkok who left a unique legacy called Krom.

KC: Thanks for being so candid, Christopher. I expected nothing less. Shifting gears for a moment, talk to me about your role in disability awareness and disability sports in Cambodia.

CM: Ah, the disability work – easy answer to that one. "Keeps a man's feet firmly on the ground, and him, properly humble." Eighteen years have been spent working with rural-based Cambodians with a disability via sports and other small-scale socio-economic developmental projects based on poverty alleviation. These persons with a disability are truly inspiring people who put one's own life very much into a proper, less selfish perspective – an ongoing humbling experience whereby I have truly learned one core rule about life, – "We are all disabled". After all, who the hell has the ferkin right to define normality? Disability sports are still embryonic in Cambodia, however we have reached great heights over the years, despite the odds, including reaching current No. 2 in the world in volleyball (men's) – beating Australia, Canada, USA, Korea and everyone else except for the Germans. That's yet to happen, but it will – rest assured.

At the moment my disability work focuses on assisting women with a more severe disability (women in wheelchairs) through wheelchair basketball ... and we now have 32 highly committed women, 16 of whom will, for the first time ever, represent Cambodia at the Korea 2014 Asia Para games.

Most of all – like I said – keeps a bloke very humble. Probably keep doing this work part-time until I die, as it's simply remarkable work with very dignified people who have so little – yet have so much. You can see the impact and strength of the women in the photos. In their own odd way, somehow, the disability/social justice work and the music of Krom go beautifully hand-in-hand.

KC: It's interesting to me how you stated that the disability/social justice work you do in Cambodia and the music of Krom go beautifully together. That leads to an idea you and I have discussed before, and it seems appropriate to discuss here. That is the possibility of a goodwill wheelchair basketball game being held in Thailand between the Cambodian women's team and the Thailand women's team. Let's talk about why it is such a good idea.

CM: Both Krom and the Women's Wheelchair Project are linked to social justice/poverty alleviation, and a very interesting note: sexual trafficking and sexual abuse are also a common theme. Few realize that sexual abuse against Cambodian women with a disability is seven times higher than with non-disabled women – they are easier to exploit. Many of the CNVLD [Cambodian National Volleyball League, Disabled] women are survivors of this form of abuse.

We all know that sport can be a powerful vehicle when it comes to fostering healing goodwill and harmony amongst nations. One only has to refer to Mr Mandela and his use of sports as a mechanism to heal wounds between black and white South Africans as an excellent example of this. All of us recognize the long and ever ongoing animosity between Thailand and Cambodia, so what better way to start the ball rolling than to organize that the Cambodian Women's wheelchair basketball team go to Thailand?

Such a project would be, as you say, a definite win-win for both nations and one would hope that this would lead to an annual exchange between Thai and Cambodian athletes with a disability.

KC: I've just re-read an excellent article about Krom, written by Christopher G. Moore, which he wrote late last year and has been published in two periodicals already, called 'Paint It Black'. As I've stated before, I like Christopher's writing on a number of levels, one of which is he helps me understand and bring attention to subjects that I intuitively know and agree with, but may not have articulated in my mind nearly as well as he does on paper or computer screen. Here is a quote from that article written by Moore which, as you might be able to tell, greatly influenced my introduction to this interview:

"Krom is such a scream from a wounded soul. The lyrics consolidate into a dark pitch blasting our sensibilities in an echo chamber of pain. There is an existential scream and nothing prepares us for it in our cozy world of shopping malls, social media, offices, clubs and homes." Christopher G. Moore.

I am a fan of noir fiction. I can handle it because, for the most part, I know it is fiction. But the Krom lyrics are not fiction. I know that – you know that. I have enjoyed the songs of Krom many times, even though they made me uncomfortable at times. But it is precisely the un-comfortableness that Krom evokes, in some, that makes your message all the more important. Your songs are the antithesis of pop songs because what you write about, the horrors of child sexual exploitation and human and social injustices, are not popular subjects, but they need to be. Why is it important for you to write about and sing about these social injustices? What good has come from your work (musically and in the area of disability awareness), and what more needs to be done – and I speak of the social injustices which you put your time and effort into exposing, particularly those that are occurring in Cambodia, Thailand and the region?

CM: Man, you throw them at me. Hey, the hardest question comes last – onto it. Okay, firstly, fact – human slavery (labor, sex and other) is at its highest point ever in the history of humanity. That's a fucking tragedy – some of this I attribute to the horror of unbridled capitalism, particularly since the collapse of communism, whereby we now have a world dominated by greed and selfishness, an ever-widening gap between the rich and the poor (which allows even greater exploitation of the poor) and power elites addicted to the worst traits of ego-driven madness found in humanity.

The sex industry – nearly everyone sidesteps the issue, they smile about it, joke about it, participate in it and waltz around it, but the blunt truth is this is an industry built on the sale of human flesh as an object of sexuality with exceptionally high profit margins and a high turnover of deaths as the women spiral quickly into a world of dependency on drugs and alcohol to numb the sale of their bodies over and over to aging and old men.

However, the real tragedy reveals itself when one sees how mainstream and integrated into society prostitution has become in many Southeast Asian nations over the past five decades – an industry that flourished during the Vietnam War and was recognized by the ruling masters as a viable and very profitable commercial enterprise, where the commercial benefits of a foreign clientele needing to purchase sex were recognized and a subsequent hospitality industry purposefully built around catering for the "sex tourist" was allowed and supported at the highest of levels.

No matter how mainstream this trade has become, one can never ever deny, or justify, that behind the scenes, it remains a brutal world of young women and girls forced by poverty and entrapped, enslaved or even kidnapped into a criminally led machine that constantly needs to be fed with new young stock to satisfy the ever growing international appetite for commercial sexual services.

As I sing in *Tango Traffic Tango*, these are nations that quite willingly sell their daughters into the sex industry. As nations they are not yet mature enough to confront the tragedy that they impose on their own people – that requires real courage and real change, unlike the ego and profit-driven political charade currently taking place in the streets of Bangkok.

So many observe the noir. How many live the noir, I ask? How many can truly acknowledge the brutal reality that 98 per cent of these women do not want to participate in this trade but have no other choice due to poverty and very often family pressure – often sold by their very own parents as part of the so called "poverty alleviation" process. Again, just take a walk down Sukhumvit and look at the numerous deluded old white boys in their 60s on a Viagra overdose drinking the morning beer with a scraggy 16-year-old girl hanging on their wrinkled arm. It says it all in its obvious brutality, and I want these deluded old fools to hear these Krom songs in order to make these people feel uncomfortable, as uncomfortable they should feel.

And in its own way I can't deny a morbid philosophical fascination with what I find is the ultimate exercise in nihilism – a nihilistic exercise that involves that most sacred of human entities we call "love", an existentialist drama that plays itself out every day in thousands of bars, brothels and hotels through Southeast Asia, and the rest of the world. Here we find lonely, pathetic, ancient men looking to purchase romantic love in much younger Asian women. Yet this love is an unattainable objective, as the very women they court are no longer capable of love, as the brutality of the process of endlessly selling one's body has destroyed these women's ability to genuinely love – a bitter irony if I have ever seen one, yet thousands of misguided fools each year embark on this fruitless and tragic journey.

The blunt truth is the Krom songs need to be sung and need to be heard, and there will be more Krom songs that touch on these uncomfortable themes. However, the reality behind the current tragedy of the sex slavery industry is that these women are not only rendered incapable of love, their lives are destroyed, including often a very early death. The more we speak out about these injustices the better, in a world that's gone stark raving mad.

What good comes from the work? I have devoted a lifetime to the causes of social justice and will continue to do so now, focusing on Krom as the main vehicle for this along with maintaining the disability work. The bottom line is the world's a shithole in so many ways – you can either try to do some good and effect positive change or you can selfishly turn your back on it all – I just try to do my best with my music and with my disability work, and hopefully achieve some good things in a rather complex world, acknowledging life's horrors and beauties are so intermingled as to be beyond all understanding.

In finishing, I give you the best example of all that negates many of the bullshit arguments supporting prostitution and the sex trade through a myriad of questionable excuses. Look at Krom and Sophea and Sopheak, the Krom vocalists, who are a brilliant example of what can happen when a 12-year-old girl is given educational opportunity rather than being steered down the path towards commercial sexual exploitation. Both Sophea and Sopheak grew up in one of Phnom Penh's most notorious slum/drug/prostitution quarters – the legendary White Building. Yet they managed to avoid the horrors that surrounded them through becoming pupils of the renowned Cambodian Living Arts program, and now at the ages of 22 and 23 they are fast becoming internationally recognized musical stars. What I am saying here is that every 12-year-old girl deserves a chance of an education, and nearly always, chances are they will go on to lead productive lives as contributing members of their respective communities. After all, look what Sophea and Sopheak have achieved, and imagine if all 12-year-old girls were given the same educational opportunity.

KC: Thank you, Christopher Minko, for your blunt truth in this most interesting and for me most memorable interview. Keep doing what you're doing, mate. I hope to see you on a basketball court, at a recording studio, or at a live Krom gig soon.

[XXX]

Cambodian Band Krom
Come to Bangkok

KROM — Photograph by Jonathan van Smit

AFTER CONDUCTING THE interview in the previous chapter without ever meeting Christopher Minko face to face, I was pleased to learn that in December 2014 the Cambodian noir band Krom, led by Minko and lead vocalist Sophea Chamroeun, would play a historic three-night run in Bangkok. I was fortunate enough to be in the audience for two of those three performances – the first at the outdoor bar of the Hansar Hotel and their final gig, enjoying the great ambience at the Overground Bar, just off Sukhumvit Road, in front of an overflowing, standing-room-only crowd. The Overground gig was a fitting finale for the Phnom Penh-based bilingual band, whose songs are performed in a mixture of Khmer and English. The unique sound of Krom is always original, with an unambiguous message of ugly truth.

The other two band members of Krom are the versatile Jimmy Baeck, who plays either a soulful slide guitar, accordion or saxophone, and back-up singer Sopheak Chamroeun, the sister of Sophea. Minko reminded the Overground crowd of the genocidal atrocities inflicted upon Cambodians by Pol Pot and the Khmer Rouge, which had a particularly horrific effect on those involved in the arts. The newest Krom member is bass guitar player James Mao Sokleap, who also serves as record producer for Krom's upcoming third album.

Krom was born from a place of darkness and the band's songs frequently touch on personal and dark themes. Krom's debut 2012 album is titled *Songs of the Noir*. The following year, their *Neon Dark* album also became a success, particularly with listeners in the United Kingdom. In mid-2015, Krom were due to release *Mekong Delta Blues*.

"The bottom-line is the world's a shithole in so many ways – you can either try to do some good and effect positive change or you can selfishly turn your back on it all." – Christopher Minko, in a February 2014 interview (see previous chapter).

The above quote by Chistopher Minko is worth repeating. It should give you some concept of the man and the message he wishes to convey in his work and his music even if we have to accept, as he reminds us in song and lyrics, that we live in a world that has gone "stark raving mad".

The three venues that Krom played in Bangkok could not be more diverse. The beauty of Krom is that their language of music can be understood by anyone, anywhere – even if the Khmer lyrics cannot always be. From the under-the-sky, 19th floor outdoor platform at the five-star Hansar Hotel, where they opened, to the Toot Yung Art

Center, highlighting works by other artists, to the second level walk-up of the Overground Bar, Krom has a message to tell. They tell it with dignity and clarity: It's not a pretty world out there.

Woven into the Krom experience is respect. You saw the respect in the eyes of Sopheak as she listened to her sister, Sophea. You sensed the respect as Christopher Minko graciously and literally took a back seat to the Khmer singers at times during the performances, to appreciate not only their voices but their culture, which is being preserved and expanded by performances such as these. And you heard the respect when John Gartland introduced the band to the audience and later when Christopher Minko took the time to thank his good friend, Christopher G. Moore, and some of the many members of the talented Bangkok expat community in attendance on closing night.

Connections were re-established and bridges were built. The journey for Krom from Cambodia to Bangkok will be easier and hopefully more frequent in the future. Bangkok has no shortage of things to do, musically and otherwise. Yet Krom created a genuine energy by their presence in Bangkok. There are more travels and more countries ahead for Krom in 2015, including Germany, France and Australia. Those who have experienced Krom tend to become fans, of both the music and the message. Both are worth exploring further.

[XXXI]

"Not all those who wander are lost."

Interview with Jim Algie, Author of The Phantom Lover

JIM ALGIE HAS done what many do not believe in and fewer still achieve. He has reincarnated himself and stayed alive in the process. The former punk rocker from Canada, known in those days as Blake Cheetah, spent eleven years playing bass guitar and touring with various bands before deciding to change careers at the tender age of 28. An age that Jimi Hendrix and Jim Morrison never reached. After a two-year stint in

Spain, where his focus on writing accelerated, Algie found himself in Bangkok with the intention of heading to Taipei.

In Jim's case, the road to Bangkok was paved with good intentions as Thailand has now been his home for more than 20 years. During that time he has observed and investigated all things not mundane in the kingdom.

As with any good detective, he hit a few dead ends along the way. But as the saying goes, patience is its own reward. Jim patiently studied what was in front of him and sought adventures off the beaten path. That produced enough material to publish a variety of short stories, earning the writer several awards, including a Bram Stoker Award – a recognition presented by the Horror Writers Association for "superior achievement" in dark fantasy and horror writing. Jim Algie has had two books traditionally published – *Bizarre Thailand: Tales of Crime, Sex and Black Magic* (Marshall Cavendish, 2012), a collection of non-fiction stories, and his recent collection of fiction, *The Phantom Lover and Other Thrilling Tales of Thailand* (Tuttle Publishing, 2014). Jim's also an accomplished journalist, editor and travel writer, having contributed to many periodicals and travel guidebooks and authored *Tuttle Travel Pack Thailand*. In 2015 he was one of five writers featured in the history tome, *Americans in Thailand*, and his next book, *Punk Is Dead As Joey Ramone*, is a collection of musical tales due to be published soon. In addition an album by his last band, the *Asexuals*, recorded live in the CBC studios, is scheduled for a 2015 Canada release. Jim graciously agreed to have his interview appear in *Bangkok Beat*.

KC: What makes Southeast Asia a good setting for writing?

JA: It's all the myriad paradoxes and extreme juxtapositions. You've got these ancient sites like Angkor Wat and the Temple of Dawn, as well as hyper-modern malls. There's incredible hospitality jostling with every sort of barbarity. You've got arcane superstitions counterbalanced by a whole new wave of thinkers and artists; some of the most colorful festivals I have ever seen, in stunning contrast to the shabbiest urban blight. And then there's the hotpot of ethnicities and all sorts of eccentric expats. So you're never short of stories, backdrops and characters.

KC: What books and or music influenced you growing up?

JA: My first writing influences were Edgar Allan Poe and Jack London. My taste in tunes also strayed towards the darker side of the spectrum, with Alice Cooper, Black Sabbath and the New York Dolls leading the savage wolf pack. Even today I still revere those bands and authors.

KC: What's the last record you can remember listening to?

JA: I've been listening to Wilco again, and their scandal-plagued magnum opus, *Yankee Hotel Foxtrot*. It's one of those rare instances when a group actually took no shit from the corporate rectums of the music business. Their label dropped them because they thought the album was anti-commercial, then the band sold it back to a different subsidiary of the same company for even more money and it became the biggest-selling album of their career. To my ears, Wilco is the best American band of the past 20 years, and Jeff Tweedy is America's greatest singer and songwriter since the late Kurt Cobain and Paul Westerberg of The Replacements.

KC: Tell our readers about the musical chapters of your life. Your ability allowed you to travel a bit. Where did you go? What did you experience that stays with you from that time?

JA: For the first out-of-town shows we played with a surf-punk band called the Malibu Kens, we had to drive 200 miles to the city of Calgary in western Canada, to play four sets a night for seven nights in a row at a skid row tavern called The Calgarian to largely hostile or indifferent crowds of truckers, junkies, alkies, wretched-looking prostitutes and a few punks who also hung out there. All four of us stayed in a small, mildew-smelling room, full of silverfish and other vermin, in the hotel. During one gig, a guy got stabbed to death in the bathroom and his bloody handprints could be seen on the walls for months afterwards. Another night there was a 20-men-and-four-whores brawl in the bar with people smacking each other over the head with chairs and tables while we played. For a bunch of middle-class boys, still only 18 and 19, that was our indoctrination – our baptism of hellfire – and real life on the dark side of the street.

Jerry Jerry and the Sons of Rhythm Orchestra George Wall, Paul Paetz, Jerry Jerry, Paul Soloudre,
Jim Algie/Blake Cheetah (Photograph by Steve Kravac)

KC: Is there a book laying around your home that you haven't gotten around to reading?

JA: Many, but the new biography of China's Great Reformer, Deng Xiaping, is especially huge and daunting.

KC: Complete this sentence. I write to…

JA: …communicate something to the world and myself that cannot be communicated in any other way or through any other medium.

KC: Make the case for fiction over non-fiction in 207 words or less.

JA: What's missing from so much journalism and non-fiction is a sense of humanism and heart. When journalists strain for superlatives they resort to the same geriatric clichés about "triumphs of the human spirit" or "tragic demises" or "losing battles against cancer" while labeling serial murderers as "monsters". Dead language does not elicit any lively reactions. One of my favorite parts of Timothy Hallinan's *Breathing Water*, a superbly suspenseful Bangkok thriller in his Poke Rafferty series, is how the Thai cop and his wife deal with her terminal illness. In journalism these days, human-interest stories are disappearing in place of celebrity gossip and business stories. By contrast, all great works of fiction put people first and human concerns at their core.

To borrow another example from *Breathing Water*, Tim has a great paragraph about how the light in Bangkok around dusk, which is the protagonist's favorite time of day and mine too, changes about five different times. I sensed that was true, but it really opened my eyes to something that I hadn't seen before. In this way, fiction and poetry enrich our lives and perceptions. By contrast, in most non-fiction – except for maybe memoirs – the editor would cut all those descriptive details as irrelevant.

KC: Tell us about your latest collection of stories, *The Phantom Lover and Other Thrilling Tales of Thailand*, and why book lovers should read it.

JA: If they don't read it, I can't say their lives will be greatly impoverished or they will come down with any loathsome diseases, but those who are interested in Thailand and Southeast Asia will find a different set of stories and characters, often with Thai protagonists, that deliver some different insights into the lives of young high-society women, ancient folklore with modern twists, the rural downtrodden, and what will probably remain the biggest natural disaster of our lifetimes, the 2004 Asian tsunami.

KC: Please tell me about your current favorite dead author.

JA: Raymond Carver. I just re-read a kind of greatest hits collection of his short fiction called *Where I'm Calling From*. He was the most heralded short fiction author when I was studying creative writing in the late 80s. So I wanted to revisit those stories to see how he achieved those incredible effects with the most unadorned prose and lack of sensationalism, combined with very ordinary characters caught up in entirely plausible situations. 'Errand', his story about the death of Anton Chekhov, who was the writer he was most often compared to, and which he wrote while dying of a similar disease, is one of the great masterpieces of contemporary literature. It's most likely way beyond anything I could ever achieve, but there's no point in aspiring to mediocrity. There's already enough of that on TV as it is.

KC: What is your approach for a book launch? You've had two now, for *Bizarre Thailand* and *The Phantom Lover*. Were they similar or different?

JA: I am not an orator. I don't do readings or impersonations. So my approach is similar. I present a slide show of travel pics, book covers, personal shots, "Hell Money Banknotes" from the Chinese festival of the hungry ghosts, and talk about all sorts of influences that were melded together to form some of the stories, from serial slayers like Ted Bundy and Jeffrey Dahmer to lesbian erotica, European artworks, snake-handling shows in Thailand and black magic from the time of Angkor Wat.

KC: Let's talk about shadows and demons, just because they are fun to discuss. How important are they to a writer? Are they one and the same thing? Should a writer have demons of his own in order to create fictional ones? If a writer hasn't struggled with his shadows or demons is he/she in denial?

JA: Everyone has their own shadows and demons. Since we can't talk about them in polite company we have to find other outlets like books, music, TV shows and films. From any artist's perspective the demons are slippery and the shadows immaterial, so they are not easy to write or sing about. Either it comes off like macho bravado or like self-pitying whining. Ultimately, you need to strike a balance between the two and not give any easy solutions or sermons about conquering them. For the most part, I try to stay away from those first-person confessional sorts of stories, though I did write one long novella, *Obituary for the Khaosan*

Road Outlaws and Imposters, in the last book that features some demon wrestling and shadow hunting.

KC: You were a drinking buddy of Thailand's last executioner, Chavoret Jaruboon, and attended his funeral in 2012 after he died of cancer. Chavoret was personally responsible for executing 55 inmates. I understand a movie about his life has just been released. Can you tell me about it?

JA: I just reviewed the film for the *Bangkok Post* ('Biopic Takes No Prisoners') It's a pretty accurate depiction of his life from being a teenage rock n' roller to becoming a prison guard, so he could take care of his family, and then working his way up to executioner. As I mentioned in the review, "conflicted characters make the best protagonists and hinges for dramatic tension", so that's why I've written about him in *Bizarre Thailand: Tales of Crime, Sex and Black Magic,* as well as the *Phantom Lover* collection. He was a fascinating man, deeply tormented by guilt and karma, but in Thailand, and this is not mentioned in either the film or in my books, the executioner can be seen as a heroic figure too, freeing prisoners from their bad karma to be reborn again. Tellingly, the death chamber at Bang Kwang Central Prison is referred to in Buddhist terms as the "room to end all suffering."

KC: Any plans for the Year of the Horse?

JA: As with every previous year I am trying really hard not to die, and to finish some new books and a bunch of stories. I'm still breathing, making toast and typing words on a keyboard, so I take these gifts as good omens.

KC: I'll toast to all that. Thanks, Jim.

Review of The Phantom Lover and Other Thrilling Tales of Thailand

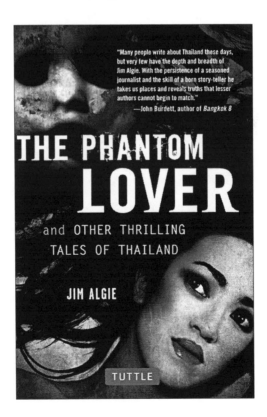

CAN YOU PICTURE your favorite Thomas Kinkade painting? That was a trick question. Can you picture *any* Thomas Kinkade painting? If you can do either, you'll need to deviate 180 degrees from where you are to enter the bleak, dark world Jim Algie has painted, with brutal honesty, in his fine collection of short stories, *The Phantom Lover and Other Thrilling Tales of Thailand*. (Tuttle Publishing, Singapore 2014).

The Phantom Lover is composed of nine stories, the shortest being a mere 10 pages about a love affair regarding a male feline temptress with a hair fetish – *The Vicious Little Monk*. The longest and last is *Tsunami* at 113 pages, or more than a third of the book's total 319 pages, detailing the devastation – physical and emotional – of the 2004 earthquake and subsequent tidal wave in Phuket, Thailand. While the first eight stories can be read in any order, *Tsunami* is best read last as it uniquely serves as an epilogue, returning many of the previously introduced characters we have gotten to know in an ambitious, imperfect and entertaining novella-like finale.

The book starts off well, with a personal favorite: *Death Kiss of a King Cobra Show*, featuring a Thai snake charmer, Yai. For this dear farang reader, Algie's writing style is refreshing in that he creates believable back-stories for the Thai people we may have seen many times but never gotten to know or, sadly, made no effort to know. Algie's prose makes us glad we finally did, whether it is a fictional or semi-true tale – the blanks are filled in beautifully. It came as no surprise to me that the two blurbs on the book are from Thailand's A-List of fictional prose, John Burdett and Christopher G. Moore. Yes, the book has the occasional jar head, bar girl, writer/English teacher who doesn't stretch the reader's imagination much, but even they tend to be rougher, tougher and more emotionally intelligent than your standard fare. It is the unique Thai characters, like Yai, that stand out for me in this Haunted Mansion ride of a book.

The Legendary Nobody creates a believable character and biography of Thailand's infamous mass murderer See Ouey. Mr Ouey is now famously preserved at the Songkran Niyomsane Forensic Medicine Museum in Bangkok's Siriraj Hospital. Another real life character that stands out is found in *Life and Death Sentences*, a story about Chaovaret

Juruboon, whom Algie memorializes in the beginning as "a rock n' roller, a drinking buddy and Thailand's last executioner". Both characters are fascinating, based on information anyone could Google, but it's the details, some imagined and some true, filled in by Algie, which gave this reader such an entertaining ride. You may feel nauseated on occasion but you're glad the ticket stub is in your pocket.

Algie's brush strokes include a once-innocent bar girl who connives retaliation for all the wrongs inflicted upon her by the sordid, perverse and deviant behavior that exists in the Land of Smiles. It ends badly for one customer. Others describe fruit fornicators, necrophilia jokes, criminal philanthropists, a conflicted photojournalist, an honest but corrupt Bangladeshi human trafficker, and farangs living with their illusions and denials. Or worse yet, not living with them.

Carl Jung was purported to have said: "Knowing your own darkness is the best method for knowing the darkness of other people." If true, Jim Algie's shadow must be pitch black – and if not a constant companion, a friend he can call upon when needed. In all that darkness are characters trying to make sense of what appears to be a senseless world, sometimes with sardonic wit, sarcasm and black humor, other times with the old reliable qualities of kindness and caring coupled with an occasional bout of optimism and faith.

My quibble with Algie's storytelling is that he places some great lines in the narrative that would read well in dialogue. As a result, the book is light on dialogue. For example, in *Tsunami*, a paragraph starts out with: "Big tragedies ask huge questions." It concludes with more narrative around a crackling campfire scene about "God and country, death, democracy and in the end what it all came back to was good friends, family loyalties, and the simple dignity of doing an honest day's work for an honest day's pay."

Those are moments that convey good values, but I would have liked to have seen more conversation going on, as you can read later in the story when Wade confronts a gloomy Yves: "No offense, bud, but I'm kinda getting the feeling that you've, uh … lost it."

The exchanges from that point on are great at recapping the effects and affects a mass tragedy like the tsunami of 2004 had on hundreds of thousands of people. Of all the stories, my favorite was *The Obituary for the Khaosan Road Outlaws and Imposters*. It recalled a time on Khaosan Road in Bangkok, before it became trendy, when people still used pay phones. The backpackers, adventurers and petty crooks who lived there found the living was cheap but not always easy. The 47-page story is a ripper of a yarn about the lives and inhabitants of what is now mostly a bygone era in Bangkok. The scene at the airport depicting the committing of an international felony in a pre-technology boarding pass scam is superb. You feel the fear as you read about the knocking knees.

The *Phantom Lover and Other Thrilling Tales of Thailand* has something for almost everybody. If you're the one with the Thomas Kinkade painting above your couch you'll probably want to give it a pass. But if your tastes run closer to an oil painting by an artist with a severed ear, a Henry Miller watercolor, a Dali pen and ink, a Chris Coles acrylic or even a thumbtacked poster of Dogs Playing Poker, these thrilling tales are framed beautifully and make for a great read.

[XXXIII]

Review of Kicking Dogs - A Novel by Collin Piprell

T HIS COMIC CRIME fiction novel, set in Bangkok, has a hilarious beginning which includes an unexpected swim in the Chao Phraya River, an ending that had me guessing wrong on a major whodunit plot point, and a middle chock-full of Thai cultural nuances that any expat living in Thailand will find useful today. Moreover, it was the cover art by Colin Cotterill that influenced my choice to use Colin to draw the cover of Bangkok Beat.

Kicking Dogs by Collin Piprell is unlike any Bangkok-based book I have read, and I have read a lot. It has colorful characters, insightful prose and laugh-out-loud moments. My only criticism is that the protagonist is a journalist, which is never my favorite choice, and the book reads at times like a journal – heavy on narrative and light on dialogue. I prefer a balance – you may not care. Set in the boom times of the pre-economic crisis Thailand of the 1990s, the storyline holds up well in 2015.

It's a bit of an odd couple story, with Jack the journalist and the city of Bangkok trying to figure out how to live with each other. Hot-headed Jack has the tougher time making the needed adjustments.

The journey takes you up-close and personal into the lives of two-bit hustlers and crooks who may have a second job working the third shift as a bargain basement assassin. Also featured is your better-than-average despicable heavyweight champ of a villain, who goes by the name of Fat Fat. This is an intriguing, often comic look into the underbelly of Thailand, where rank has its privilege and if you have no ranking you haven't got much. Lessons to be learned are plentiful, but the one that springs to mind is: "Neither a borrower nor a lender be." A first-time read for me by author Collin Piprell. I would definitely seek out others. A fun, quick read at 240 pages.

Collin, who has also written under the pseudonym Ham Fiske, has written a number of other books including the thriller *Yawn* (2000), essay collection *Bangkok Old Hand* (1993), *Diving in Thailand* (1993), *National Parks of Thailand* (1991), *Thailand's Coral Reefs* (1993) and *Thailand: The Kingdom Beneath The Sea* (1991). He has also recently completed a futuristic novel. Look for publishing updates at his website: www.collinpiprell.com

[XXXIV]

Each One his Own Direction, Each One his Own Way / kon-lá tít kon-lá taang /

An Interview with Malcolm Gault-Williams

MALCOLM GAULT-WILLIAMS is the father of three grown sons and lives in the northeastern province of Nong Bua Lamphu, Thailand. He is a former radio disk jockey, a surfer for more than 45 years while living around Santa Barbara, California, a writer and author of *Legendary Surfers*, which now runs three volumes and growing. You can learn more about Malcolm living in the Thai countryside from his blog "The Isaan: My Life in a Thai-Lao Village."

This interview initially had the working title of "The Most Interesting Facebook Friend I Have Never Met". After spending thirty minutes with Malcolm on a Skype video call, I knew I had to change the title. Not because my opinion had changed – far from it. It's just that the new title fits Malcolm and his story so much better.

Living in Santa Cruz, California as I have done for much of the past 22 years, I know that surfing is a soulful pastime. And Malcolm Gault-Williams, not surprisingly, comes across as a very soulful man. The type of soul Henry Miller tells us is out there, if we look for them. Malcolm has been going in his own direction since he first took to the waves in the mid-1960s and is still going his own way, in an Isaan village near the Laos border in 2015.

KC: I've never been an investigative reporter, Malcolm, but since you have authored books on surfing, and your email contains the words "legendary surfer", I am going to guess you were pretty good and knew other great surfers. When did you start surfing, how old were you and what memories do you have of that first year in the water on a board?

MGW: Kevin, you are too kind. I am far from being a "legendary surfer". I just write about them. I have been writing since 1963. I began writing about surfing's heroes, history and culture, when I was in the midst of a career change. I asked myself: given my abilities and interests, if I had six months to live and had to make some money somehow, what would I do?

Well, I knew I could write okay and I loved to surf, plus I've always had an interest in history, so writing about legendary surfers seemed like a no-brainer. And that's the way it's been. Of course, I've had to have "day jobs" along the way, but I've always worked toward who I wanted to be when the chips were down. I was 18 when I got interested in surfing. My first board was a Weber Performer.

KC: When did you first begin writing about surfing history? Who or what inspired it? How many books have you written since? Have you written or do you plan to write a book on anything other than surfing?

MGW: I began research on surf history in 1993 and throughout the 1990s had several notable articles published in surfing's best magazines. I finally self-published my first volume in 2005, after a decade as a contributor to the online community. Some people have, as a result, dubbed me "the most plagiarized surf writer of all time".

I was inspired to write about the history of surfing due to the work of surfer and writer Gary Lynch, whom I later worked with on the definitive history of Tom Blake. I was also inspired by Steve Pezman, a former editor of *Surfer* magazine and the genesis behind *The Surfer's Journal*. I have written three volumes on surf history, in chronological order, and will continue working from day to day, until my time comes.

Other publications include articles about East Timor and West Papua, and a history book on the student protests during the Vietnam War in Santa Barbara entitled *Don't Bank on Amerika*.

KC: Most parents, if they are lucky, give their children roots and wings. Most expats who end up living in Thailand have the necessary wings to get here, but not necessarily the roots. Tell me about your roots, your family.

MGW: My foster father is a retired Methodist minister and he was the one who got me into reading, doing well in school, and constantly trying to improve my thinking and my actions. These lessons kind of set the tone for my own nuclear family.

I'm fortunate that I have never really had a problem with my [three] sons. My first wife nurtured them well and I give her a lot of credit for how they turned out. Of course, I'll take some credit too. I think that if you are true to yourself and treat your kids as your true embodiment, everything's gonna go good.

I came to Thailand via my third wife Thiphawan, who is Thai-Lao and absolutely the sweetest person I have ever known. We initially met via the Internet and have been together now for 13 years.

KC: I have heard stories that you were a bit of an activist in your college days at UC Santa Barbara. And yet now you are the proud father of a

California State Assemblyman. What similarities, if any, do you see between activism, which you participated in during the turbulent 60's, and present day politics in California?

MGW: During what Americans call the Vietnam War, the United States grew very polarized. You had to pick sides. I chose to be counter-cultural and active. In later years I was active in the anti-nuclear movement and much later than that served on a couple of governmental boards.

My eldest of three sons, Dohassen Gault-Williams (aka Das Williams) grew up with politics part of his daily life. When he grew older, he volunteered in a county supervisorial campaign and saw that a good candidate can lose by as little as one vote (in that campaign it was four votes). That spurred him on to more political involvement and to where he is today. He serves as the California Assemblyman for the 37th District, which comprises principally Santa Barbara and Ventura counties. His progressive position on issues is excellent. He likes his work and it comes naturally to him. You can imagine how proud I am. I just wish there were more people like him in governments all over the world.

KC: Tell me more about those three volumes of *Surf History*. What are their names? How far back did you go, and what is the most surprising or interesting thing you learned in your research on the history of surfing? What's the current volume you are working on? How long did a typical volume take from start to finish?

MGW: With non-fiction, I usually write chronologically. Volume 1 of *Legendary Surfers* covers 2500 B.C. to 1910 A.D. Volume 2 of *Legendary Surfers* takes it from 1910 to 1930. Volume 3 of *Legendary Surfers* is all about the 1930s. I am currently working on Volume 4 and that will cover the 1940s. It's hard to guesstimate how long a volume takes to write because when I get down to putting it all together, it's really just a matter of pulling in what I've already written and having it make sense as a whole. I'd say a year per volume.

I build my writings on the history of surfing around the quotes of the people who lived it. Not afraid to include excerpts from other surf writers, my work is heavily footnoted not only for the reader, but for future historians. My stuff is not for the coffee table. I write for surfers who want to know the details of the heritage we are blessed to be part of.

The most interesting thing I've learned in all of this is that we really do not know how old surfing is and that it is probably much older than we imagine.

KC: You mentioned being plagiarized a lot. Discuss the pros and cons of publishing in a digital age. Are your books available in print and e-books or only one format? Is plagiarism always a bad thing? Is there any benefit, like there often is in the music business?

MGW: Plagiarism isn't a big thing for me, really. I write to be read. If I'm not credited, *lao boa die* [a Lao expression meaning something like 'whatever' or 'never mind']. It would be nice to be credited, but my ego's not so big that I would go hunting down the people who copy my work without attributing it. My time is much more valuable to me than to waste it on something like that.

I self-publish paperback books and e-booklets. I haven't put together an e-book yet, but plan to soon. What's held me back is the lack of control when things go viral. I had a friend once who asked for one of my books in a digitized format that she could use in her classroom. So I made it for her and then discovered that almost 100 of her students also downloaded the file and I didn't get a baht or cent out of it. I felt a bit burned by that.

Nowadays, you can distribute digitized works that have a unique identifier with a unique password, so if you're careful it's much easier to protect your work than it used to be.

"Malcolm Gault-Williams is on a mission to record oral histories as told to him by as many of our great surf elders as possible, in scholarly fashion, before they are lost forever." Steve Pezman, publisher of *Surfer Magazine* 1971-1991 and editor of *The Surfer's Journal.*

KC: Contrast your life now with how it used to be living in a California surf town, and talk about your own blog. What do you like best about Thailand? What do you miss most about California?

MGW: Well, I used to be a surfer/writer and now I'm a country boy/writer; very different realities. I miss the ocean and wave weaving, and I also miss my sons and parents. Not much I can do about the saltwater thing, but with family I do my best to stay connected via the Internet. I particularly like Skype video calls.

Yes, I'm having fun with my blog, The Isaan: My Life in a Thai-Lao Village. I've always written biographical vignettes, but this is the first time I've ever put personal stuff up for everyone to see. Similar to my surf writings, I like to write about the details of everyday life. They are SO interesting to me because my daily life is so new to me. It's like the title of one of my posts: 'Learning a New Way.'

KC: Malcolm, can you talk about the benefits of writing, for you? I started this blog with an idea that came from Henry Miller about how best to engage the world:

> *"Develop an interest in life as you see it; the people, things, literature, music – the world is so rich, simply throbbing with rich treasures, beautiful souls and interesting people. Forget yourself."* – Henry Miller

Do you agree with the Henry Miller quote, and how would you sum up your own philosophy of living?

MGW: Well, I agree with most of that quote by Henry Miller, except for the very last part. Anybody can write, but not everyone can craft. And in order to be a good craftsman, you have to put yourself into it. It has to be part of you in some way. If you "forget yourself", as I understand the quote, you are not adding that special ingredient that makes your writing unique.

As I mentioned earlier, I'm 64 and have been writing in one form or another for the past 50 years. It's just something that I'm driven to do. I don't know why, really, except that the more I did, the better I got and now I really appreciate the skill I've developed. I'm not a very creative or entertaining writer, but I can put a story together that makes sense to the reader by the time they're done reading it. Not everyone can do that.

KC: A final question: who are some of your favorite authors? What authors influenced you growing up? What authors do you read now? What percentage of your time is spent reading on the Internet as opposed to real books or even e-books?

MGW: Growing up, I was most influenced by the writings of Jack London, Charles Dickens and Alexander Dumas – in that order. Later, I was very much influenced by the writings of Jack Kerouac, Baba Ram Dass, Mao Zedong, Carlos Castaneda and James Willard Schultz (Apikuni).

My absolute favorite writer is David Cornwell (John Le Carré). In recent years, I have enjoyed the Vincent Calvino series by Christopher G. Moore and the Bernie Gunther series by Philip Kerr.

I'm embarrassed to say that I don't read much these days, nor do I watch TV. Last year, I think I only read three books. With the exception of *Carthage Must Be Destroyed*, which I read in America on my son's iPad, I haven't read anything thus far this year, although I am working my way through *A New History of Southeast Asia*.

I write several hours each day, but am in a phase right now where I'm not reading for fun or pleasure. When I do, it's most always on paper.

[XXXV]

Jim Thompson Is Alive!
An Interview with Thomas Hunt Locke

THOMAS HUNT LOCKE is, among other things, a husband, a father of a young daughter and a newborn son, a businessman, an adventurer, an expat living in Thailand and an author. Not necessarily in that order. He's a transplanted American. An East Coast guy with Boston ties. It is my impression that he has his life priorities in order. Plus he and his protagonist, Sam Collins, both like Checkinn99 and visit whenever they get a chance to come to the City of Angels. What's not to like? His second Sam Collins mystery, *Jim Thompson is Alive!* is available on Amazon.com and in paperback. This follows his debut Sam Collins erotic historical mystery, *The Ming Inheritance.* If that were not enough, Thom, as his friends call him has begun a second series involving a Chiang Mai newspaper man, Declan Power. Declan is a good old boy in the Mike Hammer tradition, and Thom's writing has some similarities with that of Mickey Spillane.

KC: Welcome, Thom. When was the first time you came to Thailand, when did you settle here permanently and what was the attraction to the northern part of Thailand, specifically the Chiang Mai area?

THL: Hi Kevin. I first came to Thailand in the early 1990s. I was finishing up my grad school work and delivered a paper at a conference in Singapore. I had a few days free afterward so hopped on a bus and headed north. I'm now coming on my 10th anniversary residing in Thailand. Other than a couple of months in Bangkok, I have been permanently settled in the north. I don't live directly in Chiang Mai any more but my family and I still make frequent forays into the Rose of the North. The best thing about Chiang Mai, a city I love dearly, is the balance between culture and modernity. I lack for nothing in the modern context, yet I still can meditate in the ancient temple Wat U-Hmong.

KC: I enjoy hearing about expats who have chosen to set up a business in Thailand, as well as enjoy the culture and terrain. Tell me about your business, what do you do exactly? Is it full-time, part-time or somewhere in between? What do you like best about it, and how is running a business in Thailand different than it would be back in the USA?

THL: I have set up the N.U. Test Prep Center. My main service is to prepare young university lecturers for the IELTS or TOEFL exams [English proficiency tests]. I also prepare doctors for the United States Medical Licensing Exam. In addition to that, I do quite a bit of work in business communication with the local government agencies. I'm not sure if there is a category above full-time, but if there was I would check that box. Most foreign teachers in Thailand don't want to teach test prep, so it is difficult to find good help. So in a way I've become the 'go to' guy for that in my community. It is rewarding. The best aspect of my job is the quality of people I come in contact with on a daily basis. It provides me with a very optimistic outlook on Thai society. In the States I was a community college lecturer, so I've little experience with the business field stateside. My experience here has been fantastic.

KC: Your protagonist, Sam Collins — what would readers find admirable and likable about him? Does he have any flaws? I don't like too many standard questions, but I'll give you one here: how much of Sam Collins is really Thom? Is he a product of your imagination, part you or a composite of many people you have known?

THL: Sam Collins is a retired Boston City police detective. He was forced into early retirement due to a scandal within the force and the city as a whole. He exacted revenge on a drug lord who had murdered his wife and son. Sam is deeply flawed but I believe readers can admire the way he has put back the pieces of his shattered life. He'll never be whole again. Still, he's making an effort to lead a productive life. One reviewer tabbed Sam as being half Indiana Jones and half James Bond. I'll live with that. Through Sam I try to also shine a mirror on expat life. Many 'farang' come over here to either forget, escape, or otherwise forge a new life. Sam is not Thom, however.

KC: The title of your upcoming novel: *Jim Thompson is Alive! A Sam Collins Mystery*, is a great one. Most farang who have spent any time in Thailand and certainly most expats living in Thailand year-round know at least something about the Jim Thompson real-life mystery. I have taken the tour of the Jim Thompson House in Bangkok, on a very rainy day, and it was fascinating, not to mention a gorgeous house. For those readers not familiar with the real-life mystery, give us a brief history of the real Jim Thompson and then carry that over into how your storyline came about. Did you have to do a lot of research?

THL: Let me begin with the last question. This novel has taken approximately two years to complete. A great deal of research has been put into my latest work. To step back, Sam Collins novels are erotic historical thrillers. I take each part seriously. The history needs to be well-researched otherwise the structure of the plot is weakened. I won't go into too much detail, but I conducted several interviews with people who were active in Thailand in the 1960s. You may know Mama Noi from Checkinn99. Mama was quite the hot item back in the day and she gave me some fantastic information to provide me with a flavor for that era. The most interesting, surprising perhaps, aspect of the research is the portrait of Jim Thompson which emerges when one digs deep. He is not the person one would expect. My admiration for him grew extensively, and in this novel I try to deliver that portrait in a way that has not been done before. The William Warren book can rightfully be called a vanity effort. Other efforts as well fall way off the mark. I believe if you read *Jim Thompson Is Alive!* you'll find you discover a great deal about the man and his motivations. In addition, much of the novel investigates the United States involvement in the Indo-China war, a conflict that Thompson himself was heavily invested in and at odds with US interests.

KC: What are the benefits of writing, for you? What do you like most about the process from start to finish to publishing? Tell me what you see as the pros and cons in the current publishing climate for independent novelists like yourself?

THL: Everything I do in my life is something that I absolutely cherish undertaking. From my family to my business to my hobbies to my writing, I'm invested in something I completely dig. I am not the tortured artist. More directly, the benefit of writing for me is that I'm able to carve a good story from history. I love stories and I like history so, I figured, why not give it a go? What I adore most about the process are the characters that emerge. Gemma from my first novel was a complete surprise, and Tukky from *Jim Thompson Is Alive!* is a big surprise to Sam and me as well. In the end, writing is something that I absolutely love in the same way some people are passionate about scuba diving or other challenging hobbies.

That being said, my books are not free. So it is important to develop a strategy, a business plan if you will. For me there are no downsides in the DIY publishing age. I'm responsible for everything. I am independent by nature so the way the industry is trending is something that is gratifying. That's not to say I haven't made mistakes on the business end. I'm still sorting it out. But it has been fun learning from those mistakes. For example, there is absolutely no upside to signing a contract with a company to put your book online. I can upload the novel directly to Kindle with no middleman. Smashwords I have found to be quite good in that they can connect you to many outlets such as B&N and Sony etc., while charging only a nominal fee. In the end, I find the Amazon age to be a blessing for writers such as myself.

KC: Who are some of your favorite authors – and you can play it safe and name me only the dead ones or take a risk and name the live ones. The middle path is always good, so a mix of the two is also fine. And start with your earliest memories of reading, please.

THL: I've been an avid reader since I broke my ankle as a 10- year-old. I had to sit out baseball that year. My world had come to an end. But out of the abyss came a boy clutching a book in one hand and his treasured baseball glove in the other. As for my favorite writers, well Umberto Eco would have to top the list. Unfortunately I don't have a great deal of time to read nowadays with my busy schedule. I recently finished *Dissolution* by C. J. Sansom. I quite like the Matthew Shardlake series. When I was younger I was addicted to Robert Ludlum novels. Truth be told, I don't have a favorite writer in the sense I have a favorite rock n' roll band.

KC: I've heard it advised that being a writer is like doing the laundry – it never ends. You finish one book and pretty soon it's, "What have you done, lately?" So I am guessing that after *Jim Thompson is Alive!* another project may be in the works? If so, what's the working title and how will it be different and how will it be similar to the first two Sam Collins mysteries?

THL: I'm folding and pressing my latest as we speak and yeah, I'll begin work on my next project come September. I have a total of 10 novels loosely outlined. My next effort will be set in the summertime home of my youth, Cape Cod. It will not be as sexually charged as the Sam Collins Mystery Series, though it will be a historical thriller. The working title is *Vinland*. I'll follow that up with another Sam Collins thriller. This will be interesting as it will take Sam out of Thailand. I don't want to be tied to one locale and I believe Sam gives me great flexibility in that regard.

KC: There is a lot of turbulence in the world right now. A lot of dissatisfaction in many different areas – the economy, the political climate, an increasing police state that has been eroding freedoms that you and I have taken for granted for a lifetime as Americans. And yet you come across as a very satisfied individual, who like a lot of expats living in Thailand has taken the road less travelled. Does what is going on in the world today have an impact on your life, in any way, shape or form? And I ask the question because I am genuinely curious about the answer. Some people confuse apathy with focus. I see you as a focused individual.

THL: It's an interesting question, Kevin. Tip O'Neill once said all politics is local. Let me just say that I keep my life local. So, in that sense, there is little turbulence or dissatisfaction for me to contend with. Often people involve themselves in so many things they cannot control and in many cases don't understand. I can control being a good husband/father, a hardworking and successful business owner, and a better writer. Those are my priorities and I try to focus on those pursuits. I also try to have fun in life! Making new friends and developing solid relationships takes precedence over worrying about the state of the global economy. Basically I try to not be an asshole and live the heck out of the one life I've been given. In any case I'm an independent, so both sides of the political spectrum piss me off!

KC: You talked about how your experience with a business in Thailand has been fantastic. Tell me what you like about the Thailand geography, what you like about the Thai people and what you like about Thai culture. Of those three areas, what don't you like?

THL: First, as you know, Thailand is an exquisitely beautiful country. I like to get outside and there is so much to choose from. We try to get into the mountains of Mae Hong Son at least once a year, and life would not be complete without at least one trip down south to Krabi or Phuket. Bangkok gets thrown in a couple of times a year as well. That covers a lot of real estate. My wife, being Thai, likes to visit the local shops, markets and restaurants when visiting such locales. It's a great way to experience the many different cultures that exist within the Thai borders. I think Thai people are generous by nature. Living where I do, off the tourist map as it were, I was a bit of an oddity being one of the few farang around. It was a great way to learn about Thai culture and people. Consider me impressed. If there is one thing I hate about Thailand it is the lack of civility on the roads. Thai drivers are barbaric! And this coming from a Bostonian, where bad driving has been elevated to an art form.

KC: Thom, we've had some fun today. I have a tremendous amount of respect for writers and those writers, like yourself, who write fiction. As my guy John Grisham says: "It's harder than paving asphalt." So please tell me anything else you would like that I may have missed about your latest book. While I am at it, what is your favorite rock n' roll band? And don't tell me Boston.

THL: Well thank you, Kevin, for having me as a guest. As for my favorite rock n' roll outfit, that is an easy one. The Kinks! I've been a Kinks Kultist since my mid-teens.

Jim Thompson Is Alive! is now available on Amazon. The paperback will follow in September. I'm beginning work with a Thai film director exploring the possibility of turning this novel into a movie. He's a good friend and I was happy to hear of his interest. We will meet tonight over 100 Pipers!

Tracking Down Tom Vater, Author of The Man With the Golden Mind

THERE ARE CERTAIN writers in Thailand who, if they were not writers, would make excellent fictional protagonists, because the real-life lives they lead would make for an interesting read. Joe Cummings is one such writer. As is Tom Vater. There are many things I like about Tom Vater, the writer and the person. The latter has been known to drop off the grid from time to time, which no doubt helps the former. Tom has published three novels, *The Devil's Road To Kathmandu*, *The Cambodian Book Of The Dead*, released by Crime Wave Press in Asia and Exhibit A worldwide in 2013, and his latest, *The Man With The Golden Mind*, set primarily in Laos, recently released by Exhibit A in the USA and UK as well as being available in Asia and online. In 2014, Tom participated in the Irrawaddy Literary Festival in the legendary setting of Mandalay, where he met at least one legend, Aung San Suu Kyi.

Tom Vater is the co-owner of Crime Wave Press, along with Hans Kemp. Crime Wave Press is a Hong Kong-based English-language crime fiction imprint.

In addition to his fictional works, Tom has published several non-fiction books, including the critically acclaimed *Sacred Skin* and the more recent *Burmese Light* with photographer Hans Kemp. Tom has written for *The Wall Street Journal, The Guardian, The Daily Telegraph, The South China Morning Post* and *Penthouse*, to name just some.

Tom is also the co-author of several documentary screenplays, most notably for *The Most Secret Place on Earth*, a feature on the CIA's covert war in 1960s Laos, which you will recognize in *The Man with the Golden Mind*. Tom kindly agreed to be interviewed in early 2014.

KC: What makes Southeast Asia a good setting for a crime novel?

TV: Given the culture of impunity that reigns even more freely in Asia than where I come from, or at least in a more visible manner, the amount of salacious material is never-ending. Open the papers and stories too hair-raising to be made up tumble from the pages every single day. Southeast Asia is a treasure trove of human divinity and depravity, and as the weather is always good a lot of it spills out into the open to be scooped up by writers, journalists or voyeurs. That said, almost anywhere is good to set a crime novel. I just happen to know this corner of the world a little.

KC: What book(s) or music influenced you growing up?

TV: *Treasure Island* was a big book for me. Long John Silver was and is one of my great literary heroes, a bad man but not a man without compassion. My teenage years were taken up by Jack London, Edgar Allen Poe, William Golding, George Orwell and H.P. Lovecraft. Then I discovered the Beats – Kerouac, Bowles, Burroughs and Bukowski – and the hardboiled noirs – Chandler, Himes, Goodis, Thompson, Highsmith and Ross MacDonald … and everything changed.

But I also took an early liking to literary garbage – I obsessively read Enid Blyton's adventure novels and still suffer from the fallout.

When I was 14, I saw Elvin Jones play a show in my home town. After the first song they had to nail his drum kit to the stage. That always stayed with me.

But I didn't get into jazz until I was older. From the age of eight or so, I listened to rock n' roll, and from 15 I tried to play in bands. I first got into Black Sabbath and Deep Purple and then advanced (or regressed, depending on your point of view) to Elvis, Jerry Lee Lewis, The Rolling Stones, The Velvet Underground, the MC5, The Stooges, Black Flag, The Cramps and CAN.

I always liked the monotony and repetitiveness of rock n' roll. Three minutes of high energy. Very different form of expression from fiction of course, but I somehow have an affinity for both.

KC: What's the last record or book you can remember listening to or reading?

TV: I listened to *Get Yer Ya-Ya's Out* by The Rolling Stones and *Rubber Legs* by The Stooges today. Also really into British band Fat White Family at present. They got the spirit. Best bands I have seen in Bangkok recently are Degaruda, The Sangsom Massacre and Dead Town Trash.

I am reading *The White Flamingo* by James Newman, a sleazy slice of gutter-style hardboiled with great Beat-style stream of un-consciousness writing.

My other favorite recent read is *The Gwousz Affair* by Gary Anderson, a sci-fi noir novel Crime Wave Press has just put out. It's set in 2042 and humans have made cows intelligent, the planet is run by bovines, the US government has moved to Nebraska, all humans are vegetarians and inter-species sex is permissible. Enter a hardboiled PI who is to find the killer of the female offspring of the bovine president. Think *Animal Farm* getting into bed with *The Big Sleep* and *Bladerunner*.

KC: Is there a book out there or laying around your home that you've been meaning to read but haven't gotten around to yet?

TV: There are stacks of those lying around. I've had a David Goodis and a Massimo Carlotto sitting on my shelf for months – no time to take a look yet. On the next long flight.

KC: Complete this sentence: Amazon.com is ...

TV: ... symptomatic of the way business has gone in the early 21st century.

KC: Make the case for fiction over non-fiction in 100 words or less.

TV: It's often easier for me to get at a larger truth in fiction. And the process of writing fiction is the most beautifully obsessive skill I have. I basically move in with my characters and every day I start writing I find that they have done stuff during the night I didn't ask them to do. In a way, the writing process becomes like an intense love affair, but with a whole bunch of people craving my attention while they slowly reveal themselves to me emotionally, physically and intellectually. When this happens, I am very, very happy.

KC: Tell our readers about your latest crime novel, *The Man With the Golden Mind* and why they should read it.

TV: Julia Rendel asks Detective Maier, whom I introduced in last year's *The Cambodian Book of the Dead*, to investigate the 25-year-old murder of her father, an East German cultural attaché who was killed near a fabled CIA airbase in central Laos in 1976. But before the detective can set off, his client is kidnapped right out of his arms. Maier follows Julia's trail to the Laotian capital Vientiane, where he learns different parties, including his missing client, are searching for a legendary CIA file crammed with Cold War secrets. But the real prize is the file's author, a man codenamed Weltmeister, a former US and Vietnamese spy and assassin no one has seen for a quarter century.

Almost a decade ago, I co-wrote the screenplay to *The Most Secret Place on Earth*, a feature documentary directed by my brother Marc Eberle, about the CIA in Laos. Between 1965 and 1973, the US secret service ran a clandestine war against the Laotian communists, secretly recruiting 30,000 ethnic minority mercenaries, many of whom died in battle. The agency partly financed its efforts with drugs and eventually bombed the country to bits.

During the making of the film, I met some of the people involved in that conflict – CIA case officers, Air America pilots, USAid staff, Hmong rebels, Thai mercenaries, journalists and academics – and I had always wanted to write a fictionalized account of what we felt was a war crime committed by the US that had almost been forgotten.

Oh, and in *The Man With the Golden Mind*, the most infamous former US Foreign Secretary makes a cameo appearance. Who'd want to miss that? As I said, in fiction it's sometimes easier to go after larger truths than in non-fiction.

KC: Please tell me your three favorite dead authors. Or if you are feeling confident you can throw some live ones into the mix.

TV: Dead ones: Joseph Conrad, William Burroughs, Jim Thompson. Live ones: Katherine Dunne, Philip Kerr, Gary Anderson.

KC: Tell me about your publishing house. What are the challenges of a boutique publisher in an Amazon age?

TV: I run Crime Wave Press with Hans Kemp and we have been publishing crime fiction, in eBook and POD format, for a year and a half now. We started off with Asian-based titles, but soon noticed that we couldn't find enough good manuscripts in the region to publish the number of books we need to make the enterprise worthwhile. That said, our Father Ananda Mysteries by Nick Wilgus, a series of clerical thrillers featuring a cop turned Buddhist monk in Thailand, are doing quite well, as is our international thriller *Gaijin Cowgirl* by Jame DiBiasio. And my first novel, republished by CWP, *The Devil's Road to Kathmandu*, is selling okay and is also available in Spanish.

Now that we read submissions from all over the world, we are releasing titles more frequently, and – hallo writers out there – we are reading manuscripts at present. So get in touch.

Any subgenre of crime fiction will be considered, novels and novellas, but no true crime, no short stories and no children's books or graphic novels.

[XXXVII]

Interview: Simon Palmer

SIMON PALMER WAS a screen-writer and novelist who lived in Bangkok. He was born in a small fishing town called Whitby, in North Yorkshire. After writing short stories, monologues and duologues, he went on to write and sell two screenplays. His first novel is called Lost Innocence.

Simon Palmer died, unexpectedly, on January 28, 2015, a little over five months after this interview was first published at *Chiang Mai CityNews* in August of 2014. He was involved in a train accident in Bangkok, Thailand.

I spoke with Simon Palmer on three occasions. The first time we spoke was at Hemingway's Bangkok and the other two times were at Checkinn99. On each of those three occasions I enjoyed Simon's conversation and company. He always struck me as a sensitive man with many good qualities. We didn't agree on everything, nor should any two people have to. I hope he has found some peace. We traded some good stories and shared some smiles and laughs together. Those are good memories. The last question in this interview remains particularly poignant because of his premature death.

KC: You've written your first novel. Tell me about it.

SP: It's called *Lost Innocence* and the idea for the story came as a vivid outline in a dream. It's about a young artist who comes to Thailand for the first time to sketch 'street girls'. All was going well until he was allegedly tricked by one of the girls and ends up in prison waiting to be sentenced for a crime he claims he didn't commit. He's offered a way out through a cash payment and an admission of guilt, but declines and decides to stay and play things out. Inside the prison he meets a convicted drug smuggler and together they await their fates. Meanwhile his grandfather, a once brilliant lawyer, flies out to save his grandson but with the extreme heat of Bangkok and a weak heart, Nigel has problems of his own. He hires Harvey, a PI who is assisted by Bo, a beautiful Thai who was once a working girl herself, but the deeper they delve into the corruption of the city, the more dangerous things become.

KC: The legendary 'Night Owl', Bernard Trink, once wrote, in the process of doing a book review of a first-time author, that people who have been to Thailand for any length of time between two weeks and 20 years feel impelled to write a book about it. He then goes on to be pretty tough on those individuals who fall in that category. What sets your book apart from the herd of first-time authors and self-published authors found in Thailand? Put another way, why should people give a hoot about your book over all the others?

SP: I'd like to think that *Lost Innocence* is a little different because it reads as a true crime initially, but it's actually fiction. Although some of the characters are based on real people and actual events, the story itself is completely fictitious. It starts off with all the grit and grime of a Thai prison and its dire conditions, but then family values and friendship come into the mix with a twist of romance, comedy and a hint of erotica.

It's extremely difficult to sort it into one particular genre, which I believe makes it appealing to a wider range of reader, and the fast pace, heavy dialogue and simple style of writing makes for an easy read. Also, there is not just one main character to follow all the way through, there are several, so you as a reader get to choose who you really want to follow.

KC: You mention one of the settings is a Thai prison. From what I understand, unlike a few non-fiction authors who have written about Thai prison experiences, you've never been incarcerated in Thailand. Is that true? Why choose a prison setting?

SP: It's true I have never been incarcerated in a Thai prison. I initially wrote *Lost Innocence* purely from my imagination. I then had the opportunity to meet an ex-convict from Australia, who opened up to me and shared his experiences inside over the last seventeen years. I interviewed him on several occasions, so some of Michael and John's experiences in the book did actually happen. I also researched online and was inspired by other true crime books that I'd read in the past.

I didn't choose to write the book in a prison setting. The story was so vivid in my dream that I knew I had to write it. I've never felt sympathy for criminals before, but I do feel the conditions in prisons here and in many other countries in the world are inhumane.

KC: James Thompson, the Nordic noir writer who died tragically and unexpectedly in 2014, once said: "Writing books is a funny game. You're a fool and a dreamer as long as you haven't published anything, and when you're successful, you turn into a genius." In your case, your first book actually originated from a dream. Tell me more about your dreams, figuratively and literally. How important are they to a writer to get them to the genius stage?

SP: I think creativity can come in many ways. We all dream, we just don't always remember what we do dream. I sleep next to a huge whiteboard stocked with markers and often wake up and start scribbling something in the middle of the night. As a writer you never know where and when inspiration will strike. I write onto my iPhone when I'm out, describing people I see on my travels. I find it easier that way and certainly more believable to the reader to describe from real people. As far as getting to the 'genius stage', I don't feel I have a right to comment. I'm certainly not there and may never be. It's more about the journey for me, not the success or the big pay check at the end of the month. Having people enjoy what you do is success in my eyes, and I've already had a good share of reviews with my first book. In my eyes, I'm already 'living the dream'.

KC: You and I share a favorite author who sells a ton of books every year – John Grisham. What do you think Grisham does well?

SP: Grisham was one of the first authors that I read who, for me, broke the rules. In *The Testament*, the main character narrated the story and then killed himself, in the very first chapter. That hooked me for the rest of the book. He wasn't afraid to take chances and I think in such an over-crowded writers' world, to stand above the rest you need to take chances.

KC: Tell me your two favorite British or Irish authors, dead or alive, and why you like them?

SP: I like so many. Stephen Leather was a major influence with his Thai-based book *Private Dancer*. I read that a while ago and loved how he threw the reader right into the action, and loved the style and the mix of characters. When I first read that, it inspired me to write a Thai-based book. I've currently written two and have two more to come. I also really enjoyed Jeffrey Archer's prison diaries. I loved the style and simplicity in which he wrote them. I tend to steer away from over-descriptive books. I'm all for the story.

KC: The seven deadly sins are: wrath, greed, sloth, pride, lust, envy and gluttony. Pick an instance in *Lost Innocence* where one or more of these sins are committed, and tell us why the sin occurs?

SP: Lust. Stan comes over and forgets what he's actually doing in Thailand. He ends up in quite a predicament and it occurs because there is so much temptation and Stan, quite frankly, is a weak, horny guy.

KC: In all societies, illusions and truth play their prominent roles, perhaps even more so in prison society. Without getting into the guilt or innocence of your character, what illusions did he fall for in Thailand and what truth does he learn by the end of the book?

SP: Michael was totally engrossed in his art. So much so that it overcame any lust towards the ladies he had before him. He trusted his models too easily, and once he was in trouble and offered a way out, he didn't take it. He was stubborn and set in his ways. Without giving too much away, I'd like to think that he learned regret by what he lost but also gained strength for what he went through. He's such a stronger character in *Two Years Later*, the sequel to *Lost Innocence*. I've already written the outline and I think it's looking good.

KC: Talk more about the craft of writing. When did it first occur to you that writing would be a pleasant avocation or a dream vocation? How different is screen writing from novel writing? What did screen writing teach you that you brought to your novels?

SP: I think you have to love storytelling to be a writer, or at least to write fiction. It takes time, energy and so much patience to get it right and even when you do get it right, or you think you have, you need to be able to handle criticism and rejection. Again, for me, it's about the journey not the reward. I'm grateful for the opportunity and time to write and am loving all the feedback, positive and negative. You can learn from the negative and hopefully only improve. I have still so much to learn.

I was always writing something, since my father was a singer-songwriter and writing lyrics. For me it was either writing poems or lyrics. Ever since school I was telling stories and writing dialogue.

Screenplay writing is very different to writing novels. It's a lot less descriptive and very dialogue-heavy. I prefer to write screenplays but then you can easily lose control once the movie is made. With a book, you can keep most of what you write. That is why I turned to novels. I wanted the control. Screenplay writing taught me how to write tight, compelling dialogue which hopefully I have brought over to my novels.

KC: If you were to die, unexpectedly, next month give me an original quote that you would like to be remembered by?

SP: "Damn, he's dead. Now we'll never know what happened…"

KC: Thanks, Simon. Good luck to you.

SP: Thank you, Kevin.

[XXXVIII]

Review: Tone Deaf in Bangkok, by Janet Brown

ENRY MILLER HAS been quoted as saying: "No one can write the absolute truth." And I do feel it is a lot harder than most people might think. That would explain the abundance of fiction writers in the world today. The irony is, I get a lot of my truth from fiction, which is mostly what I read.

Deviating from my norm, I read *Tone Deaf In Bangkok (And Other Places)* by Janet Brown. (Global Directions/Things Asian Press, 2009). It is a collection of short stories, real, lived by Ms Brown. There are stories of humor, stories of courage, stories of friendships made, travel stories and most of all stories of a female expat living in Bangkok between 1995 and 2001 – the operative word being 'living'. In these essays, Janet Brown does her absolute best to tell her absolute truth. And she succeeds. It is quite an accomplishment. What makes it unique, for me, is the adventurous, middle-aged female perspective she brings to the table. It was a fun read. It reinforced many truths of my own about the Land of Smiles. There were even some shared experiences.

If you bring an open mind to Thailand, as Janet Brown did, Thailand is sure to leave a lasting impression. The story about ghosts I particularly liked. Twelve years ago, when I first came to Thailand, I took a western, scientific view of ghosts. I didn't believe in them. Now, after being around so many people who do, I am open to alternative theories. It's one of many transformations that can take place in a person who chooses to live in Thailand long enough. I've concluded that alternative theories about ghosts are, if nothing else, just more fun. Had I read Janet Brown's story 'Ghosts In The City Of Angels' 12 years ago I would have been shaking my head thinking, "Who is she kidding?" Over a decade later, I just smile and nod my head up and down.

One of my favorite stories was 'Today, Where Do You Go?' about Janet's trip to the disputed temple of Khao Phah Viharn on the Thai-Cambodia border. It told me a lot about the author. It is short and sweet and sour all in one. Just like a good day, lived.

Her concluding story, 'Fireweed and Jasmine', about the lasting effects of growing up in Alaska as a young girl and getting an early lesson in impermanence makes it worth having this book in your travel collection, for those words alone. I read the story aloud. I recommend it. I also recommend it for anyone with an interest in Thailand, adventure, travel or living. That just about covers it.

[XXXIX]

Review: God of Darkness by Christopher G. Moore -

A Crash and Burn HiSo Thriller

THERE WAS A military coup in Thailand in 2014. At the time of writing, martial law is in place. Tough decisions have to be made – like what to read. A recent choice for me was *God of Darkness* by Christopher G. Moore (Heaven Lake Press, 1999, and second edition by Amazon, 2010). The Canadian author is best known for his Smiles trilogy, beginning with *A Killing Smile*, first published in 1991, and his Vincent Calvino crime series now going 14 strong – the most recent being *The Marriage Tree* (Heaven Lake Press, 2014). Moore's standalone fiction is also worth consideration.

When it comes to fiction or movies, there is no shortage of choices out there, with many of them being bad or mediocre. As for cinema, you can stay at home and watch an HBO movie, go out and catch a blockbuster with a matching McDonald's plastic cup, or head down to your local art house and view a foreign-produced film. Reading *God Of Darkness* was like watching an art house film, for me. And that wasn't always good, because I have the attention span in those films to wonder if they are still selling the buttered popcorn at the halfway mark, or why all theatres don't save on labor by having the same person who sells you the ticket tear it in half as well. I found either the book or my mind meandering at times during my reading of *God of Darkness*.

And yet, just as when you walk home after the conclusion of a good art house film that confused you for a scene or two, I was completely satisfied at the end of this 320-page novel, which I would categorize as both a thriller and historical fiction. What Moore does so well is to parachute the reader into hostile territory that would otherwise be inaccessible. In *Pattaya 24/7*, Moore takes you into the lush estate of a wealthy concert pianist and the lifestyle that goes with it. In *Zero Hour in Phnom Penh* you are admitted into the despair of a Cambodian prison. In *Gambling On Magic* you are inside the heads of bookmakers, winners, losers, high rollers and low rollers. In *God Of Darkness* you are behind the high walls of the compound of a wealthy Thai family. One that just happens to make frequent offerings to Rahu, the god of darkness.

God Of Darkness is set mostly in Bangkok in 1997, during the Asian economic crisis. Thailand is no stranger to crisis, as the current times reflect. Moore has written a wonderful time-capsule of this roller-coaster, crash-and-burn period. You land in a Bangkok high society family compound where the central character, Hurley, has been convinced by his girlfriend's family to leave the comfort of Seattle, Washington to become part of something he had not anticipated and never experienced in his young life. The drama unfolds when Hurley moves out, and it is unclear whether he will return and marry the beautiful May under the heavy-handed influence of powerful potential in-laws. Additional characters include Hurley's 73-year-old former professor flying into Bangkok in order to find a Thai wife, a masturbating monkey, a cold-blooded hit man and a ditched *mia noi*.

Moore is not a cookie-cutter writer. He takes chances. An example would be his use of settings. A short-time motel room is not particularly clever for Bangkok fiction, but Moore chooses to use that scene twice, two years apart. The same mirrored room. Once for the scene of a murder and a great education for the reader in the realities of privilege, face, ranking and *Thai Criminology 101*. A second time the unlikely room is used as a safe house, a rapid-fire courtship and a marriage proposal. It is all believable in the good times and bad times of anything-goes Bangkok.

Another of Moore's strengths is examining what is right in front of us every day in Thailand. An example: 'Ancients', Moore's term for old people. He uses the word with aplomb dozens of times, and each time it seems better than before. Moore saves some of his best writing for last. As he puts it: "Life is swimming to shore with cowboy boots on." We get a good slice of that life in *God of Darkness*. It's a bit of a reverse Cinderella story, with plenty of good intentions and malfeasance to go around.

God of Darkness is not for everyone. If you like your protagonist to be 6ft 5" and 250lbs and to roam around the United States a lot in lonely fashion, only to be played later by a 5ft 7" ex-high school wrestler on the big screen, then there are other choices for you. If, on the other hand, you prefer accurate interpretations of Thai behavior, and want insight into the Asian economic crisis of 1997, or just want to know what goes on behind those high walls in those expensive Bangkok neighborhoods while getting a good thriller of a ride, then read *God of Darkness* by Christopher G. Moore. You'll be glad you did.

[XL]

Review: The Age of Dis-Consent -

A Book of Essays by Christopher G. Moore

CHRISTOPHER G. MOORE IS, to put it simply, my favorite living essayist. So I was pleased to learn that his fourth book of essays, *The Age of Dis-Consent*, is available in e-book format and in paperback. The paperback can be ordered on his website, which also has information on where to find it on Amazon, Kobo and Smashwords.

With endorsements from one of my newly discovered and favorite political analysts, Kong Rithdee, who many readers will know from his work at the *Bangkok Post*, and Thitinan Pongsudhirak, a professor at Chulalongkorn University, and prominent political analyst in his own right, readers will find themselves choosing from an array of essays which combine Thai politics and societal issues. The topics affect every man and woman, regardless of where they might call home, while blending in literary elements, which I particularly enjoy about Moore's writing style. Individual essays are devoted to George Orwell, Kafka and Henry Miller.

As Kong Rithdee succinctly puts it, the book is "An intelligent deconstruction of the world's nameless chaos."

This is the fourth book of essays penned by Christopher G. Moore, also known for his Vincent Calvino crime series. *The Age of Dis-Consent* follows up on *The Cultural Detective, Faking it in Bangkok* and *Fear and Loathing in Bangkok*.

The title is well thought out. These are not agreeable times we live in, and permissions have been taken away, not granted, worldwide – particularly in Thailand, the country Christopher G. Moore has called home for decades. Moore helps identify not only the permissions known to be taken away, but the ones not thought of by everyone.

> *I'm going to be a happy idiot*
> *And struggle for the legal tender*
> *Where the ads take aim and lay their claim*
> *To the heart and the soul of the spender*
> *And believe in whatever may lie*
> *In those things that money can buy*
> Jackson Browne – *The Pretender*

If you are one of the happy idiots that my favorite poet, Jackson Browne, writes about in his song *The Pretender* then the *The Age of Dis-Consent* is not meant for you. If, on the other hand, you want to make a bit of sense out of a very foggy world, Moore shines an effective fog-light into the distance, which simultaneously helps the reader see the world better, while reflecting on the fog particles as well.

The book is broken down, conveniently, into seven sections: Thailand in the Age of Dis-Consent; Thai Law Enforcement and Cultural Mindset; Evolution of Violence and the Borderless World; Crime Investigation in a Changing World; Space, Time, Technology and Cultural Gravity; Information and Theory of Mind; and On Writing and Authors.

One of my favorite essays in the book is 'Personalized Swat Teams for the Filthy Rich', about the growing wealth inequalities in the world. You don't have to read the 700-page book by Thomas Piketty, *Capital in the 21st Century* – read Moore's 11-page essay and you'll learn plenty. In 'Violence: The Next Big Leap', Moore writes of the great experiment of domestication, drone warfare, and how the inevitable technological blind spots may pave the way to where it all began.

Moore saves another favorite for last – 'Man With A Scarf', an essay about the legacy of artists in general and one fascinating one in particular, Lucian Freud – the grandson of Sigmund Freud and one of the most important painters out of England in the last century. Moore writes: "Our tragedy is we fail to train ourselves to pay attention to the fine details around us. We gain our identity, ourselves, our information from instruments and machines, not from nature or each other."

As Moore reminds us, it takes endurance to pay attention. There are many people out there beating a drum, with no shortage of followers. Christopher G. Moore deciphers the beats of those drums as well as anyone, and makes readers realize the tune is more complicated than mere vibrations. There are more than enough reasons to add *The Age of Dis-Consent* to your reading list and bookshelf. To steal a line from both Lucian and Christopher, found in the final chapter, I had a lovely time reading it, and so will readers who enjoy thought-provoking essays.

[XLI]

Interview with John Burdett

JOHN BURDETT IS a British crime novelist. He is the bestselling author of *Bangkok 8* and its sequels, *Bangkok Tattoo, Bangkok Haunts, The Godfather of Kathmandu and Vulture Peak*. The sixth in the series, *The Bangkok Asset*, is due out as a hardback in the USA and UK on August 4th, 2015 and will be available world-wide on eBooks starting September 3rd, 2015.

KC: Your first novel was a murder mystery and love triangle titled, *A Personal History of Thirst*, featuring James Knight, an English barrister as your protagonist. It was published by William Morrow and Co, which is now an imprint of HarperCollins. It came out in 1996. You followed that up with *The Last Six Million Seconds* in 1997 published by the British publishing house, Hodder & Stoughton – now an imprint of Hachette. That novel is set in Hong Kong during the historically significant British handover of sovereignty to China. What did you learn in writing that first novel that was most helpful to you in writing the second?

JB: On the first novel you realize it can be done, the mountain within can be climbed. This is not necessarily positive. Before there was always the possibility that one was simply not capable of that kind of concentration sustained over a period of years. Now there is no excuse. On the second novel you learn that it doesn't get easier. For me writing a novel is like building a house, and takes a similar length of time. It's human nature to say, after completion: Wow, now I can build any house any time. Then, when you come to try, you find the same problems, the same blocks, but now you have to carry on because you know that with enough time, sweat and tears you can solve all the issues.

KC: Both of those books came out more than 10 years before the Kindle debuted in November of 2007. *A Personal History of Thirst* is not available in eBook format, despite being well received. What are your thoughts about eBooks – do you read them?

JB: At first I had no particular feeling about eBooks except relief that they didn't weigh anything. All my life I've had to hump books around, both as a lawyer and as a writer. Now, though, I find I use eBooks entirely for reference purposes, looking up a quote here a favorite passage there. I simply cannot read a whole novel on Kindle. This may not be romantic, it may simply be that my eyes just don't like having light shone directly into them. But there is a great tactile pleasure in print, there's no doubt about it. If anything Kindle has made me more appreciative of print, now that there is an alternative.

KC: Your father was a London policeman. You have stated you never really had a strong desire to be an attorney. You have a degree in English and American Literature. Yet you spent 14 years as a lawyer – twelve of those years were a combination of government and private practice in Hong Kong where you were very successful, becoming a partner in a large firm. You had the wisdom to retire, early. I have known many lawyers economically able to retire who lacked the imagination to do as you did. What lessons did you learn at a young age from either of your parents?

JB: The policeman was my step father, a wonderful fellow who kept my mother and me and saved us from disaster for fourteen years and to whom I owe a great deal. My natural father, who I met for the first time in my early twenties, was a wild man who lived on a boat and had his head firmly in the stars. I owe him a lot too. The cop taught me discipline and the kind of things society expects. The wild man taught me that there's something infinitely greater than all that, something that challenges us to take a dive into the unknown. Put the two together and you make a novelist.

KC: You've traveled to Nepal many times, even going there prior to your first visit to Thailand in 1986. You wrote about Nepal extensively in *The Godfather of Kathmandu*. It seems to be a place and people whom you hold dear. They have been hit hard recently, twice. For those unfamiliar with Nepal, and who have never been there it can be confusing on how best to help. What memories of Nepali people do you carry with you fondly and can you make any recommendations on how interested people might help those affected by the recent earthquakes?

JB: Himalayan people are a race apart. Their resilience and resourcefulness looks superhuman to the rest of us. And of course those mountains do seem to be the origin of every kind of spiritual awakening. (I find quite persuasive the recent evidence that Jesus studied in Kashmir as a Buddhist monk before beginning his ministry). I think the greatest help is to take the time and trouble to understand. Theirs is a very ancient culture, sometimes Hindu, sometimes Buddhist, with quite different values to ours. Noble as our young people are in going over there to assist, they do not always understand or appreciate the difference in cultural values. Why it might be as important to give a dear relative a proper burial as to save the living, for example. It is only when we start to understand and value difference on a deeper level that we can ever be of real use – to anyone, actually.

KC: You are best known for your Bangkok thriller series, featuring the truth and justice seeking Eurasian, devout Buddhist, Royal Thai Police

Detective, Sonchai Jitpleecheep. The novels tell stories of immorality and crime that are set in Thailand and the region. You've described Sonchai as an everyman. A conflicted everyman, which reinforces the point. The series debuted with the internationally released *Bangkok 8* (Knopf – 2003), which sold over 100,000 hardback copies and continues to sell well today. The most recent novel is *Vulture Peak*, which deals in organ trafficking among other things. You once said you were horrified to learn of the realities of organ trafficking, particularly how the poor were exploited by the wealthy. It's been over three years since Vulture Peak was released. What tops your list of horrors, about humanity, in 2015 globally and/or locally and where, if possible, can blame be apportioned?

JB: I am horrified by the increase in differentials between the super-rich and the rest of us. This has happened before, but nowadays the very wealthy have an increasing advantage in being able to purchase cutting edge technology, especially in the field of security and medicine. One has to look back to the Dark Ages to find an appropriate analogy. In that time only the very wealthy, the barons, could afford horses and iron weapons. The result was a terribly cruel form of feudalism that kept humanity in a state of fear and poverty for centuries. Now, for the first time in my life, young people in the UK are working for nothing except to gain experience. They often have no choice. This is servitude close to slavery all over again. I blame the myopia of the neocons and the economists who inspired them. Anyone who knows anything about people, especially rich people, knows that wealth does not trickle down. The rich get rich by not sharing. All economics should start with that universal principle.

KC: You've been fortunate by receiving a film option for your first novel and also having the film rights for all your Sonchai Jitpleecheep novels optioned as well. *Bangkok 8* got deep into development with a big name director at one time committing to the project. I can recall listening to you at the Foreign Correspondents' Club of Thailand during your time on a panel for the launch of *Bangkok Noir* in March of 2011. That evening you said having a novel made into a film was like having the nine planets align in perfect order. You stated, if memory serves, that as many as nine different things need to happen before an audience ever sees a film. Is getting a novel made into a movie another instance where sheer luck is at play? Can you talk about the differences in how some Thais perceive and believe in luck in daily life and contrast that with the western notion of luck.

JB: Luck, in the Thai mind, is very much tied up with karma, which drives them far more than most Westerners understand. To the average Thai there is literally nothing that happens to them that does not have its origin in the law of cause and effect operating in the moral/psychological field. On the other hand, they have the Asian sense of the deal. When you see a Thai, usually a woman, donating a hundred boiled eggs at a wat, it is often not in the form of a sacrifice in advance but cash on delivery: she is giving thanks for prayers answered. I suppose a farang might take a cynical view, but in fact she is protecting herself from the negative karma that would arise if she did not give thanks; ingratitude is one of the worst faults and the source of very poor karma. How this ties in with my experience with Hollywood is very difficult to say. Did I fail to donate enough eggs when they bought the option, so the film never got made? I'm not sure. Looking at it from the modern Western point of view, the fact is that Hollywood stopped taking big creative chances a long time ago. The vast investment needed to make a big movie is not sourced from creative gamblers, it comes from shrewd business people who have studied the market and will not invest unless they feel safe. Nobody knows how safe it would be to bet $100 million on a movie about a Eurasian cop working the streets of Bangkok. I think that's the problem.

KC: Generally, I sense empathy and respect for the Thai people in your writing, particularly those from the Northeast and the Thai working class. The contrast between East and West is one of many things I enjoy in the Jitpleecheep series since I first read *Bangkok 8* many years ago. I have read four of the five Sonchai novels which you have authored.

How is the education of some of the poorest Thais superior to the Western education? Put another way, what are the Thais learning that Westerners are not and where and from whom are they learning it?

JB: In Thailand Buddhism is almost always the answer, even when you least expect it. We farang often do not appreciate that Buddhism is a psychology as well as a religion. Especially in the devout countryside it is a way of thinking that is inculcated quite unconsciously at school, whether the child goes to the temple often or not. Also, in the country the only figures of moral authority tend to be monks and abbots. People really do not know who to turn to if not the local sangha. So what is Buddhist psychology? It is extraordinarily radical, taking one to regions of the mind far beyond culture/mother/father/sex, which is where our psychology is stuck. You could say that in Buddhism psychology and cosmology meet: as if Stephen Hawking could do psychoanalysis. The weakness is exactly its strength: it is far too deep and broad to take our blinkered materialism seriously, which makes poor Thais vulnerable to Western commercialism and exploitation by their own upper classes.

KC: Two of the main recurring characters in your Bangkok series are Sonchai, the struggling but fairly honest detective, doing his best to solve the case, and his corrupt boss, Colonel Vikorn, who is often more concerned with the ancillary benefits of his position. What can you tell fans of the series about the activities Sonchai and Vikorn will be getting involved with on the pages of *The Bangkok Asset?*

JB: I'm not saying anything about *The Bangkok Asset* except that it goes much further than the others in terms both of Vikorn's power and weakness and Sonchai's boggled mind.

KC: One of my favorite lines in *Vulture Peak* is: "It's a beautiful, global world, so long as you keep your eyes shut." In the promotional material for *The Bangkok Asset* a question is posited: "...why is everyone, from the Bangkok police to the international community, so eager to turn a blind eye?" I infer, correctly or incorrectly, in the first sentence, that you might think that large segments of the world are either under some illusion or apathetic to what is going on at the global level. In the second sentence one could infer institutional corruption. Would those be fair inferences? What diversions might be most responsible for allowing illusions, apathy and corruption to flourish in the 21st century?

JB: I'm afraid it's one of the bees in my bonnet, the way we are all corralled into a kind of mental playpen. In my youth in London it was still possible to have a serious conversation about serious matters with people from every walk of life. Today only football and showbiz are cool. Look at the front pages of what used to be serious newspapers, what do you get? A couple of inches of news, often badly reported by stringers who were not at the event, the rest is sport, usually football, and TV shows. Top Gear and its infantile presenters get more coverage than the massively important trade agreement between the US and Europe that will affect all our lives. IMHO this is not an accident. Humans are not ostriches, we do not normally hide our heads in the sand unless we sense the Terror is simply too awful to contemplate. When I was sixteen a number of my chums hitch-hiked from London to Kathmandu. One by one most of the countries in between have become violent, paranoid no-go areas. To suppose that cannot happen to Europe or the US is... well, to stick one's head in the sand. For example, Jews are leaving France in droves these days. Deja vu?

KC: Do you prefer reading non-fiction or fiction? Do you typically read one book from beginning to end or do you have many in play at once? What book have you most recently read?

JB: I'm afraid I hardly read novels at all. Perhaps I read too many in my youth. I hope I'm not accused of boasting when I confess I mostly read history books in French. When they are good I read them from end to end. I have just finished a masterpiece about *Frederick von Hohenstaufen* by Jacques Benoist-Mechin. I bet you've never heard of either?

KC: This is your lucky day. You are correct. Thank-you for the interesting insights into your world, John. I'll be expressing my gratitude in the Western way on August 4th.

Portrait of John Burdett by Chris Coles

[XLII]

Reviewing the Book Reviewers - Vulture Peak by John Burdett

THE ELECTRONIC MEDIA age has made it possible for almost anyone with the motivation to become an author. The pros and cons of that reality have been well-documented and we continue to see the results play out in the Amazonia region of the book world. Likewise, nowadays almost anyone can be a book critic – or if you prefer a neutral tone, a book reviewer. A case in point would be me. Again, there are pluses and minuses to leveling the playing field when it comes to the book review process.

I am an amateur book reviewer. Some may have other adjectives to describe what I do. Once I was told: "Writers and prostitutes have to compete against those who give the product away for free." That would again be me, in the case of book reviews. My audience is small. I do not have nor will I ever have the clout of a major book critic. Some people are fortunate enough to get paid to write book reviews. Other times book reviews are done by other authors. I enjoy reading book reviews written by professionals, a lot. I try to learn from them and glean what I can from the pros so that I can do a better job in the future.

Some very good authors who live or spend a lot of time in Thailand are among my favorite book critics. They include Tom Vater, James A. Newman, Jim Algie, Christopher G. Moore and Timothy Hallinan. I enjoy reading what they write, and I respect their opinions about what they read.

One of my favorite authors of Bangkok fiction is John Burdett, creator of the Sonchai Jitpleecheep series, among others, which consists of five novels: *Bangkok 8*, *Bangkok Tattoo*, *Bangkok Haunts*, *The Godfather of Kathmandu* and his most recent in the series, *Vulture Peak*.

I have yet to review a book of John's here, despite the fact that I have read, enjoyed and recommend the Detective Sonchai series without hesitation. Of the five novels, I have read four. Only *Bangkok Haunts* has escaped my radar. John is a top-tier author, published by Knopf, which still has panache in the age of the Big Five publishers. As such, there is no shortage of book reviews about John Burdett's novels. That is as it should be. Of the four Burdett novels in the Sonchai series that I have read, my two favorites are *Bangkok 8* and *Vulture Peak*. One of the primary reasons I never did review one of John's books for my blog is that others have done it much better than I ever could. *Vulture Peak*, I highly recommend. And I am going to discuss three book reviews which might further convince you to consider it.

A.J. Kirby wrote an excellent review of the novel for the *New York Journal of Books*. What makes it a good review? For one thing, you can tell Mr Kirby read the book, which always helps. In addition he includes excerpts and quotes from the protagonist. And he talks about the tone of the book. Little things add up in a good book review. Here is the concluding paragraph:

"But, of course, there are real villains whom Sonchai must chase, in an increasingly dangerous game of cat and mouse that stretches across the continents. Vulture Peak is a modern morality tale with all the requisite bells and whistles and much more: a salutary warning for the Internet age. "It's a beautiful, global world, so long as you keep your eyes shut."

Two Bangkok based authors have also reviewed *Vulture Peak*. Jim Algie's review first appeared in *The Nation* on August 6, 2012, with the headline 'The Peak Of The Flesh Trade'. It was, in part, because of Jim's review that I decided to read *Vulture Peak*.

One of the things I liked about Jim's review is that he takes John to task a bit. He doesn't pander to the author, which is probably one of the easier things for a book reviewer to do, particularly an amateur reviewer. I know I am guilty of it, at times. A case in point is this paragraph from Jim: "Not all the Buddhist details ring true, however. The way that the detective talks about his previous incarnations – an ancient Egyptian in "Bangkok 8", an American Indian in this book – sounds more New Age Californian than Thai Buddhist."

Christopher G. Moore also reviewed *Vulture Peak* and, like Jim, he did a great job, I thought, of explaining to potential readers what they had in store for them in the book. The review can be found on the International Crime Author's Reality Check website. Here is a passage from the review: "When I open a crime novel my wish is to plunge inside, a full headlong immersion in another world of events, characters and drama that carry me on a white water raft of sheer joy, wonder and adventure. Once the raft is pulled from the river and you think about the experience, the rush of letting one's self go and be carried away is the memory imprinted."

"Reading John Burdett's *Vulture Peak* is that kind of literary white water rafting rush I alluded to above. For those who seek the safe comfort of categories – genre and literary – Burdett's novel will cause you to rethink such a flat, arbitrary and meaningless distinction."

So now you know why I have never written a lengthy book review of a John Burdett novel. It is not because I don't like them; I like them a great deal. It is just that others have written excellent reviews already. Why reinvent the wheel when the wheels out there are rolling along so smoothly?

But I was pleased to come across an entry I made about *Vulture Peak* on John's Facebook page, the morning after I finished reading the 306-page hardback edition in December 2012. I write my best reviews when I do them within 24 hours of finishing the book, for all the obvious reasons. Here is what I had to say less than one hour after reading *Vulture Peak*:

"Just finished *Vulture Peak* this morning. Burdett blends his imaginary world with the real one in cynical fashion as well as anyone. Told with a Buddhist slant through the narrative of Thai detective Sonchai. *Vulture Peak* is about organ trafficking run by two identical twin Chinese sisters. I'd tell you their names but like Burdett's imagination and his accurate commentary on the global experience, it really doesn't matter much what your preference is; it's all entertaining. For expats living in Thailand, his breakdown of the Thai word *kikiat* (lazy) is worth the read alone. Here is a passage I liked that sums up your typical human living with failing organ(s): "Now you have a true citizen of the twenty-first century, a totally confused human soul with no identity, no direction, no faith, no religion, no politics, no instinct other than to survive." Burdett's not for everybody but I enjoy him a lot. Body parts everywhere in this book, along with ample commentary on East vs. West. I find myself laughing out loud at the accuracy of the human condition John describes, which isn't at all funny. That's the beauty of his writing to me. Bangkok 8 is still my favorite in the series."

So there you have it. A review of *Vulture Peak* from a top level literary journal, two well-known Bangkok based writers and an amateur blogger. Take your pick. Any way you look at it, Burdett and *Vulture Peak* go four for four.

[XLIII]

Dean Barrett, Man of Mystery?
Yes and No

DEAN BARRETT WAS one of the first two authors living in Thailand whose name I knew and could spell for you when I first arrived in the Land of Smiles in the early 21st Century. He was not, however, one of the first half a dozen "Bangkok authors" that I read. I can explain: Let's face it, Dean seemed like he was having too much fun in Bangkok to be a good writer. From the first time he was pointed out to me in a second-storey Nana Plaza establishment 10 years ago, to his five-minute YouTube video *Dean Barrett's Guide to Soi Cowboy*, to a few years ago when he climbed into a boxing ring for a charity event, at a time when a lot of guys his age were playing shuffleboard in Florida and collecting their Social Security checks, Dean has been enjoying life. Not to mention that one of his two websites, with the dominatrix on the enter page, will trigger the porn blocking software on any computer in China.

The first time I saw Dean's star ratings on Amazon, I was surprised how highly his books were rated. I'm not sure why I was surprised, as I still hadn't read any of his books. I suppose I wanted my authors pudgy, with pale skin, bottle-rimmed glasses, and home alone, writing 12 hours a day for my benefit. Stephen King, I knew, was a good writer, even if not a personal favorite. Dean Barrett, I still had my doubts. One should not judge a book by its cover, but I made some judgments, based on the titles of Dean's books. If Groucho Marx didn't want to join any club that would have him as a member, I wasn't sure that I wanted to allot my valuable reading time to any author who liked so many clubs. Hey, we all have our biases. I was wrong. Dean Barrett writes well.

He has written a number of novels including *Memoirs of a Bangkok Warrior*, *Kingdom of Make-Believe*, *Permanent Damage*, *Skytrain to Murder*, *The Go Go Dancer who Stole My Viagra and other Poetic Tragedies of Thailand*, *Murder at the Horny Toad Bar & Other Outrageous Tales of Thailand*, and *Murder In China Red*, which all score consistently good reviews on Amazon.

I have since read three of Dean's books from the above list and have enjoyed them all. I also like his poetry. Keep in mind, Dean Barrett is old school. These reviews are real reviews, written by real people who actually took the time to read the books they reviewed.

There are other aspects about Dean's writing not as widely known as, say, his YouTube video. Dean was a professional writer, as a librettist and lyricist, in New York City for many years. His credentials are too long to mention here. I have a theory about talent and self-deprecation: only the talented are good at it. Dean Barrett is good at self-deprecating humor. He is also a first-class public speaker. If you have an opportunity to hear him speak about literature, go. He is well-read, well-traveled, erudite, honest and humble. He's John Grisham with a more interesting personal life and a few less books sold than John.

Another lesser-known aspect to Dean's writing career is his historical fiction set in China. His talent, coupled with his background as a Chinese linguist with the Army Security Agency during the Vietnam War made his China novels a fun discovery. The first Barrett novel I ever read in the Chinese historical fiction genre was *Hangman's Point*. As James A. Newman once pointed out, Dean's work has been studied in libraries and read in bars. *Hangman's Point* is a great historical fiction novel, which will be read 100 years from now – probably in both.

Dean's latest book is one I read recently, *The China Memoirs Of Thomas Rowley* (Village East Books, 2013). It is unlike any previous Dean Barrett fiction I have ever read. It is historical fiction, a love story with plenty of erotica. I've never been a particular fan of erotic fiction, not since I stopped reading 'The Penthouse Letters' 35 years ago. Some of the erotica scenes I enjoyed more than others. Set in 19th century China and finishing in New York City in 1922, it is a story that takes place during a tumultuous period in China's history – the Taiping Rebellion. Female warriors known as "the silken armies" were common. I always enjoy the historical and literary aspects of Dean's novels, which pay close attention to detail. The love story was fascinating in how it evolved. Dean also has a knack for writing female fight scenes better than any author I can recall, perhaps because he finds a way to have women fighting. Why not? It was realistic and well-written. The ending was believable and satisfying. There were no loose ends. If you want to try an outside–the-box Dean Barrett novel, read *The China Memoirs of Thomas Rowley*.

Dean writes mysteries, among other novels. But he is not mysterious. He is as straight a shooter as you will find. You may not like what he tells you, but you can be sure he will tell you the truth according to Dean. Be prepared.

[XLIV]

What if Henry Miller had changed destinations to Siam?

A FEW PEOPLE HAVE wondered why Henry Miller is included on my blog and in this book. The reasons are numerous. Henry and I do have a few things in common. Both of us were born in America; both took to a beautiful place along California's coastline at some point, and both have been expats of sorts in foreign lands. Henry to France and European travels, and me to Thailand and Southeast Asian travels. Fantasy leagues are popular in sports, although I never got into them. They could just as easily be applied to literature. What if Rocky Marciano had fought Cassius Clay? Fun for some. What if Henry Miller had come to Thailand? Fun to think about or not?

The truth of the matter is, in this literary fantasy, I think I would have blown Henry off had I ever crossed paths with him. I think it is highly likely I would have created distance with myself and him ASAP, whether the fantasy occurred in 1931 or 2013. My mistake. It gets back to practicing, forgetting yourself. It is harder than it sounds. But it is worth practicing. It pays dividends.

I've just completed listening to, not reading, *Paris 1928 (Nexus II)* by Henry Miller, an abandoned writing project of his which was only recently published in English, in 2012. I'm really glad I listened to it as one of my first choices on Audible.com, an Amazon company. I'm equally glad I did not read it. It is more for the Miller historians or Miller buffs. I'm more of a student or a fan. I've never found Miller's stream-of-consciousness writing style particularly easy to read. Hence I have not read a lot of Miller. I find the author and what he said about living, and how he lived his life, more interesting than his books. But that may change, as I do plan to listen to more of his books on Audible.com in the future.

In *Paris 1928*, Miller recounts the events of sailing to France on a steamer with his second wife, Mona. His recollections of Paris at that time are vivid, along with the characters, cafés, conversations, literature, authors, money consciousness, food and wine along the way. I don't like everything I have learned about Miller in the past year, nor do I feel it is necessary to like everything about him. But I did like him a lot in *Paris 1928*. Little things like how he asks a friend not to use the word "nigger" when speaking about a black American living in Paris who had helped them when money became tight as they waited for an American Express transfer – I found that refreshing, considering the time and place. Miller is not a passive guy. He's an active guy. I like that. At one point he laments the need to find a male companion willing to explore the streets of Paris on foot or bicycle, not merely sit on one's butt in a café and talk the day away, like so many.

At another point a Parisian friend suggests to Miller and his wife that perhaps they should consider other countries to live in and visit, besides France, and Siam is suggested. "I bet you never considered Siam?" the friend asks Miller and his wife.

What would Miller's life have been like had he gone to Siam or Thailand in 1939 instead of returning to the USA or "the air-conditioned nightmare", as Miller famously referred to America in his book of the same name, published in 1945, six years after his return?

We'll never know, of course, just as we'll never know how Marciano would have fared against Clay, but it is fun to think about. In *Paris 1928* we certainly get glimpses into Miller's thinking and psyche, and I enjoyed what he revealed. He saves his risqué erotica for the last two chapters, recounting a flashback episode that takes place in New York's Central Park and leads to a 36-hour sexual romp with not one but two wholesome neighborhood women, despite him being flat broke. It seems every young man's fantasy of the 1960s summer of love actually took place for Henry in the summer of 1928. Good for him. You'd think that might be cause to stick around Brooklyn. But the next day, a cablegram is received from Mona, and Henry is soon on a steamer headed to France, and the Paris experiences.

I enjoyed my first Audible.com listening experience, and think Henry Miller is one of a few authors that I will be listening to more of in the future, rather than reading. Progress.

[XLV]

Observations of a Bangkok Expat

A poem by Kevin Cummings

"WALK ACROSS THE soi, you'll save 10 baht," he said
Seems like a lot of trouble on a street known for the dead
Illusions are flying like bullets and hot air
Children are dying, does anybody care?
What's it all about? Power and greed
There is no glory in doing the good deed
I hate you. But I hated you first
But I hate you more
But you are the worst
Liars call people lunatics
To try and save face
Everyone has a Plan B
To get out of this place
Burmese Fortune tellers tell a good tale
While Rohingyan refugees face rotting in jail
Is this a farce? Can this be happening now?
Don't burst my illusions and I won't burst yours, pal.

[XLVI]

City Pulse

A poem by Alasdair McLeod

TONIGHT WE'LL LIGHT the neon. We'll bring the wanderers home.
Spark up the coals and call the ships to port.
Come light up your contours from the inside and the shadows will
    fascinate the crowd.
You'll see your will is marked when it's lit from within.

The panic zone is all four walls, a melting realm of mirrors.
Complication is the comfort zone, mania the state of grace.
We are worms, pilgrim, we are tarnished coins.
It's show time, your darkest hour.

You edge along the gills of the night, among slow-burning songs.
You turn from your past for a more compelling now.
Facts are abandoned for superior fantasies, and who can stand to miss
    the fun?
Skiffs and brigantines glide like underwater shadows to ply the trade.

Come and set your fever loose to run between electric islands.
Welcome lucid trance where quickening blood turns to ink.
The patient night is waiting for all you have to give.
It's you again, walking into our midnight arms to create us.

You prowling sifters are mining the tangled yarns,
Paralyzing them in the amber strobe of your art.
You darken the doors, then you darken the rest of the street.
You invite us, and we follow your sense of journey.

A wheel has finished spinning – to pause and then reverse.
This blazing gyre is a vision of exhausted motion.
The city is busy erasing its inhabitants and their seasons.
You are only done when we are done with you.

[XLVII]

Raining Jane and Jason Mraz

Mona Tavakoli, Mai Bloomfield, Jason Mraz, Chaska Potter, Becky Gebhardt

"ISN'T SHE MAGICAL?" My sister Roxanne asked about her daughter, Chaska, who had raced down the hall and hung a hard left. My mom was dying of cancer on my king-sized bed in Mountain View, California, and Rox had come up as part of the hospice team we had put together. My roommate Sam had moved out of the two-bedroom apartment. I was staying in his room so my two sisters and me, plus an angel of a hospice nurse, could manage the unthinkable.

Chaska knew Marion was dying. She just didn't care. She was happy to be seeing her grandma right now. She was about six years old and her clean dirty-blonde hair, with no exaggeration, almost reached her ankles. Except when she flew down that hallway. Then it wafted behind her, waist high. Chaska had hopped up on the bed of Grandma Marion Cunningham by the time I got to the somber room. Only it wasn't somber any more. Because Chaska was happy. And for some precious moments, so was everyone in the room.

Chaska Potter (T) Serena Potter (B)

Singing always played a big part in Chaska's family. I remember singing Cyndi Lauper tunes with her and the clan: *True Colors* and *Time After Time* come to mind.

Chaska usually made me happy when I saw her. And I would see her a lot over the next 30 years. As she got older, you could tell – early – that she was going be a great athlete. Even better than her brother, Jeremy, and Jeremy was no slouch. In her sophomore year of high school, she averaged 19 rebounds a game on her varsity basketball team. The next highest achiever in the entire county averaged 14. I was a basketball junkie and an uncle, so I wrote to the legendary Stanford women's basketball coach, Tara VanDerveer and told her about Chaska. The assistant coach wrote her back. I offered to pay for her basketball camp between her sophomore and junior year at the prestigious school. There was just one problem: Chaska didn't love basketball. She loved volleyball. You can't win them all, but you can try. Chaska loved volleyball enough to be a third team High School All-American and play on a Junior National Championship team that featured future

Stanford All–American Keri Walsh. She was not only named Santa Cruz County Female Athlete of the Year – she got it for the decade. Chaska got a full ride to UCLA, where she was all Academic Pac 10 Conference. All was going well until she blew out her rotator cuff, learning to serve left-handed by her senior year.

When she graduated from UCLA, I thought she still could have made a WNBA team. I really did. But once again she went with love, and a career much easier on the knees and shoulders – music. She joined an established band of female musicians called Raining Jane. They were good, I thought. Why wouldn't I? Over the years I saw Raining Jane – composed of Chaska, Mai Bloomfied, Becky Gebhardt and the cool-as-Antarctica cajon player Mona Tavakoli – play at coffee houses, free concerts outside a bookshop in Santa Barbara and at a high-tech firm in Silicon Valley. Then they opened for Sara Bareilles at Moe's Alley in Santa Cruz, California, among no more than 50 people while Sara's mom sat on the bar. The bar itself smelled of stale beer and dusty hardwood floors.

Another great memory I have of Chaska is of a very large family gathering at a Ramayana play in Salinas, California when I introduced my wife to the family. Later, Chaska uttered what is now one of my favorite quotes:

"Everybody's here … How awkward."

You've gotta love honesty. Then Raining Jane played the Hard Rock Café in Las Vegas, The Great American Music Hall and Fillmore West in San Francisco, and Ratree and I were there for those too. Things were looking up, after 14 years and 200,000 miles logged on a van they toured in (granted, I do not know how many miles were on the van when they bought it). After January concerts in Anchorage, Alaska, skidding on icy mid-western highways, playing before college crowds of as few as 60, Raining Jane got lucky. Or was it something else? Jason Mraz and his management team agreed that of all the songs Jason had written, the best 75 per cent were co-writing collaborations with Raining Jane. The result – Jason and Raining Jane collaborating on the *Yes!* album, where all five receive co-writing credits.

The *Yes!* album has done well, at one point being the best-selling album in the world for a week. The tour dates usually sell out quickly.

Whatever you think of Jason Mraz, he is the rarest of entertainers. As the saying goes, he puts butts in the seats. His voice and lyrics are also amazing, as is his showmanship and concern for people and the earth. In high school back in Virginia, Jason was the lone male cheerleader, traveling with the girls to different schools. He gets to do it again, at a different level, with the ladies now. Lucky guy.

On January 30, 2015 – shortly before the publication of this book – tickets went on sale for a Saturday, March 21st 2015 concert of Jason Mraz and Raining Jane. We were in the line. It's part of a world concert tour that has seen them play over 90 times already in cities around the globe on six continents, often in historic venues. My wife and I were at the Impact Arena in Bangkok that night, along with the poet and photographer Alasdair McLeod. It never hurts to reach out to family. It was a great concert.

Six months to the day from when Jason Mraz played Bangkok in June of 2012, Jason and Mona Tavakoli headlined the Milestone Concert in Myanmar to raise awareness of human trafficking. They were the first international artists to play an open-air concert in Myanmar, drawing 70,000 people to the venue near the Shwedegon pagoda, and among only a few major American artists to be invited to play in Myanmar in the last 80 years. The others being Count Basie, Duke Ellington and Charlie Byrd.

Henry Miller said: "Forget yourself." And his message is a good one. National pride is mostly silly. But there is a place for family pride. If you made it this far, thanks for reading about one of the things I am proud of – my niece. I'm also very proud and very happy for every member of Raining Jane and Jason Mraz too. It's lucky for me to have a rock star for a relative. But then, I think all my nieces and nephews are rock stars. Every one of them.

[XLVIII]

Interview with Colin Cotterill

COLIN COTTERILL WAS born in London, England, and has dual British and Australian citizenship. He spent several years in Laos, initially with the United Nations Educational, Scientific and Cultural Organization (UNESCO), and currently lives in a small town on the Gulf of Thailand.

He is the author of the award-winning Dr Siri mystery series set in Laos, and the Jimm Juree crime novels set in Chiang Mai and southern Thailand. Colin trained in and taught physical education early in his career. He has also taught and been a curriculum writer at Chiang Mai University, was the project director of Child Watch, an NGO for itinerant children in Phuket, and worked at refugee camps along the Burmese border.

In 2009, Colin received the Crime Writers' Association 'Dagger in the Library' award for being "the author of crime fiction whose work is currently giving the greatest enjoyment to library users". Cotterill won the Dilys Award in 2006 for *Thirty-Three Teeth,* and was a Dilys Award finalist in 2010 for *Love Songs From a Shallow Grave*. The Dilys Award has been presented every year since 1992 by the Independent Mystery Booksellers Association to the title its members have most enjoyed selling.

Since 1990, Cotterill has been a regular cartoonist for national publications (and he does cool book covers). He is also the cartoonist who drew Gop, the frog in the coconut shell for Thailand Footprint. I am pleased to welcome Colin here today for a *Bangkok Beat* interview.

KC: In an essay by Jong Jie in 3:AM Magazine titled 'Literature and Politics', Jie states: "Where politics seeks to obscure, literature seeks to uncover; it insists upon a scrupulous rendition of reality, and on the courage to face up unflinchingly to it, no matter what it holds."

Southeast Asian politics obscures in its own particular way. You're a novelist who has interwoven politics into your stories from many countries. I wish to focus on three – Laos, the setting for your Dr Siri novels and a standalone novel *Pool and Its Role in Asian Communism*; Thailand, the setting for your Jimm Juree series; and Burma, which you've written about in one of your earliest novels focusing on child abuse and pedophilia, *Evil in the Land Without*. What, if anything, do you set out to uncover about the political societies of those three countries? Or put another way, what rendition of reality do you wish to convey? How is the politics different among the three countries and how is it similar?

CC: Jesus H. Trueman, this is like a bloody university exam. What happened to the good old 'Where do you get your ideas from?'

Okay, start. I know nothing about the penthouse of politics. Or, rather, I know what the newspapers and websites tell me, which is the same thing. But I live down in the basement where the garbage chute comes out. I think that's why I write about the dregs and orts of policies and doctrines rather than the people who randomly make them up. I describe how people are affected by bad decisions. I started writing because I wanted readers to know about the seedy child abuse issues in Southeast Asia. The first hurdle I hit was that people don't want to read about the seedy child abuse issues in Southeast Asia. It took two more books before I learned how to cleverly disguise my issues in a jolly yarn (*Pool and its Role in Asian Communism*). And that has become my signature. You get to the end of my books and ask: 'I wonder if there's any truth in that.' With a bit of luck you might even look it up. I write fiction but I tend to stay faithful to history. I may move buildings or shift dates for convenience, but my characters are always directly influenced by the politics of the day and they're not afraid to have opinions.

Similarities? A country with no freedom of speech run by a military dictatorship. You tell me which of the three countries I'm describing.

KC: Your SoHo Crime colleague Cara Black has said: "We write to give a voice to those who aren't heard." You've told me why you started writing; why do you still write?

CC: I don't really like writing that much. It isn't my outlet of choice but how many people in the world are doing what they truly want to be doing? In the beginning (and I was a very late starter), I wrote to see whether I could write and whether I could write well enough to make a living out of it. It was one of the challenges I set myself. I've been doing it all my life. I got lucky and passed that test. There are much better writers than me today who don't even get their manuscripts on an agent's desk. My timing was right. I haven't moved on to the next challenge because none of the others involve paying the grocery bills. So the answer to your question is 'to feed the dogs'.

KC: You seem to have made a conscious decision to live a reality-based life over a virtual one. There is no shortage of authors of varying abilities utilizing social media at varying levels. Are you sure that walks on the beach, gardening, riding your bicycle, playing with your gaggle of dogs and illustrating in your spare time beat receiving a slew of LIKES for posting a picture of Laurel and Hardy on Facebook or replying to a fan on Amazon who left you a 4-star review? What are your thoughts regarding technology trends in the 21st century, particularly as they relate to the publishing world and interaction with your fans?

CC: What do you mean? I have email. Since when is that not technology? But even that's a little too convenient for me. I miss the days when you sat on the front step waiting for the postman and cursed under your breath when he walked past. I have an email account now so the postman walks past virtually and there's nobody to swear at when I have nothing in my in inbox. If anyone wants to get in touch with me it doesn't take a lot of detective work. I appreciate the effort. But they can't do it by clicking. I don't have Facebook because I think it's dumb. In my universe, 'friend' is a noun and 'befriend' is a verb, and never the twain shall meet.

I was lucky in that I rode the last wave of print publishing. That public is dying out and being replaced by a Kindle generation. And with e-reads comes pirating. I can download any of my books absolutely free any time I like. So why should I pay for them? It might not be a bad thing as people who wouldn't have bothered to pick up my books at a shop are able to take a taste of me. With that taste will naturally come addiction and, inevitably, sales. "You know? Granny might like this. I'll get a print copy and send it to her."

KC: Your first Dr Siri novel, *The Coroner's Lunch* came out in 2004. The protagonist is a green-eyed, septuagenarian coroner – the country's lone coroner – living in socialist Laos during the 1970s. This was obviously all part of a winning formula that would see the Dr Siri series remain popular for over a decade and reach 10 books strong, with the upcoming *Six and a Half Deadly Sins* (SoHo Crime) scheduled for release in May 2015. What are the joys and difficulties of writing a series of that length, given the starting age of your protagonist? Is it a safe assumption that you didn't envision either the popularity or length of the series?

CC: I was once on a panel with Robert Crais, and one of his words of wisdom for aspiring writers was to make your protagonist young in anticipation of a long series. Dr Siri started out at 72 in a country whose use-by life expectancy was 50-something. I had no idea the good doctor would become so popular, and it does present certain problems.

One of these is that I can't afford to dally too long between books. Sometimes the next episode follows on only minutes from its predecessor. Ten books on and he's still only seventy-four. I suppose somewhere along the line I should consider a prequel.

I have a horrible memory and that is a terrible affliction for someone writing a series. I'm supposed to remember every detail of every event, every character. You might think it wouldn't matter if the dog changes gender (to anyone other than the dog), or Comrade Civilai's Citroen suddenly becomes a Renault. But, to some, it is akin to misquoting the scriptures. I have fans who know my characters better than I know my own father. What do you do at audience question time when somebody asks: "It appears Dr Siri is clinically alcoholic. Don't you think it's time he gets some help?" I want to say: "He's fictional," but I look into the fan's eyes and realize he's not.

The only good point in having a regular cast of characters is that they tend to develop stories without me. In the beginning you'd say hello to them at the first script reading and they'd be nervous and uncertain. But after a couple of years you arrive late for the first editorial meeting and they'd have their parts written out already. "This is how I'd react in that situation," says Nurse Dtui. You even dare to swerve out of character and the personality police are on your back.

KC: Let's stay with character and personality. Pick any characters you have created and enjoyed spending time with, other than Dr. Siri and Jimm Juree – tell me their strengths and flaws and the novel(s) they can be found in.

CC: I'm very fond of the two main characters in *Pool and its Role in Asian Communism*, mainly because they are so diverse. Waldo is an African-American widower due for retirement from his lifelong job at a pool ball factory. Saifon is a Lao girl who was trafficked to the States when she was very young and grew up on the streets. Both are flawed in their own sweet ways, but they develop an unlikely friendship that endures. It was a fun relationship to write and a challenge in that the entire book was written in ungrammatical colloquial English.

Of my more recent characters I think I'd have to choose Jimm Juree's Granddad Ja, a retired Thai policeman who spent his entire career in the traffic division because he refused to take bribes. I know … but it's fiction. I've just realized how many elderly characters I have in my books. It looks like I'm paving the way for my own journey down the other side of the hill.

KC: In 2004 you wrote, "We tend to notice only the atrocities that suit us." There is no shortage of atrocities going on near and far. Let's focus on two that have occurred in 2015. The Charlie Hebdo slaughter in Paris, France, which left 12 people dead, and the killing of 29 school children in Damaturu, Nigeria by gunmen from the Islamist group Boko Haram. In addition to being a novelist who has written about issues that affect African children, you're also an accomplished cartoonist. There are those who argue that the same outrage was not felt worldwide over the killing of the 29 schoolchildren as there was for the security guard and Charlie Hebdo staff who were killed. What can you say about these two sad events?

CC: Disasters have an element of 'thank goodness it's not one of us' attached to them. If Malaysian flight 370 had been full of Australian rugby players or Canadian girl guides, there would have been more of an uproar. But most of the passengers were Chinese. Sigh of relief. After the 2004 tsunami the West was shocked at the number of white holidaymakers killed. Two movies were made showing the plight of the whities, even though 280,000 of the victims were Asian. Perhaps when we see a photograph of a Caucasian massacre victim it's easier to believe it could have been us. But even so, uproar has a short shelf-life.

The Charlie Hebdo killings came as I was writing my latest Dr Siri book. The title is *I Shot the Buddha*. A few people I'd mentioned that to got in touch with me and urged me to change it for fear of repercussions. It annoyed me that idiotic violence should have an influence on my freedom of speech. The book doesn't insult Buddhism, but even if it did I reserve the right to insult any religion I wish. I welcome dialogue on the subject but I do not welcome a round of ammunition through the chest. If I were to believe in a god it would be because I loved him, not because I was scared to death of him.

KC: You live with your wife in the literary hotbed of Thailand — a fishing village located on the southern part of the Gulf of Thailand, Pak Nam. Describe Pak Nam as if you were employed with the Tourism Authority of Thailand and then again, as if to keep your most brazen fan from stalking you for your autograph of a first edition hard copy of *The Merry Misogynist*.

CC: The small town of Pak Nam (cagily non-specific as down here every town a short way from the coast has its own Pak Nam) sits on the estuary of the XXX river. As the sun rises on the Gulf of Thailand, it nudges home the squid boats, their decks piled high with the night's catch. The colourful market is vibrant with the mix of southern Thai and Burmese accents. The open fronted shops on the narrow streets offer great bargains: Malay cloth, Chinese toys and trinkets, and music CDs all the way from Myanmar. And for tourists and locals alike, the restaurants offer all the delicacies one would expect from a town so in harmony with the sea.

But, of course, nobody in their right mind would live there. The beaches are strewn with garbage nine months of the year and the shallow waters are a breeding ground for great schools of jellyfish. To break the monotony of a place with no entertainment, bodies regularly wash up on the sand, carried in on the currents from popular tourist islands. If you're really bored you can go to the high spot of Pak Nam, the 7-Eleven, and watch the Burmese being shaken down by the police, or take a drive along the most dangerous stretch of highway in the country to Tesco, where they have 34 brands of cooking oil but no wine. Better still, don't come.

KC: What can your readers expect from Dr Siri's latest adventure, *Six and a Half Deadly Sins*?

CC: During the decades of civil war in Laos, the Chinese were building roads in the north of the country under the guise of international aid. It wasn't a coincidence that the roads headed from China in the direction of the Vietnamese and Thai borders. Even in the fifties, the cunning Chinese were paving the way to international trade. But when hostilities began in 1978, culminating in a Chinese invasion of Vietnam, these roads had a more sinister meaning, providing the invaders with another front from the west. It was all Laos could do to prevent China from crossing their borders.

Dr Siri and Madam Daeng become entangled in this international intrigue whilst following a trail of clues woven into the hems of Lao skirts. Can they solve the puzzle before the invaders swarm across the border? Can they hold their own with the criminals operating in the hub of the Golden Triangle drugs trade? And whose funeral is that at the end of the story (cue kettledrums)?

KC: Peter Sellers, in his role of Chance the gardener in the movie *Being There* said, "In the garden, growth has it seasons. First comes spring and summer, but then we have fall and winter. And then we get spring and summer again." What wisdom can you add to that, and what was the last item out of your garden that you shared with a neighbor?

CC: That's my favorite movie. But Dr Siri goes one better with his immortal line: 'Forget the planet, save the garden.' It's my own pay-it-forward mantra. If everyone undertook one small random act of gratuitous generosity from time to time, the world would eventually sort itself out. But of course not everyone will, so we'll be stuck with the mess we have today. Selfishness rules. In fact, we took a bag of our mangoes to the neighbor just this morning to wish them a happy new year. The buggers threw water at us.

KC: The dogs in your Jimm Juree series get more than cameo roles – a trio even get a mention in the acknowledgments of *The Axe Factor* – GoGo, Sticky Rice and Beer. One becomes a hero and saves the day. If everyone had the desire and ability to be a dog owner, what are the first few things they would learn?

CC: Cesar Millan (the dog whisperer) reminds viewers every week that dogs are not small people. But, of course, they are. They have personalities and far more human characteristics than a lot of people I know. But they're small people who forgive easily, who don't care about our bad habits and who provide love unconditionally. After a tricky domestic upset a few years ago, I made the decision not to go back on the road but to stay with my dogs. They've repaid me a thousand times for that decision. Of course they get a part in my books.

KC: This interview happens to coincide with the two-year anniversary of my blog with the frog in the coconut shell, which you kindly drew for me. Thanks again for that.

CC: Happy anniversary.

[XLIX]

Interview with Matt Carrell

ATT CARRELL WAS born in Brighton, England more than half a century ago. Working in the investment industry involved a great deal of international travel including stints in Korea, Hong Kong and Thailand.

Matt's first published work was entitled *Thai Lottery... and Other Stories from Pattaya, Thailand*. The idea for the book emerged while watching tickets being sold by a Bangkok street vendor, and hearing from a friend about the perils of getting involved in the parallel underworld lottery. After receiving positive feedback from readers he started work on *Thai Kiss*, his first novel, this was published in May 2013.

His second novel, *Vortex*, released in January of 2014, is also set largely in Thailand and draws on Matt's extensive experience of the investment industry. In June 2014, *A Matter of Life and Death*, a novel with a football (soccer) theme was published. Breaking the Thai theme, Matt has also written a short story, *Something Must Be Done*, about a High School shooting, set in the USA, which takes on the issue of gun control or more accurately lack of control and the USA's crazy gun culture.

Vortex was very well received by critics and the public alike. As a result Matt wrote, *Vortex – The End Game,* which was launched in November of 2014.

Matt and his wife divide their time between England and the French Alps, with frequent trips to Asia. Matt Carrell is a nom de plume. In today's interview he explains, among other things, the game of soccer better than anyone ever has. I am pleased to welcome Matt Carrell here today.

KC: Let's talk football, Matt. A game you call beautiful on your side of the pond and we Americans call Super, once a year. Tell me what is beautiful about The Beautiful Game? I'm having a hard time figuring it out on my own. More people watch and cheer the game of soccer than any other. I'll leave out the word, root, for now.

MC: Kevin, I think there's been a terrible misunderstanding. I'd never call "soccer" a beautiful game, I'm just addicted to the spectacle. Humans are essentially tribal and if footballers didn't play out our proxy wars for us, I'm pretty sure we'd be back to invading each other's towns, burning houses and kidnapping folks. Fans vent their frustrations from a segregated section of the stadium and trash-talk each other on web forums. If they couldn't do that, they'd be killing each other. It's not a sport so much as a cunning method of maintaining law and order amongst those who don't buy into religion. The government loves it because it's a neat distraction. They may be running the country into the ground but their incompetence pales into insignificance compared with that referee who denied your team a goal on Saturday afternoon.

The "beautiful game" is not in my heart, it just speaks to the dark side of my head. American football is much simpler, it's something for you guys to watch between the commercials!

KC: Your writing in *Thai Kiss* won me over in the first paragraph. Tell me the first paragraph or sentence from two of your favorite books or stories you have written and then tell me your favorite opening line from any of your favorite works of fiction?

MC: The objective in any story is to make the reader want to know what happens next. If you want to upset an author here's a foolproof method. When they ask if you've read their latest book, you reply, "Well I started it." There's nothing worse than to hear that someone read a few pages and didn't feel compelled to stay up all night to finish it. The sooner you get your reader's attention the better, but you've got to maintain that momentum through the story. One of my favorite reviews of *Thai Lottery* was a single word and I'm not even sure it's a word. "Unputdownable!"

I don't consciously try to deliver an attention grabbing first line but I'm sure it helps. *Thai Kiss* starts with:

"When your best mate gets washed up on the beach with a hole in the back of his head, it's time to reflect. I turned it over and over in my mind but there was only one conclusion. If I stuck around, I'd be next."

I hope this gives the reader a sense of what will happen next. The narrator has good reason to believe he is in danger and is going to have to abandon the life he has built for himself. I'm also trying to convey that the story is pacey and action packed.

My latest novel is called *Vortex... the Endgame*, the second book in the *Vortex* series. Chapter one starts with:

"On one side of the sectarian divide, it was the brutal slaying of an heroic freedom fighter, on the other; the clinical execution of a ruthless terrorist. To an over-worked, underpaid Inspector in the Royal Ulster Constabulary it was just another ton of paperwork..."

Again I hope it gives a flavor of what follows. Violent death is an expected consequence of war. These days it happens all too often when the rest of the world is just trying to go about its business. The story is about the lengths some will go to, to further their business and political aims when others are just struggling to get by.

To answer the second part of your question I went to dig out all the books I possess which would make me look well-read and quietly intellectual. Then I realized I don't have any. I can't say they are the very best opening lines but these two did grab me:

From *Brighton Rock* by Grahame Greene – "Hale knew before he had been in Brighton three hours, that they meant to murder him. With his inky fingers and his bitten nails, his manner cynical and nervous, anybody could tell that he didn't belong…" This is a great opening line, you get the sense of danger and the particular vulnerability of the character that's being introduced. The smart money is not on Hale to survive.

From *The Day of the Jackal* by Frederick Forsyth – "It is cold at six-forty in the morning of a March day in Paris, and seems even colder when a man is about to be executed by firing squad." Again I think this is a great hook. The first time I read this I actually shivered.

For any writer who is worried that their first line isn't sufficiently catchy to deliver them a best seller, I'll offer you this, "I scowl with frustration at myself in the mirror. Damn my hair – it just won't behave…" I'm bored already but it's from *50 Shades of Grey*, which I understand has been quite successful.

KC: Let's shift gears away from sport in the interest of international harmony and away *from 50 Shades of Grey*, for this question at least. Thailand is a mixed bag when it comes to the fiction authors. The general consensus is a lot of books produced by Thailand authors are sub-par as a group. In real estate the good properties pull up the value of the bad ones in the same neighborhood. But with authors in Thailand a case could be made that all the bad authors pull down the value of the good ones. Would you agree with that? Without naming any authors, at all, give me your impressions of the books written by Thailand based authors or books with Thailand themes? What is the upside of being an author in general if there is one, and what is the downside of being an author who writes fiction with a Thailand setting?

MC: I'm an avid consumer of books set in Thailand and they certainly span the full range of the quality spectrum. Thailand is the perfect setting for a thriller. It offers a wonderful backdrop for the plot and the opportunity to introduce characters that don't fit the usual stereotypes. The best writers seize that with both hands and offer an insight into a culture that will be completely new to many readers. When I had the initial idea for Vortex, a novel that takes financial crime as a central theme, I intended to set it in London. Switching it to Bangkok and Hong Kong gave the story an extra dimension.

The disappointing books fall into two categories. The first being those that really could be set anywhere in the world. "Got drunk, met a girl, made a dick of myself." You don't have to leave home to do that. The second is where the writer forgets that someone is paying cash for their book and the editing is poor and slipshod. Thai based books seem to have more than their fair share of bad grammar and random typos. When you get one of those that falls into the first category as well, it's time to ask Amazon for a refund. Thailand is an extraordinary, complex country and the writers who help you to see what lies beyond the veneer, are giving their readers far more than those who write about their own back yard. There are plenty out there that deliver but, as you said, I'm not allowed to name names.

The upside of being an author is definitely the interaction with the people who've read my books. I often get messages asking me to bring back characters from previous stories in whatever I write next. It's a real kick to know that something I created has had that impact.

The downside is definitely that many people have a tendency to prejudge anyone who displays any sort of detailed knowledge of Thailand. My first two books focused on the bar scene and there's an assumption that I couldn't possibly know so much about it without being an enthusiastic participant. I've also written a short story about a high school shooting but, oddly enough, no-one thinks I've killed anyone.

KC: I want to talk about progress. I do not read Stephen King novels but I like, very much, what King writes on the subject of writing. What are you better at, now, than you were when you wrote your first book? How does one become a better writer other than writing a lot? Is it possible, given the opening salvo you've shared with us about *Fifty Shades of Grey* to define what a bad writer is? And finally, what is easier to recognize, good writing or bad writing?

MC: I was incredibly lucky, my first book was taken up by a small boutique publisher called Aardwolfe Books. The editor for *Thai Lottery* was only interested in making it as good as it could possibly be and he didn't spare my feelings. I'm still scarred by a note he put on one of my chapter endings, it said, "You probably think this is dramatic, it's not." He was right of course. I'd like to think my writing has always been strong on plot and in delivering plenty of twists and a good ending. With a lot of help from others I think I'm better now at creating a picture of what I want the reader to see in each scene and in fleshing out the characters so they feel like real people. I've also learned to keep the story tight, eliminating the extraneous waffle that isn't key to the storyline.

If you want to improve as a writer you have to put your ego on one side. Encourage constructive criticism and get other experienced writers/editors to go through your books with a fine tooth-comb. You might not agree with everything they say but you'll have learned something from the debate.

I wasn't inspired by the first line of *50 Shades of Grey*, and although I've read only a few lines from the rest of the book, it's not for me. That's not to say that EL James is a bad writer, quite the contrary. Anyone who has created something that people enjoy reading is a good writer. It's rare to find an author who appeals to everyone, so as long as your books work for people outside your immediate circle, you pass the test. Excluding friends and family, if everyone else reading your stuff says it sucks, then you're a bad writer.

An author's task is to transport readers to another place, to make them eager to read the next page yet not want the book to end. I get irritated if I'm reading a book where the author fails to pull that off because of implausible plot lines, clumsy dialogue, bad grammar or multiple typos. I'd hesitate before calling that author a bad writer, however. If they are selling books and getting genuine positive reviews then their stuff is working for some people, just not for me.

I think bad writing is much easier to spot than good, you may not like classical music but you'll know if the guy playing the piano is a novice. The same applies to novelists.

KC: Have you set any goals for yourself as a novelist?

MC: I don't see writing as a career, I had one of those and it left me somewhat disillusioned. I got into this because a story popped into my head that I thought would entertain people. Feedback from the publisher and from readers of my first book was better than I could ever have hoped and encouraged me to write more. As long as I think I can produce a good story and the positive reviews keep coming, I'll keep writing. Obviously I'd like to see my books in every bookstore and most writers dream that one day they'll get the call from a movie producer, but I'm realistic enough to know that is a distant dream. The biggest payoff I've had from writing has been the contacts I've made with other writers and readers of my books and everything I've learned whilst researching my stories. As long as I'm reaping those rewards, I'll be happy.

KC: What makes you angry?

MC: I just turned 55 and you don't have time for me to tell you everything that makes me angry. I'm sure it's an age thing. At the top of a very long list would be modern politics. I'm staggered at how venal and self-serving our leaders have been in recent years and appalled by the consequences of their poorly conceived actions. So many of our politicians have squandered the opportunity to make a real difference, choosing instead to ride the gravy train for as long as possible, with eye-catching short-term gimmicks rather than genuine long term solutions. I don't see much chance of this trend reversing in the near future either. My second favourite bug bear is the media, which long ago stopped holding politicians to account and can now only be relied on to push its own agenda in a desperate rush for ratings and ad revenue.

KC: Thanks Matt for doing this interview long distance. I'll be seeing you at Hemingway's Bangkok soon.

MC: Thank-you, Kevin. It's been a pleasure.

For more information regarding Matt and his novels go to:
www.mattcarrellbooks.com

[L]

Interview with Zen City Author
Jack Fielding

VOID THE RUSH and learn about author Jack Fielding, now, at
Bangkok Beat. Jack's not into self-promotion, which may be the
reason I had not heard of him, until recently. My first thought after
reading his writing: life isn't fair. But we all knew that already, right?
Jack currently resides in London and has spent a considerable amount
of time living, writing, and working in Thailand. He enjoys the theatre,
particularly if it is of the absurd. The strange worlds of Jack Fielding can
be found on his blog, where he takes a satirical look at films, books and
other things with a Zen point of view: jackfieldingauthor.blogspot.com

From his web site found at jackfieldingauthor.com: Jack Fielding has
worked and traveled throughout the world. Always drawn to the absurd
and improbable, Jack has modeled cowboy hats in Tokyo, dined with
General Franco's English interpreter in Paraguay, informally coached
Bangkok's premier Elvis impersonator and once starred in a German
travel commercial with a plastic dinosaur called Bernard. In his darker
moments Jack describes himself as a "not terribly strident Zen Buddhist."

Bangkok Beat welcomes Jack Fielding with mild trepidation.

KC: Greetings, Jack. I like your style. Your writing style. Your blog style. You even pull off wearing a hat and glasses with a certain panache. It's been said you write absurdly entertaining fiction, often with a Zen edge. How would you explain your writing style to those unfortunates who are unfamiliar with it?

JF: Thank you and it's great to be in Bangkok Beat! I seriously love books and everything to do with them – especially when they've got some kind of connection with Thailand. Digital books or trad I don't mind. Just so long as they're creative and out there!

For my One Hand Clapping stories, I guess I write in a minimalist fast-paced style. Hard-hitting. Less is more. When I'm writing I visualize the narrative being played out as a Tarantino or spaghetti western movie. I suppose I'm writing what I see. With Zen Ambulance I've tried to pare the narrative down even further, to give a stronger 'Zen' kick. I've also made up my own words, to help create a unique 'one hand clapping' world, fusing East and West.

I write across genres. Shadows and Pagodas – an outrageous gothic tale set in Old Siam – has a more traditional style. I've even thrown in the odd archaic bit of English and Thai vocab – I really love the idea of breathing life into long-forgotten words! Plus plenty of literary and movie references, too. With Neville Changes Villages I've stuck to a contemporary and relaxed style, reflecting the fact it's a straightforward comedy about a guy in real-life Thailand in the 90s.

KC: What is the focus, if you have one, for your very original blog, Pulp Zen?

JF: Because I write across genres I thought my readers would enjoy a blog devoted exclusively to the 'Pulp Zen' concept. Like the books, Pulp Zen draws in a lot of things really. Not only Zen Buddhism but samurai and spaghetti western movies, nikkatsu cinema and American/British noir. Teddy Boys, rockabilly. Retro streets. Vintage comics. Also retro Thailand, you know back to 50s Bangkok and much earlier. I'm really fascinated by it, especially as there's so little physically left. Zen City is particularly hot on breathing new life into all that long lost social history.

KC: Talk about death, just for the fun of it.

JF: One of the themes in my books is death and absurdity – always a laugh a minute around here – so I'll share what I think by way of a true story:

At one time I was keeping a low profile in a fleapit river town called Concepcion in Paraguay. Every damned night I was plagued by the same dream: I was a young German guy called Nobby Tirpitz, working on a giant airship as a lavatory attendant in 2nd class. I had this special mop, given to me by my grandfather Othmar who had run a public convenience in Hamburg railway station. Anyway, I was in terrible danger in that airship. Trapped in the lavatory while a fire raged outside, acrid smoke pouring in and the airship listing badly. Using my penknife I just had time to carve a message on the handle of the mop then shove it through a tiny porthole. There was an awful roaring noise...then I woke up.

Years later I was living in Thailand and teaching English. Porntip was one of my best female students and one night she invited me to her family house in Don Muang (where the old international airport used to be). Her dad was a colonel in the air force. Well, I met the folks and had a fantastic meal. Then her dad took me into the garage to see his collection of memorabilia. Medals, a WW2 Japanese flag and an oxygen mask, that kind of thing. And then I noticed what looked like a wooden pole. It seemed out of place so I asked him about it. He explained it was a broom handle from the Hindenburg, the airship that had exploded in 1937. Said it had some writing on it but it was in German. Well, I knew German and picked it up. I went all cold. The handle seemed strangely familiar. Then I read the writing. Incredibly it was the message I'd written in the dream – 'Anyone want to buy a cheap airship!'

You know, I've never forgotten that uncanny dream and the mysterious mop handle. Death, rebirth and multiple lives. I suppose it also explains why lavatories keep appearing in my books. In Zen City, Palmer is in one when he experiences the ghastly dream sequence. Milo the assassin-monk emerges from a weird roadside toilet in Zen Ambulance and Neville's family keep surprising him when he's sat on the bog in Neville Changes Villages.

One thing's for sure – ever since, no matter where I am in the world, I've always tipped big when I use public lavatories.

Like I said, death and absurdity.

KC: That's the best mop handle story I've heard since... well, that's the only mop handle story I've ever heard. One of my favorite fictional private eyes of all-time, Nick Danger, was once told a good line in the Rocky Rococo caper. It went, "You can't get there from here." You said earlier, it's always a laugh a minute around here. How would you describe your here? And throw in a few there's also. Where have you been? But leave out Paraguay if you don't mind.

JF: "You can't get there from here" is a brilliant line really. Love lines like that, especially when they're laconic.

Now where was I? Oh, yes. Where is 'here'? To be honest, I don't know. I've never been able to stay in one place for very long. I hitch-hiked to Normandy when I was sixteen and never looked back really. I don't own a car or property, always spending my wedge on trying to get to places – the less fashionable and visited the better. Either to live in or hang out in bars and cafes. Shooting the breeze with strangers, getting to know people. Listening rather than talking (and taking copious notes afterwards). I'm wary of trotting out a list of places I've been to – I hate that approach to travel. Going to other people's countries is always a privilege, one that most of the planet's population don't have.

Having said that, you did ask! Well, lived in Finland for a while, in a Helsinki suburb. As a genuine English Teddy Boy, in a country where 50s rock and roll was mainstream, I was briefly a legend in my own lunchtime. That was also where I met my first wife (short marriage, long story). Inspired by the final sequence in Elvira Madigan, I got my butterfly tattoo in the sailor's quarter in Copenhagen. I lived on a

Prague council estate in the 80s (during their first free elections) and hung out in the St Thomas pub with some ex-cons who wore pinstripe suits with very wide lapels. I've been shouted at in Algiers, tricked into buying an expensive pair of slippers by a blind African man in Paris and got my bottom pinched mercilessly by a Guarani Indian girl on the Argentine border. I think her name was Marina. Strong grip, too. Throughout the 90s I was forever crossing borders into Laos, Cambodia and Kelantan. Later, I spent quite a bit of time living near a sex shop in Transylvania and in Pest I ended up being a sort of unofficial therapist to a manic depressive café owner who was owned by an Arab gentleman – the girl that is, not the cafe.

Inevitably, I've also spent a fair bit of time in Britain. Although my experiences here haven't always been as positive. Getting my nose broken by an amateur boxer in a working men's club in Newcastle (he bought me a pint afterwards), thrown on the tube tracks in east London, racially abused in Leicester and completely failing to buy a Polish sausage in High Wycombe.

KC: I'm intrigued by your making up your own words in your One Hand Clapping novels. Give me some examples of those words and their definitions.

JF: Yes, one of the ways I've tried to build the One Hand Clapping world is to create a unique vocab, fusing fact and fiction, East and West. Also to provide info on retro Asia (particularly Thailand) which I thought my readers might find interesting. Here's something I posted on my Strange Worlds blog a while back:

Atomic Age – the mid to late 1950s.

Bushido/'the code' – warrior code of the Japanese samurai that drew on Zen Buddhism and Shinto teachings. I created a warped movie-trivia version of the code for the Colonel's psychopathic gunfighters, the Four Truths.

Generalissimo Vissaek – fascist dictator of Siam and ally of the Axis powers.

Iso Isetta – the iconic 'little Iso' bubble car was designed by Renzo Rivolta, a successful manufacturer of refrigerators. These wonderful cars were incredibly expensive in Bangkok because of the heavy import duty.

Kamikaze Boogie – Thai rockabilly hit penned and sung by Johnny Izu.

Kouk Moun Kid – the long-forgotten star of home-grown Siamese Westerns.

Noir Age – roughly, the 1940s and early 50s.

Siam – the original name of Thailand. It was changed by Field Marshal Phibunsongkhram in 1949 as part of his modernisation programme, along with making men wear hats, women wear gloves and everyone putting on shoes when they went outside.

Siamese salute – slang term used by some foreigners in the Noir Age. It refers to the traditional Thai greeting, which involves bringing the hands together. Properly called a wai.

Shoho – name of a notorious girl gang, it means 'Auspicious Phoenix'. The girls took the name from a famous aircraft carrier in the Imperial Japanese Navy.

'slippy shippy' – slang term for goods smuggled into the Bangkok docks by ship.

Teddy Boy – Street fashion that erupted on British streets in the early 1950s and was quickly adopted by cool yakuza. It celebrated an Edwardian look, replete with velvet-collared drape jackets and waistcoats. Die-hard Teds can still be found in remote parts of Britain.

Ticals – currency used in 1940s Siam. Plenty of references to it in Reynolds' novel, A Woman of Bangkok.

Amazingly, I'm still in one piece. Like Vivien Leigh I've always depended on the kindness of others. And, of course, being a good listener and non-judgmental helps – as does being able to retreat into my inner world. Maybe that's where 'here' really is.

KC: I have enjoyed this interview, Jack. More than I would admit publicly. What's on the horizon for Jack Fielding? What are you working on personally and professionally?

JF: Yeah, this interview has been excellent actually, and tweaking the nose of absurdity along the way always helps! Actually, on a slightly more serious note, your questions have also prompted me to reflect, not only my writing but also what I've got up to over the years. As Orson Palmer would say, No one is more surprised than me.

I'm currently finishing off the latest version of Neville Changes Villages, with the help of the author Matt Carrell. All about a dysfunctional English guy teaching in Thailand in the 90s. The basic theme isn't exactly new – but I think the way I tell it is! You know, giving it the 'Jack Fielding' treatment.

Then I'm working on a collection of short stories. They're retro sci-fi, inspired by the vintage comics of Alan Class like Creepy Worlds and Astounding Stories. But instead of being American the stories are set in Siam. They're a mix of absurdity, crime, speculation, dark comedy and just the plain weird. Inspired by our interview, there might be a guest appearance by one Nobby Tirptiz.

After that, I'm either going to get back to the One Hand Clapping stories (I've got rough drafts for about four more of those) or I might take a different direction. I've got the beginnings of a novel about a dysfunctional young guy growing up in south-east London in the early twentieth century and his involvement with the new film industry. It will link in with the mysterious Shadows of Siam film that gets mentioned in Zen City, Iso. Also it will be a bit of homage to the lost world of British silent films, which I'm quite keen on.

On a personal level, I could well be moving to Switzerland later in the year. It will be a brilliant place to raise my family. And at some point I really, really need to get back and visit Thailand. Apart from family, friends and wonderful temples, it's important my two children develop their Thai heritage. Oh, and I want to take my family to the home of Kukrit Pramoj, the author of the superb Four Reigns, to pay our respects.

My two young children are absolutely wonderful. All my creative work is ultimately dedicated to them. If they show any signs of creativity in any form, I'm determined to encourage and nurture it. I don't want them to be like me – it took me years to pluck up the courage before I finally put pen to paper. Lack of self-belief is a terrible thing. When my children are older, I hope my books will inspire them to work hard, be creative, keep moving. That's my main motivation really. And the fact that I need to get all these damned stories out of my head and onto paper!

Thank you for giving me this opportunity to talk about my books and also the more personal stuff. Really appreciated.

KC: Thank-you, Jack. Keep the Zen edge and the absurd outlook coming. And here's to hoping I never get a tip from you in my next life.

[५१]

The World According to Gop

BANGKOK BEAT IS pleased to announce a collaboration and the
addition of a new feature, The World According to Gop – a
monthly cartoon featuring Gop the frog in the coconut shell. The
drawings are by a talented, award-winning author living La Vida Loca
down in the south of Thailand. His signature is evident in its own
unique style. If and when he starts to think the strip is getting funny he
may include a second signature. Kevin Cummings takes responsibility
for the writing and humor, absent or present. Welcome to Gop's World:

World Premiere of Gop Strip #1

Chris Catto-Smith Appears in Gop's World

Paid Celebrity Endorser for Bangkok Beat

[LII]

Fictional Frog Interviews a
Pulp Private Eye

ANGKOK BEAT LOOKS to interview cutting-edge and breakout literary talent, so efforts were made to secure an interview with up-and-coming pulp fiction writer James A. Newman, author of the Joe Dylan private detective noir crime series.

Repeated calls to Mr Newman's office were finally returned by his publicist (no name given). *Bangkok Beat* was told that due to ongoing negotiations for an interview and cover photo with *After Dark* magazine, Newman would be unavailable for "bloggers". As a result, we pursued the next best thing. Gop, the literature loving, tobacco (?) smoking, sex-on-the-beach drinking, frog in the coconut shell cartoon character was retained for one purpose: find fictional protagonist Joe Dylan and interview him. Joe had last been heard from on a binge in The Zone after solving a murder mystery in Fun City for a famed ex-catwalk model, the widower Mrs Bell – also known as the White Flamingo. It's not often one fictional character interviews another fictional character. Enjoy:

Gop: Joe, you are a hard man to find. It took me days to track you down here at Last Chance Samui Health Resort & Spa, and I live in the south. Big fan, here. I read all my books on the beach and a Joe Dylan novel is the perfect beach book. There hasn't been a noir style, hardboiled detective like you since Nick Danger. Security at the main gate and the checkpoint at the front desk informed me we haven't much time before your next session. So let's jump right in: the question all your friends, fans and readers want to know is, you seemed to have it all under control – what went wrong?

Joe D: Well, I took a slide in the Red Zone following the White Flamingo caper. I guess you can fill in the details whichever way floats your lily pad. Let's just say I broke a case. When I break a case I like to celebrate. Hard. The therapy here sucks, baby. The place is full with tree-huggers and eco-warriors bringing down the tone of the establishment. The joint used to be run by some gimp called The Elf before he took the night train following a puffer fish salad served by an Aquarian temptress.

Gop: Say no more, Joe. Your true fans will stand by you and those who know the Red Zone can imagine those details. The White Flamingo case was quite a walk on the wild side up in Fun City. Congrats for cracking it. Let's talk about the therapy game. The tone may be down but this spa is superb – dragonflies are everywhere. Sliding appears to have an up-side. What are your days like here at Last Chance Samui Spa?

Joe D: You're kidding, right? That asshole Newman wrote me into this place so I could research his next book, *Synchronicity*, set inside a rehab unit. So while the author's up there in the big smoke hanging out with guys blowing their trumpets at the Checkinn99 and chewing the fat with comedians and actors, I'm here sitting in a hut shoving a rubber tube up my Harris every four hours to cleanse the colon (whatever that is), and there's no food. At least nothing solid. Two protein shakes a day and as much coconut milk as you can vomit. You wanna swap places man, say the word, give me back the city. You got any smokes?

Gop: Smokes? Sure, but they confiscated both along with my Altoids tin at the front desk. Juicy Fruit? … Negative on the swap, Joe. Sounds to me like someone needs to recite their Serenity Prayer. The pipe cleanings explain the color choice for the staff uniforms and the incense. For a second, I had a Lumpini Police Station flashback. C'mon Joe, this is not your first slip and fall. I've read all Newman's stuff – even the strange one about the lizards. Shouldn't you know the rehab drill by now after what happened to your protagonist pal, Johnny Coca-Cola, during his Buddhist temple gig?

Joe D: Talking of color – you look a bit green yourself, Gop. Johnny Coca-Cola is another one of Newman's dysfunctional creations. Let's not talk about recovery for much longer. It kinda bores me. You see, the trick is to stop trying to keep clean and then there is no conflict, works for a while. The other side of the coin is that if you take your foot off the brake too often, you may slide on the ice. We have the sea here and the beach, a couple of Hollywood types in the steam room. What could be better?

Gop: No worries, Joe. The color blonde is on my mind. Stop trying, eh? Sounds like a day at Beach Road. Let's talk about your last client – the White Flamingo. Everyone knows these spas charge an arm and a leg to stick a rubber hose up what you call your Harris. Every country has a different name for it; all I know is, everybody has one. The Fun City telegraph was burning that private dick business wasn't the only thing going on with you and Mrs Bell at her mansion on the hill. And the word on the street is, the Flamingo has spent time at this very spa. Is that a coincidence Joe, or is the Flamingo your Mrs Jones, because it seems you gotta thing going on?

Joe D: Some reviewer said recently that I have a problem with women. Well, anyone who's in a relationship has a problem and anyone who hasn't got a piece of skirt or leather vest has a problem. Money and women are the same – they mean everything and nothing … You'll have to ask the Flamingo herself if it's serious – all I can tell you about the Flamingo is she's like the bird that gave her her moniker. Each way her head turns, there's a big bill in front of it.

Gop: I figured you for a gent, Joe. And a wise one at that. I've always liked the way Joe Dylan sees the world. I don't like to pry into people's personal lives, but I am a bit concerned for your mental health. So I must tell you. There's a full moon party in two days, just a short swim from here, that will knock your flip-flops off. The here and now could be a lot worse than this seaside spa. What does the future have in store for you, Joe? What can your fans expect from you while you still have a pulse?

Joe D: Pulse? Odds are you'll croak before me, frogman. My plans? Well I'm checking out of this here new age cesspit when the doc gives the all-clear. Then it'll be swimming to the full moon, have a party, and the next assignment is something tasty. It involves a rich kid who leaves behind his promising career to live in a utopian society of naked chicks in the jungle in central Thailand. I get my assignments from the higher power. This time Newman threw me a paddle. Talking of paddles, why don't you grab yourself a paddle and hit some ping-pong balls in the rec room, Gop. I have an appointment with the enema tech at twelve. We get together this time every day and just like to shoot the shit.

Gop: Ping-pong's my game, Joe. When I was in California last summer I won a little tournament down in Big Sur. You'd love it there. Redwoods. Ponds. Beautiful. But I see you as more of a Paris kinda guy.

Joe D: Sure, in another lifetime I lived at room 25 the Beat Hotel, Left Bank. I can picture it now – gazing out that window across the rooftops and chimney pots. Up close a chimney pot's a work of art. Yeah, Paris, the 1950s – shore leave. Picked up a taste for the Chinaman's curse, and discovered my first case of the clap. Both imported from the East. But that's another story for another waiting room.

Gop: I learned a lot today. And I hope to forget it pronto. Time for you to play your game of hole-in-one with the long-haired beauty wearing the latex gloves. I need my Altoids and Camels to fuel me back to The Big Weird. It's been a real pleasure, Joe. Before I get out like trout, is there any message Joe Dylan would like me to take back to the City of Angels?

Joe D: Yes. Buy *The White Flamingo* by James A. Newman. If my benefactor doesn't come up with the readies to spring me from this joint, then we're looking at selling enough copies to spring me free. Listen, just tell your readers to buy the goddarn book.

Gop: You got it, Joe.

[LIII]

Just Visiting with Chedly Saheb-Ettaba

IN *BANGKOK BEAT* I've talked a lot about Checkinn99. But another meeting place for creative people is mentioned in an earlier chapter and it is also a regular hangout for writers, musicians and other artists. It is Hemingway's Bangkok. Located on Sukhumvit Soi 14, a narrow tree-lined alley, Hemingway's is the perfect place for creative minds to meet.

Peter Driscoll and the Cruisers, a 50s and 60s rock n' roll style band, perform there regularly and provide the appropriate mood. Peter's music is always a welcome addition at Hemingway's and goes well with the food, drinks and conversation. And, as we all know, the creative sorts love to talk.

The owner is Craig Bianchini. He is an American expat who now calls Thailand home. The general manager is Damian Mackay from Australia. Craig and Damian have always been cordial and forthcoming on every occasion I have spent time there, whether outside by the fountain in the garden area or inside the two-story restaurant and bar. Obviously, the restaurant is named after the famous American author, and is designed with the same scheme and colors as the famed Hemingway abode in Key West, Florida, which is now a museum, and home to many cats.

This unique pub is also the regular meeting place for the Bangkok Writer's Guild organized by C. Y. Gopinath. The author of an internationally acclaimed novel, *The Book of Answers*, published by Harper Collins in 2011 and shortlisted for the 2012 Commonwealth Book Prize. The Bangkok Writer's Guild has become an important presence in the Bangkok literary scene. Gopi, as he is known to his friends, is ably assisted in those meetings by his co-chairman, Mithran Somasundrum. Mithran is a short story specialist who has been published many times. The Bangkok Writers Guild offers interesting monthly topics – the most recent at the time of writing had to do with the controversy over Harper Lee's second, previously unpublished novel, a prequel of *To Kill a Mockingbird*.

This chapter is about the interview that almost disappeared. It has been my good fortune to have had conversations with Timothy Hallinan, Chris Catto-Smith, Jerry Hopkins and William Wait which all ended up, in part, in the chapters of this book. The garden has served the Bangkok Beat well. Still, there have been countless other times, gatherings with friends, which hold this intimate nook of Bangkok close to my heart. If you've never been to Hemingway's Bangkok, and are in the neighborhood, do drop in and pay a visit.

The interview that almost disappeared was with someone who I made a bit of effort to meet. And the effort was well worth it. He is, among many other things, a magician, entertainer and television personality. He is known, on stage, as Doc Penquino or Dr Penquin. Also, out of the spotlight, as Chedly Saheb-Ettaba. It was some time before fortune graced me with an interview. We were both attending the aforementioned Bangkok Blues Brothers Night. We were seated not far apart but, still the opportunity to meet was fleeting, and, like much else in Doc Penquino's repertoire, he vanished into the night.

It would be six more months before we would meet in person. Hemingway's Bangkok seemed appropriate. We made arrangements for a Happy Hour meeting one mid-afternoon. The day before my scheduled meeting with the magician, I ran into author Christopher G. Moore at the Exchange Tower building as he was coming out of his gym. I knew Christopher had been friends with Dr Penquin for decades. I told him of my scheduled meeting at Hemingway's with Doc the next day and asked if he had any anecdotes to tell about the entertainer. "Doc will be one of the most interesting people you will ever meet," Christopher told me, amid office workers walking by. And as usual, Christopher's words proved to be true.

Chedly arrived for our appointment with a pleasant countenance, looking well-groomed and freshly showered, his long hair pulled neatly back in a ponytail. He was wearing a black T-shirt with white lettering showing the silhouette of a bride and groom, which read: GAME OVER. Chedly took in the outdoor atmosphere of Hemingway's garden area near the fountain with fresh eyes. He seemed to like what he saw. We shook hands and my first question was to ask him if he was married?

"No. But I always liked the T-shirt," the magician said. I did too, so we got off to a good start. Chedly and I did have some things in common, growing up in Southern California beach communities in the 1960s and beyond. Chedly is also a Banana Slug, meaning he is a graduate of the University of California at Santa Cruz. I have lived in Santa Cruz, part-time, since 1993.

I am writing the story almost 11 months after our meeting occurred. I have no good explanation for that but I will try. This will be the very last story written for *Bangkok Beat,* and this book would be incomplete, if I hadn't taken the time to write about Chedly. *Bangkok Beat* has two chapters that deal specifically with writing. Writing a book does not make one a writer, to my way of thinking. It makes you one of the many millions of people who have written a book. It is the time I spent with Chedly Saheb-Ettaba at Hemingway's Bangkok that convinced me, once again, that I am not a writer – because I didn't take a single note that day. That is a shame in one way, but it still didn't interfere with the very enjoyable three hours I spent talking to one of the most interesting people I have ever met. Chedly is a traveling minstrel who happens to put on traveling minstrel shows.

We talked and laughed, we smiled, and we ate. Alcohol was inevitably involved. Not too much alcohol or food but a lot of talking and smiling and laughing. Here are just some of the things discussed that day: Doc's appearance on *The Tonight Show* with Johnny Carson and Ed McMahon. Ed telling him, based on stories he had heard, that Doc was the Keith Richards of magicians. His friendship with Michael Jackson and how he taught him a card trick. His royal bloodline. His family connection with British comedian/magician Tommy Cooper.

The story took a serpentine path from his earliest memories of running away from school to perform street magic at nine years old, to sleeping on Charles Bukowski's couch. His lack of anxiety about money was apparent throughout our meeting. Dr Penguin has travelled from country to country with empty pockets, relying on his brand of street magic for a bed and a meal. Travels in Nepal included a dinner invitation to the royal palace. His tales of performing magic on the radio, something I thought not possible, had me rapt. Magic tricks, performed under the influence of hallucinogenic Indian potions, kept me in awe. Adventures in Tangiers followed – or was this before? – with author Paul Bowles and artist Brion Gysin.

He told how he received his title of Dr Penguin. This followed a rainstorm, when, with his clothing soaked, he was waddling along, and the Thai locals pointed and said: "Nok Penguin." His meeting and connection with Prince Bira, which expedited his entry into the kingdom, secured a one-year sponsorship. I heard of his adventures in Bhutan, his days performing as one of the "Too Much Brothers" (with his friend, Rinchen, AKA Count Bruno the Terrible), and his one-man band. There were stories of police being called to break up impromptu street performances, only to have those same police won over by Doc and company.

The bar he was involved in, strangely, also had a dwarf doorman and it wasn't the same one from Checkinn99. That wasn't the result of magic, just odd coincidence! Descriptions of magic shows at Camillian House, (for children with disabilities) struck a sentimental chord. His story about ground-breaking magic shows in Papua New Guinea, (where one man almost lost an ear to the attentive, but primitive audience after Doc pulled some money out of that ear on stage) was hilarious. A magic show performance in 1987 for the Crown Prince of Thailand and his family at the opening of the Meridian in Phuket, revealed the elevated circles where this entertainer sometimes performed. Then again, typically, the Doc shared quarters, next door, with a giraffe.

Working with Christopher G. Moore at a charity benefit in Pattaya during the flood of 2011 led to him being whisked away, the next day, to some mysterious location to perform a private magic show on a private island. The mystery guests turned out to be Angelina Jolie, Brad Pitt and their adopted children. There was only one hiccup in the planning – Chedly had brought his adult magic kit rather than his children's magic show. Life is in the details and the details of Chedly's life are incredible but true.

As the afternoon sped by, Chedly detailed for me, decade by decade, his interesting life, tale after tale, without a trace of braggadocio, simply delight. Chedly Saheb-Ettaba is a delightful man. I didn't need a pen and paper that day. What I needed was a film crew. It was an afternoon at Hemingway's Bangkok that I will never forget. I want to thank Chedly here, publicly, for his time – and apologize for not doing a better job of documenting the fascinating details of the afternoon.

One subject I do remember better than most is a tagline you see Doc Penquino use often, and is the title of one of his many television productions: "Just visiting this planet". I asked Chedly what that meant to him. He pondered the question seriously. I sensed that Chedly understands, profoundly, from decades of experience, that people need the planet more than the planet needs people – that we should treat the planet, and people, kindly along our individual journeys. Those experiences were of much more interest to Chedly than possessions.

Chedly Saheb-Ettaba is another interesting expatriate choosing the road less traveled, by living in Thailand. I am thankful for the opportunity to include him as the final story of *Bangkok Beat*. But next time we meet for an interview I will bring that film crew, and perhaps a deck of cards.

THE END

"Appreciation is a wonderful thing. It makes what is excellent in others belong to us as well." Voltaire

VOLTAIRE GOT IT RIGHT

"Life is too short, time too valuable, to spend it in telling what is useless." Voltaire.

There is a whole lot of complaining going on these days. There is a lot to complain about in our time; no one can deny that, but this is not something new. It seems to me there is also a lot to be appreciated, which is going unwritten about, or worse, unnoticed.

"Every man is guilty of all the good he didn't do."
                                        Voltaire 1694-1778.

Everything starts with an idea. This book, *Bangkok Beat* started as an idea while enjoying the ambience of Checkinn99. They were important stories to tell, for me. It's an eye-opener to realize how many people the making of *Bangkok Beat* involved. I hope you have found it interesting and found something or someone you could appreciate. If you haven't, well, you can always complain. Thank you for taking the time to read it – in whole or in part. Reflecting on Voltaire's remark, I'll say, at least in a small way, not guilty. Writing this book, is one thing I'm pleased I got done.

Now, to thank and appreciate those individuals who donated their time or supplied inspiration to help make Bangkok Beat a much better book than it would otherwise have been, starting off with my favorite expressionist artist.

ACKNOWLEDGMENTS

Chris Coles, Chris Catto-Smith, John Gartland, James A. Newman, Alasdair McLeod, Collin Piprell, Thomas H. Locke, Mark Fenn, Dean Barrett, Christopher Minko, Anya Minko, John Daysh, Mark Desmond Hughes, William Wait, Eric Nelson, Jim Algie, Timothy Hallinan, Cara Black, Janet Brown, Kevin Wood, Bernard Servello, Kevin Conroy, Ted Lewand, Melissa Ray, Jerry Hopkins, Malcolm Gault-Williams, John Marengo, Patti Roberts, Will Yaryan, Matt Carrell, Kaewmala, Tom Vater, Robert Carraher, Grahame Lynch, James Austin-Farrell, Chris Wegoda, Philip Cornwel-Smith, Paul D. Brazill, Arthur Hoyle, Jonathan van Smit, Jiraporn Sriharach, Chedly Saheb-Ettaba, Uncle Wat, Mama Noi, Kiko, Cherry, Grace, Donna, April, Jesse, the staff of Checkinn99, Eminent Air Muay Thai Gym, Hemingway's Bangkok and the spirits of Henry Miller and Stirling Silliphant.

KINDEST THANKS TO A CARTOONIST AND AN AUTHOR ...

Two men in particular made Bangkok Beat a much better book. The flaws are all down to me. The two men are Colin Cotterill and Christopher G. Moore.

For all the reasons they know about, and for many more they do not, thank you.

Portrait of Kevin Cummings by Chris Coles

ABOUT THE AUTHOR

Kevin Cummings graduated from California State University at Chico in 1978. In 1999 he founded an Internet business that involves distilling words from legal transcripts into understandable summaries. In 2001 he met his future wife Ratree while traveling in Western Australia. Kevin splits his time between Thailand and Northern California coffee shops. He has contributed over 50 articles and interviews to newspapers and online magazines in Southeast Asia and California. Kevin enjoys traveling, reading, blogging, music and Checkinn99. In 2015 he began writing a monthly cartoon strip: The World According to Gop, with drawings by Colin Cotterill. Kevin's blog, Thailand Footprint may be followed at www.peoplethingsliterature.com.

FOR MORE INFORMATION ABOUT BANGKOK BEAT:

www.peoplethingsliterature.com

Bangkok Beat store:
bangkokbeat.bigcartel.com/products

Follow The World According to Gop cartoon strip on Facebook:
www.facebook.com/thefroginthecoconutshell?ref=br_tf

Follow Checkinn99 on Facebook:
www.facebook.com/CheckInn99

Email Kevin Cummings:
ThailandFootprint@gmail.com

OTHER ENTERTAINING BOOKS

The White Flamingo by James A. Newman
ISBN: 149099629X

Fun City is run by corrupt officials and respectable gangsters wallowing in luxury mansions in the hills high above the harbour, the beach, and the neon jungle.

When vice worker Tammy is found mutilated on top of a pool table, an effete pervert, son of a 1970s pin-up beauty queen, once known as the White Flamingo, is locked up. Can detective Joe Dylan find the killer before he becomes one of the hunted?

The White Flamingo is a break-neck neo-noir crime thriller from beak to tail feather. This novel, third in the Joe Dylan series, has been optioned for adaptation into a feature film.

Jim Thompson is Alive! by T Hunt Locke
ISBN-13: 978-1492794219

Jim Thompson Is Alive! A sexy historical thriller from T. Hunt Locke. Jim Thompson, the Thai 'Silk King' and former World War II spy, vanished into the mists of history on Easter Day, 1967. No trace was ever found and no clues were left behind. Enter Sam Collins.

Called by one reviewer a cross between James Bond and Indiana Jones, Sam is dragged from the halls of academia to solve the mystery of the missing silk baron. Murder, sex, mayhem! They are Sam Collins' constant companions as he cuts a swathe through Southeast Asia in search of the silk baron. Deceit and treachery lurk in each closet of Jim Thompson's past.

Will Sam break the seal on another of Thailand's great mysteries? Or will Thompson's enemies lay them both to rest?

Poetry Universe has landed. Take me to your reader....
John Gartland's poetry on Facebook
www.facebook.com/pages/Poetry/Poetry-Universe/168195569406
www.johngartland.net

Orgasmus by John Gartland
ASIN: B00UZ8OC7Y

In a world seemingly intent on its terminal crisis, the weirdest things just happened to Brian Carver as he creatively subverted a boring government job. Things like the dangerous embraces of Suzanna, his recruitment by Orgasmus, and involvement in the hottest product launch in history. Since mediaeval times, a continuing struggle of secret organisations has boiled beneath the surface of history. Now, it is computed from all the social and economic data that, unless man is saved by some unheard-of shift in his psyche, time for the species is fast running out. This dark, comic novel takes us there.....

Word-of-mouth advertising is needed by most authors. If you enjoyed *Bangkok Beat*, please consider leaving a review on Amazon. A few lines and a few minutes of your time will be appreciated.

FROG IN THE MIRROR PRESS
PUBLISHES ENTERTAINING NON-FICTION.
© 2015

24173163R00166

Printed in Great Britain
by Amazon